"More Than Mere Amusement"

On

"More Than Mere Amusement"

WORKING-CLASS WOMEN'S
LEISURE IN ENGLAND, 1750–1914

Catriona M. Parratt

Northeastern University Press
BOSTON

Northeastern University Press

Copyright 2001 by Catriona M. Parratt

Library of Congress Cataloging-in-Publication Data

Parratt, Catriona M., 1956–
    More than mere amusement : working-class women's leisure
in England, 1750–1914 / Catriona M. Parratt.
      p. cm.
    Includes bibliographical references and index.
    1. Working class women—England—Recreation—History.
I. Title.

HQ1599.E5 P37 2002
305.4'0942—dc21   2001044691

Designed by Kaelin Chappell

Composed in Caslon 540 by Coghill Composition Co.,
Richmond, Virginia. Printed and bound by Edwards Brothers,
Inc., Lillington, North Carolina. The paper is EB Natural, an
acid-free stock.

MANUFACTURED IN THE UNITED STATES OF AMERICA
05 04 03 02 01   5 4 3 2 1

To my family,
and especially to Ian and Tom

Contents

Acknowledgments

It is a pleasure to acknowledge the many people who have helped this work on its way, beginning with Mel Adelman of the Ohio State University, who supervised the doctoral dissertation from which it developed. In the intervening decade or so Mel has continued to be an unfailing source of support, advice, and perceptive but gentle criticism. For this and his friendship I thank him.

Friends and colleagues in the North American Society of Sport History—Jim Coates, Gerry Gems, Alan Metcalfe, Vicky Paraschak, Sam Regalado, Nancy Struna, and Pat Vertinsky—have been generous with intellectual and emotional support, and none more so than Nancy Bouchier. Chuck Korr kindly read and commented upon several chapters of my manuscript.

Jeff Hill welcomed me into the Modern History Workshop at Nottingham Trent University and Stephen Cann, Dean of Faculty and Head of the Department of International Studies, offered me a visiting research fellowship that made it possible for me to participate in this project. I am grateful for the encouragement and criticism that Jeff, Judith Rowbotham, Ian Inkster, and other workshop scholars have tendered.

I appreciate the guidance and nurturing that the faculty of the Department of Health, Leisure and Sport Studies at the University of Iowa has given. Susan Birrell, Ben Hunnicutt, and Bonnie Slatton have been all that mentors should be. Dawn Stephens's technological expertise has been an invaluable resource. The University of

Iowa generously gave research time and money through an Old Gold Fellowship, a grant from the Miller Foundation, and a developmental study leave. Laura Chase, Rita Liberti, Shelley Lucas, Darcy Plymire, Jane Stengl, and Theresa Walton were stellar research assistants.

Staff and custodians of various archival and library collections made the task of finding source materials less frustrating and more pleasurable. Special thanks to the head of Leisure Services, Sheffield City Council; the Inter-Library Loan department and Special Collections at the University of Iowa Main Library; Judy Burg and Katey Logan of the Boots PLC Archive; Chris Webb of the Borthwick Institute of Historical Research; Jo Parker and Anna Smith of Vestry House Museum; Adrian Henstock of Nottinghamshire Archives; Sheila Cutler of Dartford College Archive; Rob Petre of the Bristol Record Office; and Mrs. Frankie Calland of Caton, Lancashire. Ida Webb not only gave me access to the Chelsea College Archive but also generously shared the fruits of her own research. Ruby Pearson, Joan Sadler, and Ethel Thompson generously shared memories of their lives as Rowntree workers.

Elizabeth Swayze of Northeastern University Press has been a kind and patient editor, overseeing review and editorial processes from which the study has benefited enormously. Whatever flaws and faults remain lie at my door.

During numerous research visits to the United Kingdom, family members have taken me in and cared for me. My sister Jeanette also provided research assistantship. I hope they all know how much their love and encouragement over the years has meant.

My dearest debt is to Ian and Tom, for their love, understanding, care, and steadfastness—all of which I return a hundredfold—and for their humor and lightheartedness, which buoyed me up.

Introduction

On Saturday evenings and Sunday afternoons the London factory girl is to be found promenading up and down the Bow
Road, arm in arm with two or three other girls. . . . On those
occasions she is adorned and decked out. . . . She wears a gor-
geous plush hat with as many large ostrich feathers to match
as her funds will run to—bright ruby or scarlet preferred. . . .
She goes to penny gaffs if nothing better is offered her; she
revels in the thrilling performances at the Paragon or the music
halls; and only too often she can be seen drinking in the public-house with a young man with whom she may or may not
have been previously acquainted.

> CLARA E. COLLET, "Women's Work,"
> *Life and Labour of the People in London* (1889)

No one can fail to be struck by the monotony which character-
ises the life of most married women of the working class. Probably this monotony is least marked in the slum districts, where
life is lived more in common, and where the women are constantly in and out of each other's houses, or meet and gossip
in the courts and streets. But with the advance in the social
scale, family life becomes more private, and the women, left in
the house all day whilst their husbands are at work, are largely
thrown upon their own resources. These, as a rule, are sadly

limited and in the deadening monotony of their lives these women too often become mere hopeless drudges.

BENJAMIN SEEBOHM ROWNTREE,
Poverty: A Study of Town Life (1901)

Between the carefree pleasure seeker of Clara Collet's 1889 vignette of the London factory girl and the faded wives Benjamin Rowntree describes in his classic study of York were legions of women for whom there were two constants: work and want. But if, as the title of Carl Chinn's recent book suggests, these women "worked all their lives," it would be wrong to assume that there was no place in those lives for levity. Still, the question remains as to how and to what degree English working-class women were able to carve out what Kathy Peiss, in her investigation of the culture of young female wage earners in turn-of-the-century New York City, terms a "sphere of pleasure."[1] The present study examines that question for the period 1750 to 1914.

One objective of this book is to incorporate women and their leisure experiences into the existing scholarship on the history of English working-class culture and thus to begin to fill a significant gap in what is otherwise an extensive body of work. Rooted in the post–World War II democratization of British higher education, in leftist theory, and inspired by classic texts such as E. P. Thompson's *The Making of the English Working Class* and Richard Hoggart's *The Uses of Literacy*, this literature asserts the importance of leisure's place and meaning in that culture.[2] Whether understood as an expression of class solidarity and consciousness, as a mechanism of upper- and middle-class social control, or as a site for contest, negotiation, and accommodation between social classes, it shows that leisure mattered.[3] Yet only recently has the scholarship begun to register that leisure mattered not just for men but for women, too. Andrew Davies's recent book on Salford and Manchester is an important contribution to this reconfiguration of the field, as are a number of articles, but there is more to be done. There is still a need for history that draws women in from the wings and puts them at center stage, that acknowledges that they were historical agents and deserve to be the subjects of historical research.[4] And so, one of my purposes here is simply to begin to add women to the historical landscape of English working-class leisure, to offer a preliminary consideration of the nature and extent of working-class women's leisure from the late eighteenth to the early twentieth century.

I am also interested in the deep cultural significance of working-class women's leisure and, specifically, in its implications in and for gender. I have drawn upon sociological studies of contemporary women's leisure, especially feminist leisure studies, to help me frame my exploration of this issue.[5] Scholars in these fields have identified a number of ways in which gender materially limits all women's leisure, but especially the leisure of working-class women. In many families, for example, discretionary income is disproportionately allocated to men and their leisure pursuits. Women often cite economic factors such as a lack of transportation as obstacles to leisure participation. Household, family, and caring duties consume a great deal of women's time and married women continue to bear the primary responsibility for this work, even when they also have full-time, paid jobs outside the home. Because of their caring roles, women find it very difficult to secure a discrete segment of time for leisure, time that is not vulnerable to the demands that others' needs place upon it. As Maureen Harrington and Don Dawson point out in a study of this subject in the United States, women's "free" time is "nearly always open to interruption and diverted attention."[6] These material circumstances are enmeshed with ideologies of gender: what it means to be a woman, women's place and role in society, women's relationships with men, and the ways in which women are supposed to look, dress, and deport themselves. Gender ideologies that scholars identify as constraining women's leisure include "familism" and the ethic of care, both of which induce women to devote time and energy attending to others and to neglect their own desires and needs. This is closely associated with a lack of a sense of entitlement to leisure that many women express and something that Karla Henderson and M. Debora Bialeschki suggest women alone feel. These sentiments are intimately bound up with women's economic status and the fact that women's primary social role is still very much understood to be the care of home and family. The vulnerability and fear of violence that many women feel in the recreational domain is another limitation on their lives, the physical corollary of which is the actual violence that some do suffer at the hands of men.[7] Recent work in sports and the fitness-fashion industry also shows that women face strong cultural pressures to pursue activities and to behave in ways that shore up highly feminized, sexualized, and heterosexual identities; this, too, is a significant constraint.[8]

Gender can thus be understood as working to restrict women's leisure resources and opportunities, marking out what are considered to be appropriate activities, and reinforcing dominant notions of femininity. However, it does not work in the same way for all women or have the same power to limit, restrain, and contain all women. Where women have a measure of economic independence, for example, they often feel entitled to and have the means to fund active and varied recreational lives. Similarly, not all women view the dominant notions of femininity and heterosexuality inscribed in common cultural practices as problematic; indeed, they embrace these understandings and pursue such typically female-oriented activities as aerobics as a means of achieving an "ideal" female form. Still others confound hegemonic ideas about femininity by pursuing sports that have been clearly marked as "masculine": rugby and ice hockey, for example. Or they assert their right to alternative sexual identities by forming leisure communities around them.[9]

From the sociological and cultural work on the interconnections between gender and leisure I have taken two ideas that guide the present study. The first is that gender is a crucial, constitutive force on women's leisure and that leisure reciprocally builds and reinforces gender hierarchies, inequities, and identities. The second is that leisure is an arena in which gender can be confounded, interrogated, even resisted. I develop these themes here by detailing the ways in which gender circumscribed working-class women's leisure in the period under consideration, in a material, physical sense and through the medium of ideas, attitudes, beliefs, assumptions, and emotions. Uncertain, often barely subsistence-level earnings, exploitative working conditions, the double burden of domestic and waged labor, sexual divisions of leisure in the family, and the lack of leisure time and money that stemmed from these things were all important material constraints. Interwoven with them were gender ideologies that rendered women's claim to a right to leisure tenuous and shaped the nature of and meanings associated with their leisure roles, practices, and behavior in powerful ways. The reproduction of patriarchal relationships in courting rituals, the construction of ideals of womanhood through certain kinds of recreation, and the opprobrium that gender ideologues directed at women who drank, gambled, or gossiped can all be understood as expressions of leisure's reciprocal implication in shoring up gender. Yet these things did not work uniformly and they did not determine in any reductionist sense the behavior or experiences of all. Despite operating within a matrix of very real limits and limitations, working women were able to create spheres of pleasure for themselves. They achieved this in a number of ways: by dissolving the lines between work and play, by refusing to be bound by deprivation or by stricture, by resolutely finding their fun where and when they could. In short, working-class women did exercise their will to find the opportunities and resources for leisure and to take their pleasures in the manner and measure of their choosing.

Women's agency in this regard, their capacity for stymieing the gender imperatives that shaped their leisure, flowed in large part from leisure's resistive, subversive potential, a potential that is always there in its inherent openness, license, and freedom. These attributes make leisure a highly charged realm, one that historically has excited the interest of those concerned with gender order and one in which women have tested the limits and contested the sway of that order. Leisure, in short, has been a source of and a site for cultural and social tensions.

The late eighteenth to early twentieth centuries were a time when working-class women's leisure was of especial concern, though it was by no means a novel one. What women were up to when they were not usefully occupied or otherwise keeping their "proper" place had worried the patriarchs of the ancient world and continued to plague men through to the modern era. Deeply rooted and rarely questioned assumptions about women's irrational, sensual, disorderly, and downright wicked natures tumbled alongside equally perennial fears about the baser side of humankind, disposing many to see the female *homo ludens* as a creature that had to be kept in check.[10] In the context of the changes that the rise of industrial capitalism wrought from the late eighteenth to the early twentieth century, these misogynistic and dualistic sentiments came together as a heightened concern over gender and leisure, a preoccupation with controlling both, that was brought to bear sharply on working-class women.

Leisure historians have traced one line of this anxiety through plebeian and working-class culture from the customary rituals and sports of the eighteenth century to the "mass" commercial amusements and codified team games of the late nineteenth century. They agree that there was a growing, widespread distaste for and hostility to rough, rowdy, and bawdy recreations and a movement toward more orderly, sober, and uplifting forms, though they continue to debate over details such as who the agents of this change were, its extent, pace, and implications.[11] By the early to middle decades of the nineteenth century the tension between these competing visions was one of the central dynamics of working-class leisure. It converged with suspicions about women's predilection for dissolution and disorder that some scholars have indicated were being displaced increasingly upon the lower classes in the late eighteenth century. It also converged with similar anxieties about women's voracious desires and insatiable appetites for pleasure that recent work on gender and consumption has highlighted.[12] And all this built into and upon fears that social, cultural, and economic transformations were carrying working women beyond the "natural" purview of their sex, beyond the rational control of husbands and fathers. In the early phases of industrialization, these concerns and tensions were beginning to ferment into the first stirrings of what would be an enduring struggle to counter the troublesome, subversive potential of working-class women's leisure. Initially, this largely entailed exhorting women to avoid the idleness and frivolous and foolish amusements to which their slothful, sinful natures predisposed them. By the 1830s and 1840s, however, early Victorian rational recreationists were finding redemptive qualities in leisure. They recast it, in certain forms and under certain circumstances, as a prophylaxis against sin and as a prop for shoring up the gender order underpinning patriarchal industrial capitalism. And some also saw it as a means of effecting the social, moral, and political changes that would put an end to patriarchal industrial capitalism. I examine these topics in Chapters 1 and 2.

By the middle of the nineteenth century, a remade vision of working-class leisure had emerged; indeed, in Raymond Williams's sense of the term, it had become a dominant hegemony.[13] Cohering around the containing, controlling ideologies of domesticity, separate spheres, the "family" wage, and polarized ideals of femininity and masculinity, this was a sexually divided vision of leisure that was consonant with the imperatives of patriarchal industrial capitalism. Rendered in the starkest terms, it allowed men, as a due reward for their wage labor, to arrogate the right to and resources for leisure; women were expected to provide the labor and services necessary to satisfy men's leisure wants.[14] Or, as Chartist John Watkins characterized it in the cozier rhetoric of his 1841 "Address to the Women of England," "Man goeth forth to work and returneth for that rest and refreshment which his labour at once needeth and provideth. Woman, in the mean time, fitteth and prepareth the good things provided by his toil, and she cheereth his worn spirit by words and looks and deeds of love." Rendered thus as the transformer of the products of her husband's labor into his comfort, the voracious, uncontrolled woman became a safely domesticated consumer.[15] But, as Williams also indicates, no hegemony is ever complete or secure; alternative and oppositional practices and ideas continually challenge it. Always there to counter the dominant, rational, edifying trend was that unreconstructed hedonism that would continue to course through the culture of working people, tempting women to indulge in pleasures and pass their time in ways that were decidedly subversive of order. And countering the patriarchal privileges of the dominant model were expressions of mutuality and egalitarianism, aspirations that for many may never have been realized, but that also were elements in this ideological play.

Chapter 3 considers the material circumstances that worked in consort with the foregoing to shape working women's leisure in the late Victorian and Edwardian eras. This has been seen as a time when the laboring classes began to fully enjoy the fruits of industrial capitalism, among which were more time and more ample means for leisure.[16] But a number of historians have indicated recently that this interpretation does not hold for women and signally ignores the critical role that gender had in restricting their leisure. Indeed, their work suggests that the sin of excessive consumption, which by the late nineteenth century was being naturalized as a female failing, in many working-class families was to be laid squarely at the door of men.[17] In Chapter 3 I support this revisionist position by detailing the meager resources for leisure—specifically, free time and discretionary income—that women of the working classes had.

I also offer some qualifications and modifications. First, as I show, by no means did every working woman lack the means for leisure. Young, single wage earners, especially those from relatively prosperous families and those who worked in relatively well-paid industries such as cotton textiles, certainly could afford to participate in the buoyant leisure culture of the period. Indeed, some commentators felt that they did so to an excessive and worrying degree.[18] Second, even those in dire material circumstances were adept at finding ways of creatively financing their amusements. They established party clubs into which they paid pennies weekly, treated one another to drinks in the pub, assuaged their consumerist impulses by buying hats and clothes through credit and hire-purchase schemes, and the like. Finally, and perhaps most important, as Wray Vamplew has noted for working-class men, individuals could simply (if, in the view of critics, perversely and irrationally) elect to spend their income on pleasures rather than on satisfying basic needs.[19] And some women exercised their agency and free will to do just that, expressing materially their preference for a little luxury and self-indulgence over the mundane practicalities and the gnawing cares of life.

These complexities between material resources and working-class women's leisure are part of my examination in Chapter 4 of some of the forms that working-class women's pleasure seeking took in this same period. In this chapter I also offer a cultural reading, partial and mediated though it necessarily is, of the meanings that women brought to and derived from their leisure experiences. And I discuss the meanings and significance that others, men and the upper and middle classes, found in working-class women's leisure.

The transition from Chapter 4 to Chapters 5 and 6 is organized around my conceptualization of leisure as a crucial element in the transformation that the vast majority of working-class women would experience when they married and began having children. Most likely, it was in the recreational domain that women met the men with whom they would one day establish homes and families; indeed, such encounters seem to have been a core part of the social life of both young working-class women and young working-class men. But as soon as women began seriously to "walk out" (date), their leisure horizons started to contract and, come marriage and maternity, most would find that those horizons were woefully foreshortened. Thus, leisure was a pivotal part of the cultural machinery producing and sustaining gender relations among working-class people, a sphere in which many couples first came together. It was also, ironically, a realm whose very freedoms forged the constraints within which women took and made their leisure and against which some had to struggle to do so. This intertwining of marriage and leisure was one of the most basic and enduring structures and expressions of gender. It was one that could not be taken for granted, however, because in leisure was the potential for a woman to choose not to be a respectable, sober, and home-loving body who would care dutifully for her husband and children. Consequently, upper- and middle-class reformers developed schemes that would encourage working-class women to adopt the ways of a late Victorian and Edwardian version of rational recreation.

Chapters 5 and 6 examine this movement in some detail. Upper- and middle-class women were leading figures in it, but male industrialists also made important contributions, as did working-class girls and women. All were keen and impassioned participants in the heightened discourse on women, gender, and leisure that built up in the final decades of the nineteenth century. This was a period of anxiety over physical and moral degeneration, race suicide, delinquent youth, and the integrity of the empire, and upper- and middle-class rational recreationists saw leisure as being a large part of these problems. Consequently, they determined instead to make it part of the solution by trying to turn it into a mechanism for building and maintaining an exemplary working-class womanhood.[20] Chapter 5 examines one of the sites on which this attempt to construct gender through leisure was undertaken: in the community, largely through the medium of working-girls' clubs. Chapter 6 explores programs of rational, educational recreation that were based in the workplace.

In both of these chapters, I attempt to accord some agency to working women themselves and to understand their perspectives on rational recreation. There were some who held views on self-improvement and class advancement through leisure that were very similar to those of upper- and middle-class reformers and others that rejected those ideas out of hand. And there were still others for whom, as Peter Bailey has argued for the code of respectability, rational recreation was something that one could choose to take or leave as one's circumstances or inclination shifted. This element of freedom, of some choice, however limited by the meanness of material resources or cramped by ideological strictures, offered at least the possibility of a fleeting moment of pleasure in all working-class women's lives. And it was this license at the heart of leisure that fundamentally limited its potential as a means of controlling and containing working-class women, that made it the cultural battleground that this study argues it was.[21]

PART ONE

PLEBEIAN AND WORKING-CLASS WOMEN'S RECREATIONAL CULTURE IN THE LATE EIGHTEENTH TO MID-NINETEENTH CENTURIES

Historians of leisure have seen the eighteenth century almost as a laboring women's Merrie England that declined if not perished during the bleak and difficult years of the early Victorian era. This is, in part, the plot of Shirley Reekie's dissertation, among the few historical studies of British women's sport and recreation. Reekie concludes that by the mid-nineteenth century the combined forces of industrialization, urbanization, and evangelicalism had left lower-rank women bereft of the hearty physical activities and games that they had enjoyed previously. In this interpretation she follows Robert Malcolmson's more general assessment of the fate of popular recreations in the period. "Never . . . completely secure," as Malcolmson judges it, the "traditional" ludic culture of the people disintegrated during the late eighteenth and early to mid-nineteenth centuries, undermined from within and attacked from without.[1]

This narrative of decline in accounts on popular leisure is a familiar one in the historiography of the period and, as Amanda Vickery has pointed out in a recent and incisive review essay, it has been a central theme in the literature on women and gender. The pioneering studies of Alice Clark and Ivy Pinchbeck established the idea that industrial capitalism destroyed the family economy, taking production out of the home and diminishing women's economic roles. For Clark this process began in the late seventeenth century and resulted by the early nineteenth century in the cocooning of privileged women in the home and the exploitation of laboring women in mines, mills, and factories. Pinchbeck takes a more optimistic view of these developments and locates them later, between 1780 and 1850. But both agree, along with a number of more recent scholars, that by the early to middle decades of the nineteenth century, there was a pronounced trend toward excluding middle-class women from the world of formal production and dispatching them to the domestic. For the less sanguine proponents of this school of thought these transformations entailed a significant lowering of women's status and a narrowing of their economic, cultural, and social horizons.[2]

Counternarratives in both the literature on leisure and that on women and gender question the notion that the late eighteenth to mid-nineteenth centuries were decades of decline, of doom and gloom, and insist that for all the change, there were important continuities. A number of historians have interrogated the notion that industrialization had dramatic—and, with respect to women's lot, largely negative—consequences. Judith Bennett and Olwen Hufton both see the picture of low-status, low-paid, and low-skilled female work as centuries old and conclude that industrial capitalism made little if any difference to long-established patterns of gender segregation and inequity in the economic sphere. On the constructs of separate spheres and domesticity, Lawrence Klein warns against interpreting eighteenth-century understandings of "private" and "public" too schematically and thus misreading their alignment with one gender or another and their putative separation in the late eighteenth and nineteenth centuries. For the middling ranks, Paul Langford also questions the validity of the separate spheres model, insisting that women and men mixed with one another to a significant degree, both in the home and outside it. And Linda Colley believes that late-eighteenth-century declamations about women staying in the domestic realm arose precisely because so many were failing to do so.[3]

Hugh Cunningham similarly views the state of popular recreations in the same period. He interprets the hostility that they aroused as testimony to their vigorous growth and believes that rather than crumbling away, they

adapted and persisted doggedly into the nineteenth century. Dennis Brails-
ford's research on sports such as pugilism and cockfighting shows how the
process unfolded in one sphere of leisure. Brailsford argues that, although
aristocratic patrons withdrew their financial and moral backing of the
"manly art" from the late eighteenth century, publicans and other minor
leisure entrepreneurs stepped in as sponsors and promoters. Thus, a plebeian
sporting fraternity nurtured prizefighting into the Victorian era.[4]

Cunningham's vision of a popular culture whose exuberance seemed to
threaten the social, moral, and economic order constitutes one thread of the
interpretive pattern I develop in this study. In the first two chapters I draw
it together with Colley's specter of disorderly womanhood to establish a cen-
tral theme of the book: the tensions that built around the leisure of working-
class women and how those tensions worked themselves out through the late
eighteenth to the early twentieth centuries. In Chapter 1, my exploration be-
gins with plebeian and working-class women's recreational culture and the
concerns it aroused towards the end of the eighteenth century. Chapter 2
examines how working-class radicals and reformers articulated an alterna-
tive vision of popular leisure around such concerns: a vision of sobriety,
order, and enlightenment, a vision of "rational recreation," a vision that
by the latter half of the nineteenth century would be hegemonic.

Chapter One

WOMEN'S POPULAR RECREATIONAL CULTURE TO THE TURN OF THE EIGHTEENTH CENTURY

THROUGHOUT THE EIGHTEENTH CENTURY AND INTO THE nineteenth, women were visible and vital participants in popular recreational culture. In their cottages and workshops, in urban streets and on village greens, in alehouses and on farms, they worked and socialized alongside men. In the daily ebb and flow of labor and release from labor, and in the seasonal and annual round of celebrations, feasts, and holidays that more infrequently punctuated life, they shared in an array of amusements that were gregarious and open. They gossiped and gambled, took tea with friends, neighbors, and fellow servants, got drunk and got rowdy at private parties and public assemblies, feasted with and fought among each other, socialized at church and chapel, and trekked out into open fields and onto moors to listen to ranting preachers. In short, as Peter Burke comments for the secular popular culture of a slightly earlier period, a "comprehensive list" of the diverse pastimes and amusements in which women of the lower ranks engaged "would reach formidable proportions."[1]

Fairs, central to both economic and social life, were major recreational occasions. Most were commercial—"horse fairs, cattle fairs, sheep or hog fairs, cheese fairs, fairs for hardware, or leather, or general merchandise"—but even these combined business with pleasure and some were solely for pleasure. St. Faith's Fair near Norwich, for example, was one of the biggest cattle fairs in England, but its first day was devoted to amusement.[2] Farmers brought cheese, cattle, poultry, horses, and, of course, geese, for sale to the annual Goose Fair held at Michaelmas in Nottingham, but "multitudes of household articles, clothing, and trinkets" could also be bought, "and, besides all this [there was] a vast of seeing and being seen to be done." Though Goose Fair mornings were for commerce, "from noon till eleven or twelve o'clock at night, pleasure [was] the pursuit."[3] In the mid-eighteenth century there were hundreds of fairs, large and small, throughout the country, most clustered into slack periods in the agrarian calendar, between spring sowing and summer harvesting and in late summer when the harvesting was over.[4] Hiring or statute fairs were also a combination of the economic and the festive. Their original purpose was to bring under the regulatory eye of chief constables the annual hiring of servants, and they continued to function as labor markets into the nineteenth century. Malcolmson indicates that hiring fairs were widespread in the late eighteenth and early nineteenth centuries. As with other fairs, statutes generally dispatched with business in the morning and gave the rest of the day and the evening over to the equally important matter of having a good time. And there were the pure pleasure fairs, some of which—like the annual St. Valentine's Day Mart in Lynn, Norfolk, dating from the reign of Henry VIII—had commercial origins. "Immense numbers of persons" gathered at Lynn Mart "from all parts," noted Hone's 1826–1827 *Every-Day Book*. "Neither [was] there any lack of incitements to unburthen the pockets: animals of every description, tame and wild, giants and dwarfs, tumblers, jugglers, peep-shows, etc., all unite their attractive powers."[5]

Women were a ubiquitous presence in all the busy, diverse doings of the fair. They swelled the holiday crowds that in the early

nineteenth century from dawn to noon streamed along the roads
leading out of London to the Easter Monday Fair at Greenwich:
"working men and their wives; 'prentices and their sweethearts,"
"pickpockets and their female companions." They gathered at the
Cumberland hiring fairs at Whitsuntide and Martinmas, at Aving-
ham Fair in Northumberland, at Pack Monday Fair in Dorsetshire,
at Clack Fall Fair and Purton Fair in Wiltshire, and at hundreds of
others besides. "Farmeresses," tradesmen's wives and maidservants,
"girls that have been scrubbing, churning, and milking," country
"lasses with their Sunday gowns, caps, and ribands"—the fair called
to them all "with all its mirth and gaiety," and to it they "has-
tened."[6]

But fairs were central to the broader nexus of women's economic
and social activities and relationships, and they attended them in
various and multiple capacities. They were there as producers and
vendors of commodities, and as seekers of employment, and as entertainers. Nicholas Blundell's *Great Diurnal* from the early eighteenth century records some of the commercial activity of Alice
Steward, who along with her husband was a trader in sundry goods
in Great Crosby, Lancashire. She regularly traveled to regional fairs
in the course of her own business and conducted transactions for
Blundell and probably others there, too. On July 29, 1715, for instance, the *Great Diurnal* shows Blundell paying "Ailes Steward for
my Wigg-Powder as she had bought for me at Chester Fair."[7] Those
women working at fairs included farming women, smallholders, and
servants with produce for sale. Others had stalls selling drinks, gingerbread, nuts, oranges, and sweetmeats: The "spruce Mrs. or Miss
Sugarplum[s]," who, in William Hone's account, enticed visitors
with a pop of her nut canister and a " 'buy some nice nuts, do taste,
sir (or ma'me,) and treat your companion with a paper of nuts,' " and
the frowzy, fictional "Mrs. Goodenough," who tempted them with
dishes of furmity spiked with rum.[8] Those seeking work gathered
together at statute fairs where they advertised their particular skill
by donning its token—dairymaids with a tuft of cow hair in their

bonnets or at their breast, for example—and negotiated terms with prospective mistresses.[9] Women commonly featured among fairground hucksters and entertainers. Rebecca Swain, "a tall and portly dame, six feet tall, with a particular screw of the mouth," was a commanding figure in the 1820s at the Pack Monday Fair in Sherborne, Dorsetshire. Taking up her pitch, Swain would stand "with her . . . lucky-bag," bawling out: "Come my little lucky rogues, and try your fortune for a half-penny, all prizes and no blanks, a fair heart never wins a fair lady." In the early eighteenth century, a female ropedancer (reputedly the daughter of an Italian nobleman who fell in love and ran away with a "Merry Andrew") performed at the infamous St. Bartholomew Fair, held in the autumn in the Smithfield Market district of London. In 1782, the fair counted the Rochester Theatre, a "company of comedians," whose proprietress was a Mrs. Baker, among its attractions. Despite frequent declamations against "Bartlemy" Fair and much talk of abolishing its "nondescript noise and nonconformity," it was still going strong in the 1820s and in 1826 featured "a dwarf lady" and a female sword-swallower in the two-penny shows. The latter "figured . . . by placing her feet on hot iron, and licking a poker nearly red hot with her tongue" and appeared in the penny shows as an assistant to a glass blower who made "pretty little tea-cups at threepence each, and miniature tobacco pipes for a penny."[10]

The fair had a critical function in serving the women who stood on the other side of the economic equation as consumers of commodities, and those for whom the joys of "all its frivolities, . . . all its enticements & endearments " were the main appeal.[11] So generations of thrifty Norfolk women visited the Lynn St. Valentine's Day Mart to buy their prosaic stores of soap, starch, and other household goods at the booth of a London dealer who annually traded there. But trinkets, toys, and an "endless variety" of ornamental and decorative items were also among the staples on offer: "tea-caddies, work-boxes of rosewood and pearl, china, cut-glass, drums and trumpets . . . bracelets and necklaces . . . fans, and parlor bellows, figures in porcelain and painted wood; purses, musical boxes."[12] At Pack Monday Fair in Sherborne, Dorsetshire, along with the mundane mart for buying and selling livestock, were vendors "with drapery, hats, bonnets, caps, ribands, etc. for the country belles." These were the "fairings" designed to catch the eye and delight the heart of the female fairgoer, and, of course, to loosen her purse strings or those of the sweetheart, friend, or employer who might treat her. "Here stands . . . Joan," Hone's *Every-Day Book* relates of these, "with her sloe-black ogles stretched to their extremity at a fine painted shawl, which Cheap John is offering for next to nothing."[13] Fairings were among a cornucopia of amusements and diversions that drew women in "a great number . . . when the weather [was] favorable." On April 18, 1715, Blundell recorded that when his "children and the Maids went in the Coach to Formby Faire, there was a Stage Play Acted there." On July 26, his "Wife, Fanny [their youngest daughter], and some of the Maids went to Leverpoole Fair." Some half century later Thomas Turner, a small shopkeeper in the village of East Hoathley, Sussex, noted in his diary entry of Friday, May 21, 1756, that his wife, together with "Miss Day, Mrs. Fuller, Molly and Elizabeth Fuller, and Fran. Cole went for Whitesmith Fair." On Thursday, October 6, 1757, the Turners' servant, Mary Martin, "after dinner . . . went to Blackboys Fair and stayed all night." Sylas Neville, the black sheep of an affluent upper-rank family, assiduously detailed one pleasure outing that his housekeeper *cum* mistress took to a Norfolk fair in the summer of 1771. "Sally went to Martham Fair with Miss Liffen," he wrote in his journal. "She wore silk for the first time & looks very well in it." On another occasion Neville recorded, "My people [Sally included] being gone to Ingham Fair, shall be alone till tomorrow evening."[14]

Seasonal festivals and feasts were other recreational highpoints. Parish wakes, held annually to mark the feast day of the patron saint of the church, or the church's dedication, were among the most important of these. Notwithstanding the early religious significance of wakes, by the eighteenth century they were largely secular, even profane affairs. "They continu'd not in their original Purity," clergy-man Henry Bourne complained in 1725, "for the Feasting and Sporting got the ascendant of Religion, and so this *Feast of Dedication*, degenerated into Drunkenness and Luxury. At present there is nothing left but the very Refuse and Dregs of it [original emphasis]." If the religious aspects of parish wakes had atrophied, well into the nineteenth century they remained highly significant as occasions for strengthening and renewing kinship and community bonds. The annual feast was the time when family and friends who had moved away returned to visit; frequently one of the main conditions of service to be settled on hiring days was that a servant would be permitted "to go home at the wake."[15] Like fairs, wakes were widespread and numerous. An eighteenth-century study of the parishes in Northamptonshire indicated that roughly two-thirds had an annual feast. In one district of mid-eighteenth-century Buckinghamshire, fourteen of twenty-eight parishes had wakes; in Berkshire around the same period, the figure was eight of fifteen. A list of wakes from the later period of the 1840s shows a combined total of 118 (in six different counties) in the vicinity of Stamford, Lincolnshire. Again like fairs, parish feasts tended to be clustered around two seasons, late spring–early summer and late summer–early autumn, but besides these there were many other customary holidays throughout the year, Christmas, New Year, Twelfth Night, Shrove Tuesday, Ash Wednesday, Easter, May Day, and Whitsuntide among them. There were also feasts on the completion of important agricultural tasks such as bringing in the harvest and finishing the sheep shearing.[16]

WOMEN CELEBRATED ALL OF THESE ENTHUSIASTICALLY, PITCHING themselves into the heart of the rituals and merry-making. They worked hard in the weeks and days before—preparing food, cleaning homes, making holiday outfits and decorations, designing, sewing, and constructing costumes, and adorning "sacred" objects and places. They had important symbolic roles, presiding as goddesses and queens whose fecundity, purity, and bounty customary rituals both invoked and celebrated. They were "cheerful and joyous partakers of [the] flow of soul," the "mirth and jollity," the "rudeness," "drunkenness," and rowdiness that commentators judged to be the "invariable accompaniments and great attraction" of customary popular holidays and festivals.[17]

Women were especially concerned with providing food, drink, decorations, and costumes, an involvement that was consonant with their critical productive, provisioning, and nurturing roles in the family and community. Into the middle of the eighteenth century on New Year's Eve (or at Twelfth Night in Cornwall), for instance, young women ceremoniously took the wassail bowl—a bowl of spiced ale—from door to door and parish to parish, "singing a few couplets of homely verses composed for the purpose, and present-[ing] the liquor to the inhabitants of the house where they called."[18] For the Christmas holidays in Middleton, Lancashire, Samuel Bamford recalls that "the house was cleaned, the furniture rubbed . . . the ale was tapped, the currant loaf was sliced out." Mary Hardy, mistress of a prosperous and upwardly mobile farming household in Norfolk in the 1770s, gave huge Christmas dinners for her laborers and their families. The foodstuffs for the 1802 feast included "32 lbs mutton, 16 lbs pork, 16 lbs beef, 2 st flour, about 12½ [lbs.?] plumbs, 5 lbs suet, about 20 pints Milk."[19] No good hostess would fail to offer the delicacies associated with particular holidays: pancakes at Shrovetide, hot cross buns on Good Friday, roast beef and plum pudding at Christmas, "pace-eggs" or "peace-eggs" at Easter, "cymbalin cakes" on Midlent Sunday, "tharcake and toffy" on the Fifth of November.[20] The annual feast, above all other holidays, was the time for people to "have open doors and splendid Entertainments, for the Reception and Treating of their Relations and Friends, who visit them on that Occasion, from each neighbouring Town."[21] It was "a scene of a joyous gathering and a hospitable festivity," Bamford writes of the Middleton rush-bearing feast, a time when "the very best dinner which could be provided was set out." In Yorkshire the customary dinner for the wake was "roast beef, plum pudding, and an extra allowance of Yorkshire stingo [a strong, pungent beer]."[22] In Norfolk, Gloucestershire, Devon, Essex, and Hertfordshire the harvest supper was another occasion upon which the mistress of the house was expected to lay out a festive meal of this order—a "substantial, plain, and homely feast, of roast beef and plumb pudding"—for harvesters, neighbors, friends, and relations.[23]

Ornate costumes, new clothes, decorations, and displays were essential to making such occasions special, and in the days and weeks before holidays women busied themselves with these festal accompaniments. "Tinsel was purchased, hats were trimmed with ribbons and fanciful devices; shirts were washed, bleached snow-white, and neatly plated," Bamford records of women's work on the outfits men wore during the Middleton rush-bearing feast. (Women assumed the same responsibility for the elaborate dress worn by the men who danced at mayings held in parts of Wales in the early nineteenth century.) In addition, women crafted the ornaments and collected the flowers and foliage that adorned the centerpieces of holiday rituals. Nicholas Blundell records that he gave "a great many Flowers to two young Women for Flowering of a May-Powl" in June 1719, for instance. In Middleton, as in many other parts of Lancashire, communities participated in a ceremony of carrying to the church rushes that it had long been a tradition to strew on the floor. The young men undertook the selection and mowing of the rushes and loaded them onto the cart upon which they were transported to the church, but women's special charge was "the sheet" that was displayed on the front of the rush cart. This was "a piece of very white linen, generally a good bed sheet," Bamford writes, "and on it were arrayed pretty rosettes, and quaint compartments and borderings of all colours and hues which either paper, tinsel, or ribbons, or natural flowers could supply." Women designed and constructed many of the decorations that made up this framework, "tassels and garlands, and wreaths of coloured paper, tinsel, and ribbon," and within it they arranged a splendid display of "silver watches, trays, spoons, sugar-tongs, tea-pots, snuffers, or other fitting articles of ornament and value."[24] At "Cross-Dressings" at Ilkeston in Derbyshire, and at Ince Blundell and Great Crosby in Lancashire, it was the village cross that was the focal point, "dressed up with oaken boughs, with their leaves gilt and spangled."[25] "Well-Dressings" and "Well-Flowerings" were equivalent rituals in other parts of Derbyshire and in Nottinghamshire. At Tissington, near Dovedale in Derbyshire, for example, village women decorated five local springs with garlands and wreaths of fresh flowers. They cut boards to represent different figures, covered them in moist clay and inserted flowers, petals, and leaves "to form . . . beautiful mosaic work . . . tasteful in design, and vivid in colouring." Positioned carefully over the springs, these well-dressings gave the delightful, magical impression that the water flowed "from amongst beds of flowers."[26]

Customs of this kind, rooted in agrarian, rural life, persisted even when towns and cities absorbed the communities in which they originated. Thus, while only a few families observed the annual feast in Sheffield by the 1820s, people established many other smaller feasts around that period in the town's neighborhoods and suburbs. The Wicker and Little Sheffield suburban areas and the Broad-lane and Scotland-street districts held theirs on different days throughout the summer. "Scotland Feast" was the biggest, celebrated by the residents of a hilly, heavily populated part of the town on May 29, the anniversary of the restoration of Charles II. The outskirts of even a growing manufacturing center like Sheffield were rural, and on the eve of Scotland Feast parties of young women and men went into the neighboring woods and brought back boughs and branches with which to decorate the streets. "By five or six in the morning, Scotland-street . . . [had] the appearance of a grove" festooned with garlands of flowers and ribbons "gay with silver-tankards, pints, watches, etc."[27] In the final decades of the eighteenth century, the milkmaids of London observed a similar custom on May Day, adapted to the mesh of economic and social relationships within which they lived, worked, and played. Those who could afford to do so hired a "garland" from a pawnbroker and paraded with it along the route of their milk rounds. The garland consisted of a pyramid-like frame covered in white damask and decorated with "polished silver plate, and adorned with knots of gay-coloured ribbons, and posies of fresh flowers, surmounted by a silver urn or tankard." Here, city commerce met country custom—to the profit of the pawnbroker who "furnished out the entire garland, and let it out at so much per hour, under bond from responsible housekeepers for its safe return." Thus equipped, over the first three days of May, one set of milkmaids after another promenaded and danced through the streets of London, one "from ten o'clock till one," another "from one o'clock till six," and so on. There were other, more modest May celebrations in the city during the same period, such as the one that a contributor to Hone's *Every-Day Book* witnessed, in which a gaily dressed milkmaid led a cow decorated with flowers and ribbons around the streets in the vicinity of Westminster Abbey. And in Northamptonshire in the 1820s, May Day was the occasion for yet another kind of merging of rural ritual with urban life. On the morning of the holiday, girls from villages in the neighborhood of Northampton went into town exhibiting from house to house the garlands they had made and soliciting boons for a feast.[28]

In mayings, as in other popular festivals, there was often a female figure of authority, beneficence, or procreative power. A "queen" or "lady," representing the goddesses Flora and Maia and the annual rebirth with which they were anciently associated, was the most important figure in May Day celebrations.[29] A young woman or a youth traditionally took on this role in the character of Maid Marion, the Queen, or the Lady of the May. On the Isle of Man, the Queen was chosen from among the daughters of the prosperous farmers in the parish and opposed by a man playing the "Queen of Winter."[30] In the 1820s, May revelers in Hitchin, Hertfordshire, and the chimney sweeps of London usually had youths "in female attire, indescribably flaunty and gaudy," as their Ladies of the May, though the sweeps sometimes elected "a strapping girl" to the role.[31] At the end of the summer it was the goddess Ceres who appeared as the central figure in harvest celebrations throughout the country. In the Cotswolds village of Hawkesbury, for example, harvesters brought home the final load of corn on a wagon decorated with flowers and ribbons, accompanied by the men, women, and children of the village. At the head of the procession was "a damsel . . . to represent Ceres," mounted on the leading horse and dressed in white.[32] From Northumberland to north Devon, Ceres figured in other harvest-home rituals as an effigy dressed in finery and flowers, or as a doll made from the last and best of the corn to be cut. In Kent the doll was called "an ivy girl" and was "curiously dressed by the women, and adorned with paper trimmings, cut to resemble a cap, ruffles, handkerchief, &c. of the finest lace." In Northumberland it was called a "kern baby." In parts of Devonshire it was a "knack," which was "brought home with great acclamations, hung up over the table, and kept till the next year." In Hertfordshire, Shropshire, Yorkshire, Bedfordshire, Gloucestershire, Suffolk, and Norfolk, a custom of "crying" the corn doll was part of the harvest celebration. Each community enacted this differently, but its central elements were the same. The harvesters formed a circle around the figure and chanted, shouted, or hallooed three times in unison to announce that the harvest was over and to call for largesse for their feast.[33] In some places the ritual included a ceremonial elevation of the corn doll, a symbolic resurrection that, in the "Lady of the Lamb" custom observed at Whitsuntide in Kidlington, Oxfordshire, was also invoked and conjoined with references to innocence and Christ's suffering and sacrifice. "A fat lamb [is] provided," according to John Brand's account, "and the maids of the town, having their thumbs tied behind them, run after it, and she that with her mouth takes and holds the lamb is declared Lady." Processions, morris dancing, and feasting followed the race and continued through the next day, culminating in the "Lady's Feast, where she [sat] majestically at the upper end of the table, and her companions with her, with music and other attendants."[34]

WHATEVER THE SPECIFIC VARIATIONS IN POPULAR FESTIVALS, their associations with fecundity, plenty, and bounty made them red-letter days on which people put aside their usual work and obligations and came together in a carnival of fun and license. Women were inveterate parties to the revels—drinking, dancing, feasting, flirting, and (sometimes) fighting with the best of them.

Alcohol was a universal dissolvent of the restraints that governed the ordinary world and at carnival time it flowed liberally. Londoners on the way to Greenwich Fair, for instance, began drinking in the morning when they set out on their journey. On "full-sized coal waggon[s]" the wives of coal-hewers "solace[d] themselves with draughts of beer from a barrel aboard, and derive[d] amusement from criticizing walkers, and passengers in vehicles passing their own." In the afternoons and evenings, female fairgoers and holiday-makers, dressed to the nines, joined the rich human bustle of the streets, marketplaces, public houses, and inns where they kept up dances and parties long into the night—and oftentimes resumed the parties and dances on the next and subsequent days. By nightfall on fair day in Greenwich, "drinkers, smokers, singers and dancers," female and male, young and not so young, "fully occupied . . . every room in every public house." During the severe winter of 1814, when London held a "Frost Fair" on the River Thames, women and "their companions" crowded into the drinking tents set up on the ice where they "danc[ed] reels to the sounds of fiddles" or "sat round large fires, drinking rum, grog, and other spirits."[35] At Nottingham Goose Fair, farmers' daughters, who in the morning sold cheeses, in the afternoon "metamorphosed into the most extraordinary belles," each with a "dashing" beau with whom she spent the rest of the day and much of the night "eating, flirting, drinking, and dancing."[36] Once the morning's statute was over at the half-yearly hiring fairs in the north of England, young women began "to file off and gently pace the streets, with a view to gaining admirers, whilst the young men with similar designs follow[ed] them." Each "lad," having "eyed the lasses" and chosen "a sweetheart," conducted her to a dancing room, where they spent the afternoon "and part of their half-year's wages" in like company, "drinking and dancing." Groups of young women and men thronged the public houses in the neighborhood of Bamford's Middleton in the weeklong celebration of the annual feast, starting as they processed with their rush carts through the parish to church. Each cart stopped at the door of every public house on the route and the young men and "the girls bepranked [dressed] in . . . new pumps, kirtles, and bonnets" who accompanied them shared cans of ale. After depositing their rushes at the church, rush-bearing parties "repaired to the public-house . . . and there spent the night in drinking and dancing." On Sunday, "the lads and lasses again met at the public-house, where they drank, smoked, and treated their neighbors and friendly visitors from other public-houses."[37]

The bounds of behavior tolerated during popular festivities could be wonderfully elastic. At dances and parties held after the Cumberland hiring fairs in the early nineteenth century, for example, holiday spirits frequently ignited into fights in which women were not loath to join. While the "weaker portion" of the company took refuge on benches or were "cluster[ed] in corners," according to one source, "the lasses . . . often assist[ed] in the battle." The affray over, "the bruised pugilists retire[d] to wash, and the tattered nymphs to re-adjust their garments."[38] Horn Fair, held near London on St. Luke's Day, had since the sixteenth century been associated with a high degree of women's license; according to one popular myth, the horns that fairgoers delighted in donning represented the cuckolded husband to whom the fair's charter was first granted. In the 1780s, some of the women of Bishops Stortford, Hertfordshire, took advantage of an old Michaelmas custom to exercise their right to drink and be disorderly. On "Ganging Day," a large group assembled in the fields before roaming through the district and "bumping" anyone they met on their travels. This was "performed by two other persons taking them up by their arms, and swinging them against each other," according to an account of the custom in a Lon-

don newspaper that antiquarian John Brand quotes.[39] In a number
of parts of the country—Lancashire, Cheshire, Staffordshire, Warwickshire, and Shropshire—women practiced a very similar ritual of
"lifting" or "heaving" at Eastertide.[40] Thomas Loggan wrote to
Brand in 1799, describing his own experience of the custom at an
inn in Shrewsbury:

> I was sitting alone last Easter Tuesday at breakfast at the Tal-
> bot in Shrewsbury, when I was surprized by the entrance of all
> the female servants of the house handing in an arm chair, lined
> with white, and decorated with ribbons and favours of differ-
> ent colours. I asked them what they wanted: their answer was,
> they came to *heave* me. . . . It was impossible not to comply
> with a request very modestly made, and to a set of nymphs in
> their best apparel, and several of them under twenty. . . . The
> groupe then lifted me from the ground, turned the chair about,
> and I had the felicity of a salute from each. I told them, I
> supposed there was a fee due upon the occasion, and was an-
> swered in the affirmative; and, having satisfied the damsels in
> this respect, they withdrew to *heave* others.

Another of Brand's correspondents described "women's heaving-
day" in Warwickshire. "Many a time I have passed along the streets
inhabited by the lower orders of people, and seen parties of jolly
matrons assembled round a table on which stood a foaming tankard
of ale," he wrote. "There they sat in all the pride of absolute sover-
eignty, and woe to any luckless man that dared to invade their pre-
rogatives!—as sure as he was seen he was pursued—as sure as he
was pursued he was taken—and as sure as he was taken he was
heaved and kissed, and compelled to pay sixpence for 'leave and
license' to depart."[41]

THROUGH THE FABRIC OF THESE SEASONAL HOLIDAYS AND
festivals, these customary bouts of earthy, animal indulgence, sports
figured as a heightened expression and celebration of the sensual

and the physical. Malcolmson suggests that women were largely shut out of this aspect of popular recreation, but as Reekie and Allen Guttmann indicate, this rather overstates the case. At fairs and hirings and festivals, as well as on other occasions, girls and women played ball games such as cricket, stoolball, trap-and-ball, handball, and "folk" football. They ran in footraces and battled one another in prizefights, quarter-staff fights, and sword fights.[42]

Pasquil's Palinodia, a seventeenth-century poem that celebrates the joys of drink and "harmelesse honest mirth,"[43] identifies Shrove Tuesday as

> the day of all dayes in the yeare
> That unto Bacchus hath its dedication
>
> .   .   .   .
>
> When country wenches play with stoole and ball,
> And run at barley-breake untill they fall:
> And country lads fall on them, in such sort
> That after forty weekes they rew the sport.[44]

The associations continued in the eighteenth century. "Stool-Ball, or the Easter Diversion," from a 1719 book, *Wit and Mirth, or Pills to Purge Melancholy*, for example, waxes lyrical on the athletic "love-l[ies]" of the stoolball pitch:

> See at the goal Pulcheria stand
> And grasp the board with snowy hand!
> She drives the ball with artful force
> Guiding through hostile ranks its course.[45]

These representations of rustic female athletes had plenty of flesh and blood counterparts. Ball games were customarily played in the springtime, especially at Easter and on the pre-Lenten and Lenten holidays of Shrove Tuesday and Ash Wednesday, and stoolball has been considered almost exclusively a game for women. Sources also refer to challenge matches between teams of young women and young men, often for a prize of ale, cider, or "tansy cakes."[46] Blundell noted in his journal entry for May 14, 1715, that "the Young Folks of this town had a Merry-Night. The Young Weomen treated the Men with a Tandsey as they had lost to them at a game at Stoole Balle." Likewise, in a 1725 account of popular customs in Newcastle-upon-Tyne, Bourne documented an Easter "playing at Hand-Ball for a Tanzy-Cake" among the young people. Into the 1820s, the older women of Bury St. Edmund's in Suffolk still marked the Shrove Tuesday, Easter Monday, and Whitsuntide holidays with games of trap-and-ball. The twelve "combatants dexterously hurl[ed] the giddy ball to and fro," Hone's 1826 *Every-Day Book* relates. One woman, "named Gill, upwards of sixty years of age" had long enjoyed local renown as " 'the mistress of the sport.' " In 1850, in the Sussex village of West Tarring, women's stoolball was still a part of the community's recreations.[47]

Cricket, an athletic enterprise that in the Victorian period would be stamped the manliest of English sports, was in the eighteenth and early nineteenth centuries also a game for women. The earliest documented women's match was in 1745 between teams from the southern English villages of Bramley and Hambleton.[48] Representatives of the former (sporting blue hair ribbons) scored 119 "notches," the latter (in red ribbons) 127; both, according to the *Reading Mercury*, "bowled, batted, ran and catched [*sic*] as well as most men could do."[49] Like a number of other women's cricket games played from the 1740s to the 1830s, this one was well attended by spectators who paid for admission to the grounds and bet on the outcome. Newspapers and specialist sporting periodicals advertised upcoming women's matches, printed challenges from teams, and reported on the play and the money wagered, won, and lost.[50] In 1747, for example, the *London General Advertiser* announced a women's cricket tournament scheduled to be played on the Artillery Ground at Finnsbury near London to which teams from the villages of Westdean, Chilgrove, and Charlton in Sussex were invited. So large and enthusiastic was the gathering of spectators and gamblers assembled for the event that its organizers were unable to

maintain control and were forced to cut short the first day of competition when the crowd spilled onto the pitch. Play resumed and was
completed on the morning of the next day and the teams also played
a second game in the afternoon.[51] A 1768 three-game series by
women from Harting and Rogate (again, villages in Sussex) attracted
the same level of interest and enthusiasm, with crowd size for individual games estimated between two and three thousand people.
Robert Southey recorded a 1772 match arranged between a team of
eleven Hampshire women and twenty-two men, the purse for which
was an impressive five hundred pounds. At this level, cricket required the sponsorship and patronage of the aristocracy and was part
of the complex meeting of "patrician society and plebeian culture"
that occurred in other sports such as prizefighting and cockfighting.[52]
But women also played the game like their male counterparts and
stoolball players—as a local, communal affair for wagers of food and
drink: a pound of gingerbread, half a crown's worth of punch,[53] or "a
large plum-cake, a barrel of ale and regale of tea."[54] By the final
decades of the eighteenth century, women's cricket was beginning
to assume some of the characteristics that Guttmann, Melvin Adelman, and others have attributed to modern sport, such as quantifica-
tion, a preoccupation with statistics, and competition far beyond that
at the local level. On July 11, 1788, for instance, a Miss S. Norcross
scored the game's first recorded "century," and in 1793 a team from
Bury, Sussex, was confident enough of its cricketing prowess to issue
a challenge to "all England" through the pages of the *Times*.[55]

Football in its various modern codes was another sport that men
would make their own in the Victorian era, but in certain customary
forms it admitted women. They undoubtedly participated in some
of the rough, ranging games that were to be found before the nineteenth century (and into the 1840s and beyond in some places)
throughout the length and breadth of the British Isles. Football was
a widely variable game; one of its most characteristic features was
that it was something in which whole communities engaged, often
against "ancient" rivals. Contests between villages and parishes

were widespread and, in some of these, women claimed their place alongside male neighbors and kin: in Scarborough on the Yorkshire coast, for instance, women, men, and children played on the sands. Across the country in the northwestern town of Chester (and in Inveresk near Edinburgh, Scotland), meanwhile, women had their own game.[56]

The football of this period was only marginally less bloody than the animal sports that were a core element in popular culture, so it is not surprising to find a record of women's involvement in these, too. Indeed, structurally, some blood sports were very much like some local variants of football, entailing crowds of people chasing down, "playing" with, and driving an object (be it ball or bull) to a goal (the animal's death).[57] Bull-running was one of the most notorious of such sports, and a description of the annual event held in Stamford, Lincolnshire, vividly conveys its indiscriminate and tumultuous communality: "The bull is turned out . . . and then, hivie, skivy, rag-tag, men, women, and children, of all sorts and all sizes, with all the dogs in the town, promiscuously running after him with their bull-clubs, spattering dirt in each other's faces, that one would think them to be so many furies started out of hell." Presiding over all was a patroness, dressed in blue and wearing "a rare display of ribbons, and other insignia of her . . . office."[58]

A football game or a bull-running was the province of the crowd and women were caught up and immersed in the anonymity of this mass. But athletic and other contests just for women were a regular feature of the sports held at fairs and festivals. Footraces in which women competed for a prize of a smock were common, part of a varied menu that might include such diversions as climbing greasy poles, grinning and grimacing through horse collars, chasing pigs with soaped tails, and wrestling and cudgeling matches. "Smock races" ranged in distance from a few hundred yards to half a mile, a mile, or even farther, and young women and girls as well as older women competed. The Reverend James Woodforde documented the women's races that were part of the celebrations held in Castle

Cary, Somerset, for the anniversary of George III's coronation. "Great doings again to-day at Cary," he wrote for September 23, 1769: "At one o'clock there was a shift run for by women. There were five that started for it, and won by Willm. Francis's daughter Nan of Ansford—her sister Peg was second and therefore had ribbands. I never saw the Park so full of people in my life. The Women were to run the best of three half mile Heats: Nan Francis run a heat in three minutes."[59] The Hungerford (Wiltshire) Revel of 1825 offered a wider range of contests. In addition to smock races, there was a tea-drinking competition for "old women" with a prize of snuff for the one who could "drink it the quickest and hottest." There were also a "grinning" contest, at which the gentleman observing the sport felt old women were particularly adept, or "certainly . . . the most amusing," and a footrace between "twenty or thirty old women for a pound of tea." This "occasion[ed] much merriment," the same source continues, "and it [was] sometimes astonishing to see with what agility the old dames [ran] in order to obtain their favourite."[60] For some women, running was part of the regular flow of their work and play. The wife of one of Nicholas Blundell's tenants, Margarit Darby, literally ran frequent errands for him and on March 29, 1703, Blundell records that she "should have runn [a race] with Skinner Blundell."[61]

Almost without exception, these athletic contests were part of the fabric of rural, agrarian life, but some footraces and other sporting encounters between women took place in the city. James Pellor Malcolm gives an account of a race held in Pall Mall, London, in 1733, the prizes for which included a Holland smock, a cap, clocked stockings, and laced shoes. The contest "attracted an amazing number of persons," according to Malcolm.[62] In June 1744 a London newspaper announced a similar event between "The Little Bit of Blue (the Handsome Broom Girl)" and "Black Bess, of the Mint."[63]

Women also engaged in sports that may well have been unique to the city. In pugilism, the passions of rough, violent recreation shaded into the spectacle and display of a commercialized, professional sport culture that was emerging in London in the early part of the eighteenth century. Centered on long-established venues such as the bear-garden (a venue for bear-baiting contests) at Hockley-in-the-Hole, Clerkenwell, and newer ones like James Figg's Amphitheatre in Oxford Street, opened in 1719, these "rude sports" boasted some doughty female fighters.[64] For instance, Elizabeth Wilkinson of Clerkenwell and Hannah Hyfield of Newgate Market, "having had some words," arranged to box one another on the stage at Hockley-in-the-Hole in 1722 for a prize of three guineas. Attired in "close jackets, short petticoats, holland drawers, white stockings and pumps," the two "fought for a long time to the general satisfaction of the spectators."

In this age the distance between a bout of alcohol-fueled fisticuffs and a prearranged fight was not far (indeed, the latter was often merely a more formal continuation of the former), and some women willingly traveled that distance. Some were also proficient enough to earn at least part of their living through doing so. In 1725, for instance, Figg's Amphitheatre staged fights between "Sutton, the champion of Kent, and a Kentish woman," and James and Elizabeth—"his much admired consort"—Stokes of London. The prizes were "£40 to be given to the male and female who gave [the] most cuts with the sword, and £20 for [the] most blows with a quarter-staff, besides the collection in the box." The following year, two Irish fighters, Robert Barker and Mary Walsh, issued the typically colorful and bombastic challenge of their profession to the Stokes duo. "Having often contaminated our swords in the abdominous corporations of such antagonists as have had the insolence to dispute our skill," they declared, "[we] do find ourselves once more necessitated to challenge, defy, and invite Mr. Stokes and his bold Amazonian virago to meet us on the stage." The wager was for twenty guineas, put up by an "honourable lord of [the] nation," and the purse and the "benefit of the house" were to go to "they that give the most cuts." "If swords, daggers, quarter staff, fury, rage and resolution will prevail," Barker and Walsh promised, "our friends will not meet with a disappointment."[65]

Elizabeth Stokes also had a solo career as a prizefighter. In October 1728 she accepted a challenge from Ann Field, an ass-driver of Stoke Newington, to box for a purse of £10. "I do assure her," Stokes stated, "that the blows which I shall present her with will be more difficult for her to digest than any she ever gave her asses."[66]

IT IS DIFFICULT TO SAY HOW RARE AN EVENT A PRIZEFIGHT involving women was; probably it was not commonplace. Yet it was in the context of the ordinary and everyday that women found much of their leisure. This has left less extensive impressions in the historical record, but there are traces to be found.

Interludes of gossiping, socializing, drinking, and dancing broke up and enlivened women's working days and weeks. Bamford relates how, in the late eighteenth century, the women of Middleton gathered in the mornings at a house in the village to wait for the milk to be brought in from neighboring farms. "A dozen or so married women" and "two or three young ones" whiled the time away by circulating "some snatches of scandal . . . sly insinuations respecting 'this body's character,' and 'that body's conduct.' " Some treated "themselves and neighbours to snuff" or to a "whiff or so of tobacco, 'just to keep the wind off.' " Meanwhile, the mistress of the house "sat croning at her wheel, and her daughter, a flashy lass, was on her loom weaving napkins, and singing love ditties like a nightingale." At the end of the workday, the aunt with whom Bamford lived would set her spinning wheel aside, "take a pinch of snuff, hutch her chair towards the . . . hob," and entertain the children with "fearful tales of witches, spirits, and apparitions."[67]

Drinking tea or coffee or dining with a fellow servant, neighbor, or, in some households, the master or mistress was a small pleasure to be taken during the day. The memoirs of John Macdonald (1745–1779), a footman, tell of the tea parties he shared with female servants and other women of his station. Similarly, the landlady of a public house or a woman who let rooms might sit down to coffee, tea, or something a little stronger with her clientele or lodgers, or accompany them on an evening out. Carl Philip Moritz, a German visitor to England, was gratified to be invited to drink coffee with his landlady at a small, "homely" inn in Tideswell, Derbyshire, during his travels in 1782. He was all the more so because, up to that point as a foot traveler, he had met with very cool, indeed often hostile, treatment from innkeepers. Sylas Neville drank tea and porter with his London landlady on one sojourn in the city in 1767, despite finding her a "grossly ignorant" woman.[68] At another time he escorted his housekeeper, Sally, and her landlady to Sadlers Wells, although, again, he was disdainful of the company he was in and the crowd there, noting in his diary, "what odd beings the ignorant vulgar are!"[69]

There appears to have been less social and cultural distance between Thomas Turner and his maidservants, who often drank tea with him and his wife and had friends, relatives, and sweethearts over for dinner or supper at the house. Female servants also managed to arrange more intimate meetings with their lovers in the households in which they worked, though they risked dismissal if they were caught doing so. Thomas Wright remembers a maidservant "having sweethearts attending her" at his grandmother's house when her mistress was absent, and he himself once accompanied a neighboring man on a similar tryst. Wright "passed part of the night" with the daughter of the house after the family had retired to bed, while his friend "wooed the maid." For even as evidently tolerant and good-humored a master as Nicholas Blundell, assignations of this sort were too much. "I found Mary Holme & Henry Bourne in the Gatehous Chamber about four in the Morning for which I turned her out of my service," he records for December 1, 1713. Likewise, Mary Hardy dismissed both her maidservants in January 1778, "for raking with Fellows and other misdemeaners."[70]

But female servants seem to have enjoyed a fair degree of recreational agency, the demands of work and their employers' moral codes notwithstanding. They paid overnight visits to friends, held dances and parties in the evening in their own or neighboring households, or at alehouses and inns, and visited commercial places of entertainment such as playhouses. In May 1715, for example, Nicholas Blundell's maidservant Betty Latham "went to Aintry to stay a Night or two, to take leave of her Friends." On August 16, 1719, Nelly Howerd, his wife's maid, "went to lodge at Darby upon account of some Merriment as is to be there," and in June 1712 Blundell, his wife, and two of their maids went to Liverpool together to attend a stage play. On January 26, 1756, Thomas Turner recorded in his diary: "Tonight there was a dance, made, I conject by the servants, there being all the young people of both sexes in the parish." One of Turner's servants celebrated New Year's Eve of 1761 by staying "out all night a-dancing." Likewise, Mary Hardy's diary for April 1789 records that as part of the general thanksgiving held for George III's recovery from one of his bouts of mental illness, "a few young people" of the town "met in the Shirehouse and had a dance." Sylas Neville, though mortified by his entanglement with his housekeeper, was also violently jealous and possessive of her. Nonetheless, she still managed to slip away on occasion to enjoy herself in other company—as she did one night in July 1771, prompting Neville to fume: "Wednesday night [Sally] Russell broke her promise by dancing at an improper place & this day used me very ill. God knows when & how I shall get rid of my embarrassments." In the 1770s the peripatetic John Macdonald shared in a busy social life of balls and parties among the gentry servant class. Macdonald hosted balls for friends and fellow servants, male and female, providing them with suppers, wines, and spirits and entertaining them with hired musicians. At similar affairs given by others, Macdonald enjoyed country dances, cards, and drinking.[71]

In an age when the general consumption of alcohol was high, women regularly indulged in ale and liquor, and often did so freely if Thomas Turner's diary is any indication. "Dame Durrant," wife of the local blacksmith, was very partial to a little tipple. Of an entertainment hosted by Turner's neighbors in January 1760, the diarist commented, "We came home about 3.20 [A.M.] and thank God very sober, as was all the company (except Dame Durrant)." And again, for Friday, October 29, 1762, Turner writes: "[Dame Durrant], Tho., Mr. Tipper and Sam. Jenner drank tea with me. I gave the good woman also a little of that which she esteems of more value than gold, ay, of that delicious cordial, Mrs. Nant's [brandy]." "When there is too much [of that sweet delicious relish] taken," Turner judged, "it renders the most agreeable part of the creation mere brute creatures, as is too often this poor woman's case." The wife of the local excise officer, George Banister, was likewise rather fond of the brandy to which her husband had ready access. Her drinking was obviously a source of tension in their marriage, which Turner and others in the community occasionally stepped in to defuse. For Friday, June 1, 1764, Turner wrote: "In the even Mr. Banister and myself smoked a pipe or two with Tho. Durrant, purely to keep Mr. Banister from quarrelling, his wife big with child, lame of one hand and very much in liquor, being out in the middle of the street at tennis among a parcel of girls, boys etc." Drunken and rowdy behavior was not confined to women (or, indeed, men) of any particular social stratum in Turner's community. On Sunday, September 26, 1756, he records that "about 9 in the evening we were all alarmed by a drunken travelling woman, swearing and rolling about the street," but on many more occasions he witnessed village women of no mean rank in a similar state. There are numerous accounts in Turner's diary of parties at which "downright obstreperous mirth mixed with a great deal of folly and stupidity" continued from early evening to early morning and beyond, and at which the good dames of the community were among the most raucous of the inebriates. Turner describes how, at one gathering, "our diversion was dancing (or jumping about) without a violin or any music, singing of foolish and bawdy healths and more such-like stupidity, and drinking all the time as fast as could be well poured down." Included in this party were the vicar, the Reverend Thomas Porter, a local trades-

According to Hannah More's Cheap Repository Tracts, *the "good mother" raised her daughters not to be frivolous, flaunting minxes whose love of worldly pleasures would lead them to ruin. From Hannah More,* Cheap Repository Tracts, *courtesy of Special Collections, University of Iowa Library.*

man, a prosperous farmer, several gentlemen, and their wives. At dawn the next day, while Turner and his wife were recovering from the effects of the night before, Mrs. Porter and her husband, together with the local butcher and his wife, arrived, still drunk. Having persuaded Mrs. Turner to join them in another drinking session, Mrs. Porter led the group in a high-spirited assault on Turner. They drew "me out of bed," Turner complained in his diary. "Instead of my clothes, they gave me time to put on my wife's petticoat. In this manner they made me dance with them without shoes or stockings untill they had emptied their bottle of wine and also a bottle of my beer." This "drunken perambulation" continued until about half past three in the afternoon, when the revelers all finally "found their ways to their respective homes."[72]

THROUGHOUT THE EIGHTEENTH AND INTO THE NINETEENTH centuries, then, the popular recreational culture of England allowed women a fair degree of license with respect to the forms their amusements took and the manner in which they took them. In the "almost Rabelaisian atmosphere," their hedonism and high spirits met little check.[73] Women expected to be able to feast, drink, and disport themselves on public holidays, during seasonal festivals, at fairs, and in the hiatuses of their working lives. And it seems that they managed to do so without too much hindrance.

This evident tolerance makes sense in the context of the benign paternalism that the eighteenth-century governing classes liked to believe characterized their relationship with the lower orders. Indeed, it was an essential element of the cultural theater that played out and supported their hegemony. Eighteenth-century pastoral literature used the imagery of rustic, sporting "nymphs" to the same end that landscapists of the period did. The "nubile women and girls stripped for action," the "beauteous maids" who played stoolball and other games, and the "willing swains" who watched them were elements of a picture that John Barrell indicates the upper ranks favored. In this they saw themselves "as thoroughly tolerant

and good-humoured in their relations with the vulgar" and the nation as a quintessentially "Merry England," a "Happy Britannia."[74]
The libidinous overtones of this literature indicate the frank sexual
license that was also associated with women's recreational culture.
Erotic play was commonly understood as part of the fun of springtime customs such as mayings and stoolball, as Henry Bourne's qual-
ifiedly optimistic comments on the latter suggest: the game "is
generally practised and I would hope practiced with Harmlessness
and Innocence." The statistical profile of illegitimate births in eighteenth-century Westminster, London, belies such hopes. Nicholas
Rogers's analysis of these figures points to an increase in sexual intercourse over Christmastime, at Easter and Whitsun, and in late
August and early September, when St. Bartholomew's Fair was
held.[75] That such license could take frighteningly illicit shape the
infamous "cock and hen clubs" of the capital affirmed. On March 7,
1775, George Christoph Lichtenberg recorded in his travel journal
that "a club, which used to meet on Tuesdays in Wych Street, was
dissolved." The club "consisted of servants, journeymen, and apprentices," each of whom paid fourpence an evening "for which he
had music and a female gratis." "Twenty of the girls were brought
before Sir John Fielding [the magistrate]; the beauty of some of
them aroused general admiration." Francis Place remembered cock
and hen clubs as a popular and ubiquitous institution among the
young working people of London in the last few decades of the
eighteenth century, merely a more libertine manifestation of a popular recreational culture that allowed much that, in the nineteenth
century, would be proscribed.[76]

There are intimations of this more refined sensibility in the critical tone that some adopted in their observations on particular customs in the final decades of the eighteenth century. A woman's
presence could strike one as a disturbing measure of the mob's
drunken disorderliness. The woman who headed the procession of
Stamford bullards (supporters of bull-running at Stanford) was "a
bold virago stout and tall," who "by close of day generally imbibe[d]

so much of the inspiring spirit of Sir John Barleycorn, as to make her fully verify the words of Hamlet, *viz.*—'Frailty, thy name is woman.' "[77] A woman who observed ganging day in Bishops Stortford likewise risked being marked as a termagant. "The women in general keep at home at this period," a London newspaper noted, "except those of less scrupulous character." They, "for the sake of partaking of a gallon of ale and a plumb-cake, which every landlord or publican is obliged to furnish the revellers with, generally spend the best part of the night in the fields" sharing in "the cheer."[78] A 1784 witness to the custom of lifting in Manchester viewed it in the same light. It was "a rude, indecent, and dangerous diversion, practised chiefly by the lower class of people" that "the women of late years have converted . . . into a money job."[79] Disapprobation of women who cut loose and claimed the license to revel and roister was hardly unique to the 1780s and 1790s, of course. Daniel Defoe was disgusted by the enthusiasm for misbehaving that women showed when he attended Horn Fair in 1742. "The Mob take all kinds of Liberties," he groused. "And the Women are especially impudent that Day; as if it was a Day that justified the giving themselves a Loose to all manner of Indecency without any Reproach, or without incurring the Censure which such Behaviour would deserve at another time."[80] But by century's end, censures on plebeian and working-class women's leisure habits seem to have become more frequent and more severe. This may have been part of a broader shift in understanding and articulation of gender and class that some historians judge to have approached a crisis precipitated by the tumultuous and broad-reaching changes of the period. No matter its intensity, no matter the precipitating forces, no matter whether it was a long or short time coming, the late eighteenth-century assault on popular recreational culture marks an important development in the history of women's leisure.[81]

Circumstances were propitious. The spiritual and moral sensibilities of religious dissenters and Anglicans alike came together with the economic imperatives of an ascendant industrial capitalism and a rising tide of progressivism, reformism, and general earnestness to produce a climate hostile to some of popular culture's most basic features. Earlier moral improvement initiatives had included societies for the reformation of manners (1692–1738 and 1757–1766), and from the late eighteenth century there was a renewal of this kind of activity. A Royal Proclamation for the Encouragement of Piety and Virtue was issued in 1787, and 1802 saw the establishment of the Society for the Suppression of Vice. Magistrates, justices of the peace, and the new police force vigorously licensed, prosecuted, and jailed in an attempt to promote the moral elevation of the nation. The common people's assumed propensity for idleness, drinking, and dissolution became an accepted tenet of political and economic theories and justification for the suppression of those institutions and establishments that catered to these wants. Alehouses were closed, fairs were suppressed, wakes and other customary holidays were "tamed."[82]

The evangelical revival of the eighteenth century, in both its establishment and dissenting forms, provided much of the energy fueling this assault. Sensing a malaise within Protestantism itself, and fearful of the widespread, deep moral crisis they perceived in the nation as a whole, evangelicals set themselves to the task of stemming "the tide of wickedness." The way out of the spiritual morass was to seek personal salvation through repentance and faith, through moral reformation. Consumed with securing salvation and avoiding sin, constantly on guard against the temptations of the world, and fearful of succumbing to the appetites of the flesh, evangelicals shared a general antipathy toward recreation. Anything that inflamed the passions or gratified the senses was morally dangerous and thus to be avoided, for even the most innocent-seeming amusement might detract from the individual's pursuit of a state of grace or lead her or him into sin. Evangelicals subjected their own lives to constant and rigorous scrutiny, abjuring levity, indolence, and time wasting, assiduously measuring and marking their progress along the path to grace.[83] They were also indefatigable spiritual missionaries to the masses whom they believed to be especially in need of moral reformation. Wesleyan Methodists carried the joyous message of the possibility of salvation through faith alone to communities notorious for their "vice and wickedness," reaching out to the poor, the dispossessed, the "unchurched" whom the established church failed to touch.[84]

Despite the various forms that evangelicalism took and the limits of its formal influence among working people, certain common, central tenets set it in direct opposition to popular recreational culture. Forward-looking, reformist, preoccupied with sin and salvation, suspicious of worldly pleasures, concerned about the need for social and self-discipline and with the way in which individuals conducted their private lives, evangelical morality represented the forces of enlightenment and progress. Popular culture, on the other hand, harbored, celebrated even, the unregenerate, the hedonist, and the sinner; consequently, from the 1730s onward it became a focal point of evangelical campaigns to reform both private and public life. There were a number of obvious targets for attack. Customary sports, many of them involving ritualized violence against animals, were highly offensive to evangelical sensibilities on any number of counts: their appeal to the basest of human passions, their wanton and irrational destruction of life, their association with general disorder and tumult, heavy drinking, and wagering. Bull-baiting and -running and cock-throwing and -fighting were the first to be subjected to prohibitive legislation, but traditional games such as quoits, skittles, pitch and toss, football, and hurling and combat sports such as wrestling were also suppressed. The seasonal and other holidays within which such practices were enmeshed, the feast days, fair days, and market days, and the rowdy, drunken reveling and carnivalesque license that marked them underwent similar scrutiny and attracted similar hostility. Cards, dancing, the theater, drinking, and vanity in dress and personal appearance: all these amusements and diversions were proscribed.[85]

Especially opprobrious was the involvement of women in such

activities. The "many young women" who "had cast off all appearance of decency and order" to participate in the 1829 Stamford bull-running must have been a truly awful spectacle to evangelicals. The dissenting sects of the eighteenth and early nineteenth centuries had rendered certain aspects of gender identity more fluid and offered women an unusually public voice and role. By the end of the eighteenth century, however, among evangelicals of all persuasions, increasingly conservative notions of femininity and masculinity and of appropriate religious, social, and cultural roles for women and men were becoming entrenched. Even among the practitioners and preachers of "cottage religion," many of whom were young women who had cut themselves off from families to pursue their vocation, traditional gender arrangements ultimately prevailed. And while millenarian prophetesses such as Joanna Southcott claimed boundless authority, both spiritual and moral, including authority over men, their influence and renown were fleeting. Ultimately, among the predominant trends of the evangelical revival of the period that would have a long-lasting impact was the elevation of patriarchal order and a concomitant expectation of female subservience. Other major themes were the valorization of domesticity and the assertion of women's superior—if fragile—morality. These tendencies came together with evangelicals' suspicion and fear of the venal, corrupt world and distaste for the excesses of plebeian customary pastimes to contract the leisure culture of the morally earnest or pious working woman around her home, family, and chapel society or church congregation.[86]

SOME SCHOLARS HAVE POSITIONED UPPER-CLASS EVANGELICALS in the vanguard of this movement, paramount among them Hannah More.[87] More launched her assault on popular culture on two fronts: her missions to the "savage," "depraved," and "brutal" inhabitants of the Mendip Hills, in Cheshire, begun in 1789 and the *Cheap Repository for Moral and Religious Tracts (CRT)*, written and published between 1795 and 1798. In both spheres, women were a special focus of More's attention; her purpose was to "prepare [them] to be good wives and good mothers, as well as good Christians." The *CRT* offered as exemplars those whose "modesty, sobriety," and good "reputation" qualified them for this estimable standing, and offered cautionary tales of those whose moral weakness and folly condemned them to earthly misery and eternal damnation. The Mendip mission was a frontline engagement with the forces within popular culture that inclined women toward one or the other of these destinies.[88]

"What, then, causes the poor to fall?" Idleness, as Susan Pedersen shows in her analysis of the moral content of the *CRT*. For the poor wife and mother, idleness was a failing that destroyed her own family and set a disastrous example for her children. "The Two Shoemakers," "Sorrowful Sam," and "The Good Mother's Legacy" offer portraits of idle, gossiping, slatternly wives and their antitheses, and the deserved fates of each. Mrs. Williams, the wife of a master shoemaker, is an "idle and dirty," "quarelling" creature who winds up in the parish poorhouse. Susan Waters, wife of "Sorrowful Sam," "loves work as little as [her husband]." "She is a lazy, dirty, gossiping body" whose unclean and unkempt children she leaves to run wild. They all "turned out very badly," made "more wicked by her own example." Mrs. Adams, in contrast, the eponymous "Good Mother," lives a life that is "a daily lesson of instruction" marked by piety, unwearied industry, and religiosity. When she has an occasional hour's leisure in the evenings, she uses it to "instruct her servants and children" by gathering them around the fire to read testaments and sermons while mending and making the family linen.[89]

If idleness offered a vacancy into which women's weaknesses poured, popular amusements positively inflamed their worst passions. More saw in too many married women an unfortunate predilection for evils such as drinking that carried them away from the sober discharge of their duties. A good mother such as Mrs. Adams was singular in her temperance: she "never went to drink a dram when her marketing was over, as is but too customary." Vigilant on her own behalf, she was thus able—for the most part—to guide her daughters away from the dangers that lurked in the tankard and in the dance, at the feast and at the fair. Her children "were never present at any revelling or merry-making in the parish; and as a reward for their dutiful behaviour, she often made some little entertainment for them at home." No killjoy, then, was the good mother, but rather a wise guide to innocent enjoyment. Though she "love[d] to see young people cheerful and happy," she "tremble[d] to have them dancing in alehouses, which takes away their modesty—or getting drunk, which turns them into brutes—or profanely cursing and swearing to the endangering of their immortal souls." The various fortunes of Mrs. Adams's three daughters confirmed these truths: "by first yielding to small sins," she warned the unfortunate Betsey, "you will be led on to fall into even greater ones, and for the indulgence of a worldly pleasure, you may endanger your mortal soul." And so Betsey did. She "imprudently" took up with the servants of a wealthy, extravagant gentleman and lady whose household lived "as though there were no duties in this world, and no God in the next." The lady's maid, "a very dressy, flaunty body," a "tawdry minx," tempted Betsey with tales of the wonderful life that the servants in such families enjoyed in London, that by-word for corrupt delights. They "often had more pleasure than their masters and mistresses." They had their "card-parties in the hall; sometimes a dance; sometimes a concert"; and they told her, "you have a very pretty voice, Betsey . . . you will be vastly admired among us; besides, our butler is half in love with you already." Poor Betsey, her mother's careful upbringing and warnings were all for naught. In this sinful company that "made it quite a pastime" to "laugh [her] out of [her] religion," she succumbed to the blandishments of the butler, who soon cast her out to starve along with her child. In the depths of winter she found her sorry way home in time for a death-bed repentance and reunion with her family. Betsey's more sensible sisters avoided the snares of worldly amusements to which she fell

prey. Mary, "by being kept out . . . of evil company . . . was pre-
served from falling into those temptations which prove the ruin of
so many young women." Her dress was "neat, modest, and suitable
to her station." She spurned the "ruffles and flounces, long-tailed
gowns, and . . . hair curled half way down the back" that were the
downfall of others. Like Betsey West in "The Two Shoemakers,"
whose "excellent character" and "modest appearance" won her the
excellent James Stock as a husband, Mary thrived. So, too, did Mrs.
Adams's other daughter, Susan. "Sober, diligent, and faithful," she
went into service with a family of very good repute and, abjuring the
"flaunty gowns and caps" upon which "many young servants"
wasted their wages, secured a modestly comfortable life.[90]

More and her sister Martha cajoled, hectored, manipulated, and
organized the women in the communities scattered through the
Mendip Hills into giving up the ways of the Williamses, the Wa-
terses, and the Betsey Adamses, and following those of Mrs. Adams
and her two exemplary daughters. The mothers of the children who
attended the Mores' Sunday schools regularly received lectures on
their "vices and faults." "Neglect of sending the children sufficiently early" was a particularly shameful trait that provoked tirades
from the benevolent ladies: "Have you no concern, I may say shame,
that we are here from such a distance in all weathers, and often find
too many absent at nine o'clock?" Gossiping was another: "There
are still too many of you who have not yet discovered that a prating
tongue commonly slanders an innocent neighbour." "The intolerable gossiping and idle slander at . . . the bake-house, by a few idle
women, are sufficient to set a whole village together by the ears."
Self-examination might help the transgressors reform: "Let every
woman . . . say to herself, Have I watched over my evil tempers?
Have I indulged in any sinful language? Have I set my child a bad
example of pride, passion, or laziness?" With reform came the com-
pliments that the Mores were pleased to give when deserved—
though, on balance, their condemnations seemed to overwhelm
these. As inducements for the women of the Mendips to behave

themselves, the Mores set up, in association with the Sunday schools, clubs modeled on friendly societies and burial societies. Their innovation was to grant "a marriage-portion" to any "girl bred in the school, who continues, when grown up, to attend its instructions, and has married in the past year with a fair character (a rare event)." The gift was "five shillings, a pair of white stockings, and a new Bible." The sisters railed against young women attending "lewd plays" and engaging in "licentious" dancing. Of the latter, they insisted: "it must always be improper, but in the midst of religious institutions, societies, and schools it is particularly indecent and abominable." They organized events so that they could "avoid the indecency of women appearing at a public-house." They remonstrated with those who were "drawn aside by the temptation of improper company." They rejoiced at any sign of "improvement in the women's dress, as well as deportment." They breathed a sigh of relief when they could observe that "the fair just over . . . passed off with unusual quiet amongst the young people."[91]

Susan Pedersen suggests that Hannah More's missionary work and moral propagandizing prefigured the rational recreation schemes of upper- and middle-class Victorians.[92] But she was only one figure—albeit a notorious one—and like others she adapted to more elevated ends elements that were already an established part of popular culture. Decades before the publication of the *CRT* and long before the Mendip schemes, plebeian women were seeking out sober and improving social intercourse, especially those who had close religious affiliations. Attending church or chapel, teaching in a Sunday school, or walking out to listen to an alfresco sermon delivered by an itinerant preacher might well have been a recreational activity as well as a duty. Peggy Turner went to church with her maidservants and family, as did Mary Hardy, who took great interest in the quality and scriptural sources of the numerous sermons she heard, both in the establishment church and in dissenting chapels. As Moritz observed on his travels in 1782, congregations met in places of worship not simply for divine service but for social purposes. In Nettlebed, Oxfordshire, the villagers' custom of assembling in the church on Sunday afternoons, simply to make music and listen to the choir singing psalms, charmed him greatly. Deborah Valenze has demonstrated how thoroughly popular evangelicalism thus intertwined with popular culture, enriching the lives of its adherents, drawing on and adding to the passion and boisterousness of plebeian customs with its love feasts and camp meetings, its ranting preachers and female revivalists. The theater of religious dissent promised enough entertainment to draw establishment churchgoers and the merely curious, as well as the pious. On a Sunday afternoon in June 1763, for instance, Thomas Turner's Anglican maidservant, together with two female friends, went "to hear a clergyman (lately curate of Laughton but now become a field preacher) where there was . . . a pretty large congregation." Women were dominant figures in cottage religion, as preachers and members of congregations, and in early industrial centers such as Belper, Derbyshire. Primitive Methodism in particular provided young, unmarried women with a supportive communal and cultural life. For committed female members, such religious groups formed relatively enduring structures for social intercourse, an inherent aspect of ostensibly devotional and educational activity. Sarah Mayett was one. She first took up with her husband, Joseph, when she joined the small Baptist group of which he was already a member, and for a while ran the Sunday school with him. After the couple married they met together in their homes with others from the congregation, and Joseph Mayett, at any rate, chose to remember these as times "when we never were so happy . . . when we were together and we Could say the candle of the Lord Shone round about us."[93]

The women workers who came together in friendly societies also built a consciously reformed leisure culture. Anna Clark has examined records for these organizations from the late eighteenth century to the 1840s, mostly in London but also in the provinces. Of the sum total of London friendly societies registered in 1794, fifteen percent were women's, concentrated in areas and occupations with high levels of female employment. A similar pattern existed in textile-producing regions of the country where there were large numbers of female operatives. Thus, in Stockport, one third of the friendly societies established between 1794 and 1823 were for women, and in Nottinghamshire, Lancashire, Cheshire, and Leicester in the mid-1820s, female associations constituted 16, 18, 27, and 35 percent of the total number, respectively. These organizations provided important financial aid and mutual support in times of difficulty such as sickness and they offered regular opportunities for socializing and drinking. Clubs usually met on a monthly basis in public houses to conduct business and collect dues, and they held annual dinners and feasts, often during the Whitsun holiday. They set clear limits on the behavior of their membership and excluded anyone whose reputation had been compromised or who engaged in low-status occupations such as street vending. Rules typically demanded "decency," "good order," and "moral decorum" while proscribing drunkenness, fighting, and swearing; members whose infirmity or sickness was the consequence of "intemperance or vicious life" were not allowed to claim benefits. The Oxton (Nottinghamshire) Female Union Society, for example, required members to attend its annual Whit-Monday feast. On that occasion the society stipulated that members should "proceed to church in a decent, sober manner, to hear divine service, or forfeit sixpence; and when divine service is over . . . return in the same order to the society's rooms." Friendly societies mirrored and meshed with the broader culture of plebeian recreation, but they tolerated a narrower spectrum of female behavior, emphasizing order and decorum, and requiring at least outward signs of religiosity. That they had to work to achieve this is hinted at in the detail of some of their rules, which suggest that a rich variety of "mis-behavior" could be expected even of women of "good" repute. As Clark observes, "one can only imagine why the Fore Street Society" insisted that "no member shall commit any indecent act with the victuals" at its annual feast![94]

In the early to mid-nineteenth century, this more restrained culture gained ground, and nowhere more so than among the secular radicals and reformers of the working classes. Central to this was a preoccupation with order, and women were high on the list of those to be ordered; their behavior, demeanor, social and familial roles, responsibilities, and relationships were all grist for the mill. The next chapter examines this re-visioning and remaking of working-class leisure.

Chapter Two

RE-VISIONING AND REMAKING POPULAR RECREATIONAL CULTURE IN THE EARLY TO MID-NINETEENTH CENTURY

*B*Y THE END OF THE EIGHTEENTH CENTURY POPULAR recreation found itself assailed from every side: by evangelicals who abhorred its hedonism and excess, by employers who wanted their work people sober and productive instead of rowdy and recalcitrant, by reformers of every stripe who attacked its atavism and degradations. Much of this opposition came from the upper and middle classes, but significant groups of working people also had their own concerns about the manner in which amusements were and should be taken. During the early and mid-Victorian periods these reformers constructed a vision of recreation that set them foursquare against the dissolution, dissipation, and disorder with which popular pastimes were often associated. That vision emphasized self-improvement, respectability, and order: in short, rational recreation.[1]

Among the things that proponents of rational recreation attempted to order were women and gender. They delineated the preferred relationships between women and men, endorsed particular ways of women's and men's being and behaving, and assigned specific duties, responsibilities, and roles to women and men. In so

doing they lay down the threads of the dominant ideological framework within which working-class women of the Victorian and
Edwardian periods shaped and experienced their leisure.[2] The main
elements of this were female subservience and self-sacrifice, dependence and domesticity, and decency and respectability. But there
were alternative notions of how the recreational culture of the people might be reformed, too. These challenged some of the basic
tenets of the patriarchal order, spoke of and aspired to gender mutuality and egalitarianism, and offered women the possibility of claim-
ing a right to and sharing equally in the resources necessary for
leisure. There also persisted a defiantly unregenerate strain of
amusements, one that was rooted in the past and that retained the
hedonism, earthiness, and disorder that the advocates of rational recreation rejected. These various visions of working-class leisure are
the focus of this chapter.

THE REJECTION OF POPULAR RECREATIONAL CULTURE EXPRESSED
in eighteenth-century evangelicalism was something that allied
pious and morally earnest plebeians with the otherwise antitheti-
cally inclined secular radicals of the first decades of the Victorian
period. It is striking to note the consonance between Hannah More's
fulminations against women's vain and dangerous pursuit of pleasures and amusement and those of the radical William Cobbett, for
example. His checklist for the key virtues that a young man should
look for in a wife might have come directly from the pages of one
of More's tracts: chastity, sobriety, industry, frugality, cleanliness,
knowledge of domestic affairs, and good temper. "Skipping, caper-
ing, romping, [and] rattling" were fine for girls, he wrote, but when
they began to think about marriage, "it [was] time for them to cast
away the levity of the child." A woman who was "vain of her person,
very fond of dress, fond of flattery at all, given to gadding about,
fond of . . . parties of pleasure, or coquetish, though in the least
degree," promised to be a disastrous wife. To that kind of woman,
simple domestic life would never be sufficient and home would be

"merely a biding place, whence to sally in search of enjoyments."
At home such a woman would be "a dull, melancholy, moping
thing." More frightening still was a woman who relished her drink,
who tipped it off "with an appetite, and . . . a smack of her lips."
She was "fit for nothing but a brothel." "There was never a woman
who loved strong drink," Cobbett charged, "who was chaste, if the
opportunity of being the contrary presented itself to her." Vain
women promised to make woeful wives, too, so the wise man would
avoid those who preferred "the showy to the useful, the gay and the
fragile to the less sightly and more durable." And to be sure of not
being saddled with a "dirty, sluttish wife," a "sloven in one thing
[who would prove] a sloven in all things," Cobbett suggested that
the prospective bridegroom should check behind a woman's ears, or
"glance at her poll [nape]" for dirt. These precautions taken, a man
might anticipate that his wife would be able to furnish him with the
"constantly clean board, well cooked victuals," the "house in
order," the "cheerful fire" that he deserved.[3]

To give Cobbett his due, he was also exacting in his expectations
of husbands' virtues, and his sentiments in this regard aligned him
with many of his fellow radicals of the period. These, too, consciously turned their faces against certain aspects of lower-class culture, namely, the exclusionary, masculinist, and often-misogynist
spirit and customs of some of its strains. Anna Clark has argued that
this renunciation of long-standing elements of artisan, radical, and
plebeian life and associated embracing of a more inclusive, and improving, model was a rhetorical and political strategy employed by
working men to articulate and justify their demands for a place in
the body politic.[4] To achieve these ends, male radicals had to be able
to voice the grievances of a wider community of working people, a
community that extended to include women. And they had to for-
mulate an agenda for change that held the promise of improving
women's lives also.

For women in the early nineteenth century, the "pot-house" (alehouse) and libertine amusements of the bachelor subculture in

which many men (whether or not they were married) indulged contributed greatly to domestic unhappiness and the violence and sexual exploitation they suffered. Consequently, litanies of women's grievances and manifestos for ameliorating their lot frequently focused on these leisure places and practices. The most radical campaign against male pot-house culture was that mounted by socialist followers of Robert Owen in the 1820s to 1840s, and especially after 1834, when, with the collapse of the Grand Consolidated and Trades' Union, leisure rather than work became the most important sphere of socialist activism. Central to the Owenite vision of a New World was a model of popular culture built around gender egalitarianism. In the pages of the *Pioneer* and other periodicals, these early socialist feminists attacked the unequal division of labor and leisure resources in lower-class families. If it pleased a married man to do so, noted one critic, he could spend half his wages indulging himself; his wife, meanwhile, worked from morning till night keeping house. "She is bearing children, and suffering all the pangs of labour, and all the exhaustion of suckling; she is cooking, and washing, and cleaning; soothing one child, cleaning another, and feeding a third." Yet all this counted as "nothing." "She gets no wages. Her wages come from her husband; they are optional; he can give her either twenty shillings to keep house with, or he can give her only ten. . . . And it is high treason in women to resist such authority, and claim the privilege of a fair reward of their labours." To some Owenites, the relationship between working women and their husbands was as tyrannical as that between workers and masters under capitalism— "even the unionists themselves who rail against tyrants and oppressors, have the blood of the aristocrat flowing in their veins," declared one.[5] The *Pioneer* encouraged married women to assert their rights as equal partners with husbands, and supported the right of unmarried female workers to earn a living wage and be included in the union movement.

Making leisure a companionate, family affair was a crucial part of that re-structuring of working-class gender relations, which Owenites saw as a necessary preliminary to establishing socialism. Consequently, they promoted heterosocial gatherings and amusements in which all—women and children, as well as men—could participate and from which all would derive pleasure and edification, rather than exclusively male gatherings and "sottings" in public houses and club rooms. Owenites established Social Institutions, which provided "public rooms wherein the working class might assemble with their wives and children to acquire and communicate useful knowledge, and wherein they might have innocent recreation and rational amusement at so trifling an expense as to be within the means of the poorest."[6] The Worcester Social Institution was one of the first of these family-oriented facilities, and by 1842 there were more than two dozen other similar ventures, the grandest of which boasted rooms capable of holding over two thousand people, kitchens, cloak-rooms, reading rooms, libraries, and classrooms.[7] Activities included lectures, concerts, choirs, evening classes, tea parties, dances, picnics, and Sunday schools "for interested persons of both sexes."[8]

Owenites studiously eschewed "low and debasing" practices such as heavy drinking and violent, bloody sports, insisting that such activities undermined the socialist program of political reform because they reinforced upper- and middle-class perceptions of the masses as incorrigibly brutish.[9] Temperance was a strong tendency within the movement, one that spoke powerfully to women's complaints about the domestic discord and impoverishment that resulted from men's drinking. Having done away with the "excess, intoxication and noisy revelry" that was all too often a part of "old world" plebeian entertainments, Owenites were happy to note that "the old practice of excluding the ladies" was also a thing of the past.[10] The 1834 playing of the Derby football game was a particularly opportune occasion for Owenites to challenge both upper- and middle-class prejudices about popular culture and traditional elements of that culture. They called upon trade unionists in the town to refuse to participate in what the *Pioneer* characterized as a "silly exploit," a "barbarous recklessness and supreme folly." Not joining in the game was an assertion of moral superiority, "a glorious shout of moral revolution!"[11] Derby unionists' renunciation of the football games included a carefully staged demonstration of rational working-class recreation with all the hallmarks of gender and class order, decency and sobriety, improvement as well as entertainment. On Shrove Tuesday, from five hundred to six hundred female workers and upward of thirteen hundred male unionists assembled in a long column and, organized in ranks and headed by a mace bearer, marched out of the town of Derby to a small village some four miles distant. They assembled and paraded again to a different destination on Ash Wednesday. En route and on arrival, they sang hymns, listened to speeches, and picnicked. The emphasis on the order, decorum, and respectability of the processions and gatherings, and particularly the appearance and demeanor of the women who participated—that they "could look so clean and respectable"—was as striking as it was meant to be. Owenite unionists saw the event as a declaration by working people of their fitness for the political rights they demanded. Staging the demonstration alongside the traditional football game, juxtaposing it with a "bear-like custom" played only by "agricultural labourers or men of weak minds," the trade unionists highlighted the powerful contrast between the nasty, brutish pastimes of the unregenerate masses and their own eminently rational and progressive recreation. And a major signifier of that uplifting recreation was the carefully orchestrated spectacle of orderly working women.[12]

Janus-like, this vision of popular leisure both derived from past practices, in that it was gregarious and heterosocial, and prefigured what would eventually become a central, hegemonic motif of working-class culture, in that it emphasized a demure, sober, and respectable womanhood.

As Clark indicates, plebeian women and men were both "together and apart" in their culture and communities, and their relationships were often, and sometimes violently, antagonistic. By 1834 these tensions had fractured the fragile gender alliances that the

In the working-class "cottage of content" rationale, improving family leisure was a central motif. This vision, which was ideologically dominant by the mid-nineteenth century, is a consistent one in the rational recreation literature from the late eighteenth to the early twentieth centuries. From Hannah More, Cheap Repository Tracts, *courtesy of Special Collections, University of Iowa Library.*

Owenite Consolidated and Trades' Union had represented and begun to resolve themselves into the polarities associated with high Victorianism: separate spheres, and the cults of domestic femininity and wage-earning masculinity. Already in the 1830s and 1840s, when Owenites were attempting to draw women and men together in socialist leisure, women's withdrawal from the public domain, and—what was especially problematic for working-class women—from wage labor, was becoming more and more widely seen as a marker of respectable femininity. This was so for the lower as well as the middle classes. Furthermore, the Owenite emphasis on improvement and reform, and their rejection of such common practices as drinking, represented a narrowing of the range of leisure possibilities that had greater ramifications in women's culture than in men's. This contributed crucially to the incorporation of the earlier emergent vision of heterosocial, egalitarian leisure into a dominant model of patriarchal privilege. Men's enjoyment of that privilege came at the cost of a sharply delineated role and realm for women as the servicers and providers of male domestic comfort and leisure, both within and outside the home.[13]

CHARTISM, THE MOST WIDESPREAD AND INFLUENTIAL RADICAL political movement of the Victorian period, played a major role in inscribing these more restrictive gender ideologies deep within popular and working-class culture. The movement as a whole was highly conservative with respect to gender, though some proponents of the People's Charter espoused egalitarianism and women's suffrage. In fact, "the class that came into its own in Chartism," writes Jutta Schwarzkopf, "was one in which women's needs and requirements were submerged in those of men and in which unquestioned male authority and female subservience, its counterpart, became the proclaimed hallmarks of working-class masculinity and femininity respectively."[14] Chartist leaders universally condemned married women's employment outside the home, and although they acknowledged that unmarried women had the right to work to support themselves and their dependents, most asserted that by nature women were unsuited for wage labor. National figures such as Henry Vincent, Ernest Jones, Thomas Wheeler, and William Lovett all expressed this belief and painted doleful images in their speeches and writings of women morally and physically blighted by wage labor.[15] In Jones's novel, *Woman's Wrongs,* for example, which appeared as a serial in *Notes to the People,* the rigors of wage employment have a crippling effect on the health and vitality of two of the central female characters. "Anna," a young milliner, dies from a wasting illness brought on by the combined effects of overwork, starvation, and her seduction and betrayal by a scion of the "favoured few."[16] "Laura," a tradesman's daughter, laments the consequences of years of clerking in her father's concern: "From twelve years of age I was hailed to a desk, poring over figures. I grew into a form as cold, and stiff, and rigid, as the columns that I added up. From being made a machine of, I began to look like one."[17]

This degradation of literary figures bespoke Chartist concerns about the growing prevalence of wage labor among "real" women and held up the non-wage-earning woman as a norm for the laboring classes. "Will you," thundered the authors of the 1839 Manifesto of the General Convention, "allow your wives and daughters to be degraded, your children to be nursed in misery, stultified by toil, and to become the victims of vice our corrupt institutions have engendered?"[18] Prostitution represented the ultimate corruption of women forced into the wage labor market and was doubly potent as a metaphor for the vulnerability of working-class women when coupled, as it frequently was, with the antithetical image of female domesticity and motherhood. Chartist literature cherished and nurtured the social institution of marriage, and its authors frequently invoked visions of humble but happy homes and families in their writings and speeches. They gave heart-wrenching descriptions of the homes and families of working people destroyed by the forces of capitalism and "class legislation," and conjured up images of a golden past in which even the poor man's cottage was a haven of happiness. This was the iconic "cottage of content" in which John Watkins and other leading Chartists installed the respectable working-class woman. There, supported by and supportive of her wage-earning husband, caring for and educating his children, she belonged; it was her "proper sphere," and "a proper woman should be suffered to rule there."[19]

During the 1840s and 1850s, mainstream Chartism's whole-hearted advocacy of this conception of gender roles and relations, and the identification of masculinity with the "family wage" ideal, converged with similar tendencies in factory-reform movements and a more moderate reformist, rather than radical, trade-unionism. After midcentury, mass-based political activism declined and skilled working-class men organized to secure specific economic and social goals: "wages, conditions and benefits sufficient to ensure financial security for a family."[20] This pursuit of the family wage, based upon the exclusion and marginalization of women as wage workers and their idealization as wives and mothers, continued as a central plank of working-class reformism throughout the nineteenth century and into the twentieth. It carried along with it a vision of rational working-class recreation whose key features were dependency, submission, and domestic seclusion and service for women. For men, there was the expectation of domestic comfort provided by women's service in the home and the lion's share of family resources for engaging in the world of public, commercial leisure.[21]

These patriarchal arrangements crystallized into a mainstream of working-class thought through the 1840s, 1850s, and 1860s. Within "moral-force" Chartism, for example, leisure ideologies and practices similar to those of the Owenites emerged, and for much the same reasons: they demonstrated working people's sobriety, decency, and order, and—as a necessary corollary—their fitness for, and right to, full participation in the political domain. However, the moral-force Chartist vision of working-class rational recreation departed from the Owenite model in a significant regard. There was none of the gender egalitarianism that was so fundamental to Owenite recreation, but in its place an unquestionably patriarchal, if benevolent, rule.[22] William Lovett was a leading architect of Chartist rational recreation. He urged working men to give up gambling, "demoralizing" sports, brutal pastimes, and all their "vicious associations," and exhorted them to take up instead "rational and instructive" amusements like "chess and drafts." In July 1842, Lovett's London Working Men's Association opened a National Hall (boasting a library and coffeehouse) that catered to the "physical, mental, moral, and political instruction" of working people. More specifically, it was a facility for "readings, discussions, musical entertainments, dancing, and such other healthful and rational recreations as may serve to instruct and cheer . . . and *prevent the formation* of vicious and intoxicating habits [original emphasis]."[23] Lovett accorded women a position in this scheme elevated above that which they inhabited in pot-house culture, and he urged husbands to spend more time with their families. Nonetheless, women's sphere remained a limited one, subordinate to men's and supportive always of male aspirations. Lovett exhorted husbands to esteem "their wives as their equal companions, and not as mere slaves of their passions," to "cultivate" and "instruct" them, and to "let them, as far as possible, share in [their] pleasures." But this was only so that wives might then "participate in [their husbands'] views and feelings" and be better prepared "to train up their children in knowledge, virtue, and the love of freedom" and provide that "comfort, cheerfulness, and affection" upon which so "much of men's happiness [depended]."[24]

IN THE 1850S AND 1860S, THE DOMESTIC THEME CONTINUED to resound in the writings and speeches of skilled, unionized working men. Thomas Wright, "the journeyman engineer," evoked all the comforts that wage-earning men returning from the night shift might expect to command in a well-ordered home. "They will, as a rule, find a bright, cosy room, a nice warm tea, and a smiling wife, mother, or landlady waiting for them," he wrote. "They will be comfortably ensconced by their own fireside, or be 'cleaned up' preparatory to going for a 'turn round,' or a visit to some reading place or amusement, or if they are courting, for a walk with their sweethearts." In Wright's opinion, the most critical factor determining the comfort of the working man's home was his wife's housekeeping skill; "among the working classes the *wife* makes the home [original emphasis]," he stated. He cautioned young men to avoid taking a wife from the "young-lady" class of milliners, dressmakers, and shop assistants. Frivolous and shallow, "dressy and vain," such a woman was likely to prove to be a sloven upon marriage, incapable of making a comfortable and attractive home for her family. Wright contrasted her "very unfavourably with . . . the really clever housewife, who goes actively about her work, and in her clean, cotton working-gown looks to the full as comely and attractive as she does . . . after her work is done."[25] *The Working Man* concurred. "The true comfort of man depends upon his home," an 1866 article ran. "Men are capable of going through almost any labour when they have a comfortable home waiting to welcome them; but [a] wild tone and reckless liberty acquired . . . in girlhood unfits the tastes and destroys the domestic habits in woman which alone can make home happy and comfortable to her husband."[26] "It is not the daily toil in the sweat of his brow which threatens the workman's domestic peace," averred another, "it is that we have taken the key-stone from his arch by tempting his wife away from her proper and natural sphere of domestic labour." John Broadhead, a Birmingham compositor, joined the chorus with a prize-winning essay entitled "Domestic Economy" that was also published in *The Working Man*. "Home is that hallowed spot," Broadhead wrote, "where, after the toils, troubles, and difficulties of the day, we can rest our weary limbs. . . . Home is almost the only place in which we can fully enjoy the peace and comfort which are the just reward of our labours."[27]

The parliamentary investigations into various trades and occupations and the representations that short-hours advocates made show clearly that it was not just domesticity in general that men feared was under assault. More specifically, women's leisure habits and practices were a problem. This manifested itself in debate over two related matters. The first issue was that girls and women who worked outside the home did not receive proper training in the necessary housewifely skills and consequently were unable to attend to their husbands' leisure wants. The second was that women's experiences in the culture of wage work were liable to give them such a taste for amusement themselves that they would be reluctant to settle for the quieter, self-denying role of providing for someone else's pleasure. Along with this argument ran the related one that wage work encouraged a liking for particular forms of leisure that compromised the morals of working-class girls and women. Where female agricultural labor came under attack, for example, there was often a consensus that it led to a troubling lack of restraint in women's behavior. The 1867 Royal Commission noted that employers and working people in the county of Northamptonshire were convinced that young girls and women employed in field labor learned "loose and disorderly habits." A similar state seemed to prevail in Cambridgeshire and Yorkshire. One commissioner pointed out that the decline in women's employment as servants in farming families had left the daughters of agricultural laborers with no satisfactory means of acquiring domestic training. He went on to praise the industrial schools that had been established as a means of compensating for this. Commenting on one of the schools, he wrote: "It is the only instance of the kind I met with, and it is quite worthy of imitation by those who have the opportunity with the view of drawing the tastes of girls away from the license of field labour, and fitting them for domestic service and their future duties in life."[28] If working-class women were to be willing and able to perform their domestic duty of providing for men's comfort and leisure, care had to be taken that their own appetites for leisure were not piqued.

Thus, by the middle decades of the nineteenth century, Owenite socialists, Chartists, short-hours advocates, and trade unionists had conjured up visions of an "ideal" domesticity that depended on the self-effacement of women and their subservience and immurement in the home. This way of living undoubtedly had ideological tendencies that largely served men's interests while effacing, ignoring, or denying those of women.[29] Yet, it is also possible to find within the ideological disposition of Victorian working-class domesticity more idealistic, egalitarian aspirations. Domesticity was a complex bundle of ideas and practices that was a key element in both reformist and radical conceptions of a "better" world, and in some of those conceptions women's needs were represented to be as legitimate as men's.[30]

The distinctive literature of both prose and poetry, and especially poetry, of self-taught writers from England's artisan and working classes reflects just such an alternative conception. The urban, industrial culture of Lancashire was a particularly rich fount of literary endeavor, renowned for "homely rhymers" such as Edwin Waugh, Samuel Laycock, and Joseph Ramsbottom, as well as others. Dialect poetry was one of the more authentic and less mediated expressions of the culture of the northern, industrial working classes. Unashamedly "lowly" in style and subject matter, it emerged from a long oral tradition and spoke of and from the experiences of the working masses. Its main concern was the ordinary but vital stuff of their lives and culture—the people, their hard times and good times, life, work, love, and death. It celebrated community and asserted the dignity of working women and men, even as it acknowledged and poked fun at their oddities and failings. It admonished and cajoled, celebrated, protested, and consoled. It had a distinct tendency toward conservatism with respect to gender that feminist scholars have clearly elucidated, but in places it also cut across that grain and disrupted it in important ways.[31]

Edwin Waugh's "Come Whoam to Thi Childer an' Me" is one of the classics of dialect poetry. First published in 1856, the poem is structured as an exchange between a wife and husband, and in it the comforts of home and family serve as a counter to the attractions a man could find with his mates in the alehouse. The husband, having admitted that he likes to indulge in certain pleasures outside the home, confirms nonetheless that after his spree he can't wait to get "whoam" to his wife and children, that they are the true source of his pleasure and comfort.[32] Like much dialect poetry, "Come Whoam" tends to the sentimental. It is also typical in its polar configuration of the domestic and public spheres and in casting women as homemakers and men as wage earners, and thus inclines strongly to the ideological. Yet there are other dialect poems in which women do not inhabit only the domestic realm, that show women playing roles other than, or in addition to, those of wife and mother, in which they are producers of commodities for the market and wage earners.[33]

These works challenge what is often taken to be an uncontested element of the ideology of domesticity: the belief that woman's only fitting social role was as a non-wage-earning, dependent housewife. William Baron's "Yon Weyver As Warks t'Beam to Me" and "Hawf Past Five at Neet," Joseph Burgess's "Neaw Aw'm a Married Mon," Samuel Laycock's "Sewin' Class Song" and "Bowton's Yard," Joseph Ramsbottom's "Coaxin'," and the traditional songs "Th' Owdham Weyver" and "Rambles in Owdham": all these figure women as men's co-workers in cottage industry or as waged factory workers. "Rambles in Owdham," for example, describes the industrial town of Oldham in the 1850s, by which period, Anna Clark suggests, the notion that wives should operate simply within the domestic sphere was pretty much triumphant in working-class culture.[34] The song suggests otherwise, with its glimpse of female operatives hard and skillfully at work in the kind of environment that domestic ideologues considered too hostile for women's "tender" sensibilities: work that the rambling narrator not only accepts with equanimity, but also seems to celebrate:

> I went into a weavin' shade,
> Un' such o clatter there!
> Wi' looms un' wheels all going so fast,
> I hardly durst go near;

> Then the lasses were so busy
> Shiftin' temples—shuttling cops;
> One shuttle had liked o given me
> O devilish slap o t' chops. (ll. 72–80)[35]

"Coaxin', " a love poem first published in the Lancashire journal *Country Words* (1866–1867), opens with a similar image of a young female weaver absorbed in her work. In this instance, however, it is cottage industry that is depicted, not factory production. It might be argued that this "domestic" setting is what gives the poem its ideological thrust; but, equally, the woman's action as a skilled, productive, and committed worker serves to defuse the power of that ideology.[36]

One way in which dialect poetry's treatment of the work identity of women is more consistently in line with a constraining ideology of domesticity is in associating wage labor with unmarried women rather than granting much possibility that wives and mothers might also work for a wage outside the home. The vast majority of female wage earners depicted in dialect verse are young and single (as they were in real life).[37] But there are two poems by Joseph Burgess, whom scholars judge to have been considerably more radical than most Lancashire dialect poets, that do feature women who combine marriage and maternity with factory work. Burgess's "Neaw Aw'm a Married Mon" is atypical for several reasons, one being its assertion that "woman's work might be a man's work as well."[38] In this poem, the poet accepts the notion of a wage-earning wife and mother and embraces the idea that husbands should assume childcare and other responsibilities in the home:

> Un as hoo's a factory lass
> Un me a factory lad,
> We'en noather on us brass—
> Aw nobbu' weesh we had;
> Soa we'st booath ha' to work,
> Un it wudno' be so fair

Happy domesticity could be threatened by a husband's dissolution as well as by a wife's. In this illustration, the mother and child in their home are clearly to be read as victims of the man's inability to resist the blandishments of male "pot-house" culture. Domestic ideologues often laid the blame for a husband's resorting to the public house at his wife's door, however: slatternly, nagging, "sotting," and "gadding" women were all likely to drive a man to drink. From Hannah More, Cheap Repository Tracts, *courtesy of Special Collections, University of Iowa Library.*

If aw began to shirk,
Un didno' do mi share.

Soo aw'st help to mop up stone,
Help to scrub un skeawr,
Un do everythin' aw'm shown,
If it lies within mi peawer;
Fur, neaw aw'm a married mon,
Aw'm beawn to be soa good,
Un do the best aw con,
To be o' a husbant should.[39]

Burgess's "Ten Heawrs a Day" is of a different cast in that it seems to ascribe tragic consequences to maternal wage labor and thus warn mothers away from working outside the home. The poem tells of the death of the child of a female weaver so exhausted by her statutory ten hours of work in the mill that she is unable to care for the infant. But Burgess, far from using this story to inveigh against women's wage labor, instead uses the female operative and her child as symbols of the depredations that working-class people as a whole faced under laissez-faire industrial capitalism. He proceeds from recounting her tragic story to calling on working men to unite in political action that would secure a shorter workday, not just for women (a strategy which, a number of historians show, some male workers used to control female labor), but for all workers.[40] Thus, in an inversion of dominant Victorian constructions of gender and work identities, "Ten Heawrs a Day" makes the representative wage-earning worker a mother.

There were few women among the ranks of dialect writers, but more than a few male poets tried to assume the perspective of women in some of their work, which also tended to disturb the smooth surface of ideological domesticity in the genre. Waugh wrote a number of these songs and poems, but there are plenty of others, all by different writers. More than merely sympathizing with women's lot (though they obviously do that), these poems positively counter the ideological notions that housework isn't really work at all but a "natural" function like breathing and bearing children, and is too far below men's dignity to warrant them performing it.[41] James Standing's "Wimmen's Wark" is one example. It is structured as a line-after-breathless-line account of a harassed mother's round of domestic chores, chores that demand superhuman faculties and with which her husband never deigns to trouble himself:

> Aw think sometimes aw should be made
> To do beawt rest or bed,
> Wi' double hands at ether side,
> An' een all round mi yed . . . (ll. 78–81)

> An' as for him, he takes no part
> I' keepin' corners square;
> Heawiver heedless th' childer be,
> He niver seems to care;
> An' stead o' leyin' on a hand,
> An' helpin' what he con,
> He leovs all t' bits a jobs to me,
> Whol mi warks niver done. (ll. 122–129)[42]

In "Th' Coartin' Neet: Part Second," Samuel Laycock also invokes the image of a husband who is a wastrel, but uses him as a foil for his young narrator who, newly engaged to be married, rejects an ideal of masculinity that precludes housework and child care. Lines 31–32 offer a wonderfully appealing version of working-class masculinity:

> Yo'll noan find me like some; for lo!
> As soon as th' weddin's o'er,
> There's sich a change, they're nowt at o
> Like what they wur before.
> Aw'll turn mi hond to ony job,
> Keep Johnny eawt o'th' dirt,
> Or sit bi th' hob an' nurse eawr Bob,
> While Rosy mends mi shirt.

Aw never wish to be admired
For handlin' broom or cleawt;
But when aw see th' lass gettin' tired
Aw meon to help her eawt.
Aw'll try an' save her o aw con,
An' when hoo's noan so well,
Aw'll poo mi coat off, like a mon,
An' wesh an' bake misel' [emphasis added]. (ll. 17–32)[43]

Fitton's "Th' Childer's Holiday" is patterned like "Wimmen's Wark" but is more patently comic in intent. Still, the humor does not negate the central thrust of the poem: the assertion that a "tidy whoam"[44] and "rook o' childer"[45] demanded a degree and kind of hard work too rarely characterized as "real" labor:

Eh, dear, I'm welly off my chump!
I scrub, an' wesh, an' darn;
Eawr childer han a holiday,
An th' heawse is like a barn.

Yo talk abeawt a home sweet home!
My peace is flown away;
I have to live i' Bedlam for
A fortnit an' a day. . . . (ll. 1–12)

I'd lock 'em up i' thi' schoo for good
If I could ha' my will;
I'd see they had another clause
I thi' Education Bill.

I've clouted 'em an' slapped 'em till
My honds an' arms are sore;
I'st fancy I'm i' Paradise
When th' holidays are o'er. (ll. 57–64)[46]

Among the Lancashire dialect poets, Laycock often raises his voice in condemnation of men's behaviour and denunciation of the

baneful impact it could have on women and family life. "Owd
Fogey," "Eawr Jim," "Uncle Dick's Advoice to Wed Men," and "A
Little Bit o' Boath Sides"—all either sympathize with the hardships
wives endured in marriage or criticize the way in which husbands
failed to meet the obligations marriage placed on them.[47] "Eawr
Jim" similarly decries a husband's drunkenness, the damage it
causes his family, and the despair it brings to his wife:

> Aw hardly know what to do wi' eawr Jim,
> For he's drunk every neet of his life;
> He's crackin' a skull, or breakin' a limb,
> An' often ill-usin' his wife. . . . (ll. 1–4)

> If [Jim]'d some wit, an' would put it to use,
> He'd buy [his] lad a pair o' new clogs,
> But he'd rayther be spendin' his time at "Th' Owd Goose,"
> Makin' matches wi' pigeons an' dogs.

> It pains me to look at his poor, patient wife
> 'At wur once so good-lookin' an' fair:
> Sich a harassin', wretched, an' comfortless life
> Must drive her to hopeless despair. (ll. 13–20)[48]

Not only were poets such as Laycock not loath to represent failed
domesticity and attribute it to men, they were ready to point out
possible remedies. Zlotnick has shown how a distinct subgenre of
dialect advice poems placed the burden of achieving domestic content on wives. But Laycock penned a series of these, each directed
to either a female or male agent who he insisted bore equal responsibility for establishing and maintaining domesticity. "Uncle Dick's
Advoice to Sengle Men" and "Uncle Dick's Advoice to Sengle
Women" counsel on the qualities for which prospective wives and
husbands should look in their betrothed. Laycock cautions young
women "To try an' foind aewt if he's fond ov his books, / Never
mind what he wears, nor heaw pretty he looks."[49] Young men should
also beware of being drawn by superficialities, but must

> . . . look eawt for a lass
> wi' some brains an' good fingers, care nowt abeawt brass,
> For iv that's o tha gets ta'll repent o thi loif
> At tha' didn't get howd of a sensible wife. (ll. 37–40)[50]

In his advice to those already married, Laycock declaims against drunken, brutal husbands and slatternly, bad-tempered wives and exhorts both to try to "mend a bit." "A Little Bit o' Boath Sides" is a slightly more oblique admonitory poem in two parts that presents a marriage successfully made into an ideal of domesticity through just such a dual effort. Significantly—for Laycock was a teetotaler—the first step in the transformation is the husband's signing of a pledge of abstinence.[51]

This all suggests the complexity of working-class understandings of domesticity as represented in Lancashire dialect poetry. Some poets clearly did not shrink from acknowledging the dark side of marriage and yet could also write as fondly and lyrically of the joys of home life as any of their peers. Laycock's work especially exemplifies this duality and tension. Domesticity as an ideology is challenged, domesticity as an ideal is shown as a fragile, precious thing toward which both women and men should strive. The vulnerability of the domestic world is a consistent theme. Endemic poverty, disease, death, unemployment, underemployment, hard-hearted landlords, and bullying bailiffs: in addition to the fallibility of wives and husbands, these are all identified as representing a threat to even the most modest working-class aspirations of domestic security and cheer. It is the genre's general tendency to avoid articulating a political analysis of these forces that has led scholars to see it as conservative and consolatory. "The invocation of the pleasures of domesticity" has been identified as one of the main strategies that dialect poets used to defuse social and political tension.[52] But it is also feasible to see domesticity as something that working women and men were struggling to construct and to read dialect poetry as an expression of that struggle. Some dialect poets articulated a vision of domesticity that did not preclude a wage-earning wife, that did not insist upon female subservience and self-sacrifice; that recognized women's desires and acknowledged men's failings, that allowed for, indeed insisted upon, the necessity of equity and mutuality between wives and husbands.

IT IS IMPORTANT TO RECOGNIZE THIS DIVERSITY AND ITS DIS-turbance of what otherwise seems to be a smoothly efficient ideology of patriarchal comfort and leisure privilege within Victorian working-class culture. Another disruption is also persistently present, that of the hedonistic, dissolute customs associated with an unregenerate popular culture, from which rational recreationists had begun to turn in the first few decades of the nineteenth century. In a series of essays on various aspects of working-class life ("Out of Work," "Getting Married," and "Saturday Evening in Victoria Park"), *The Working Man* delineated some of the particulars of this oppositional leisure culture and underscored the ideas about gender implicit within them. The strategy employed is the familiar one of setting the model of a hedonistic, fairly egalitarian, and thus disreputable model of working-class leisure against its antithesis: the respectable, gender-ordered model of thoroughly domesticated, rational recreation. After work, a "steady-going sort of fellow" reflects, "I do like to enjoy myself." "If my enjoyments are found at home, in a chat with my wife, a game with the children, and a little odd jobbing about the house and bit of garden, a walk in the lanes in summer, or a stroll along the streets to show Nelly the shops . . . they certainly have one or two advantages over the amusements which are sometimes run after." The advantages of these simple, domestic pleasures, the narrator goes on to reveal, were their cheapness, the fact that wives and children could share in them, and the fact that they could be indulged in without regret. Not so the attractions of the beer shops and low theaters that appealed to very different sorts of working men, those "who are so far on the wrong road that I am afraid they will never get on the right one. If their wages were doubled, they would be just as wretched, and they would have only so much more to spend on beer and pipes, and in betting that some scoundrelly skittle-sharp would not take the lot in two." In another piece on New Year customs, the same contrast is made. After tea, "Tom" gathers his wife and children around the newly swept hearth, where they chat about their day. "I told mother [I always call her mother when the children are about; she likes it, and says that, as a title, duchess, no, or even queen, is not to be compared to it] what a big engine we were making on a new construction, and she told me how she had thought she had lost little Billy." "Charley," on the other hand, Tom's workmate, married to a girl with a "pretty face and a liking for artificial flowers . . . and a queer home they have, that's a fact," spends the holiday evening with his wife, in cheap finery at a low theater: "that's their notion of enjoyment . . . but not ours." Other shopmates see the old year out "over a tripe supper and cards. There will be too much drink about, mother; and if they don't lose at least half a day tomorrow, I shall be surprised."[53]

Formulaic as they are, these writings provide insights into the extent to which the dominant vision of working-class leisure was penetrated by particular and, for women, often limiting ideas about gender and respectability. The rhetoric made much of the mutual benefits that women and men would derive from spending time together in the pursuit of sober, homely pleasures, and in the early nineteenth century, when Owenites began to craft this conception of leisure, it did offer the possibility of an egalitarian, companionate working-class culture. By the second half of the century, however, and certainly by its final decades, the promise of that emergent rational recreation had faded, leaving most working-class women with little means and little time for leisure. Indeed, they were left with only the most tenuous of claims to any leisure at all. Numerous complex and shifting forces contributed to this circumscription of women's lives, but a central and enduring one, as I have indicated here, was gender, which, to paraphrase Clark, profoundly shaped the making of working-class rational recreation. And, ironically for a movement with its origins in radical politics, it did so in profoundly conservative ways. In the next chapter I will examine some of the material structural forces that similarly served to circumscribe and shape working women's lives and leisure.[54]

PART TWO

NINETEENTH-CENTURY
WORKING-CLASS WOMEN'S LEISURE

The British people were able to concern themselves with more than mere subsistence; they had a surplus to spend on more and better food, on a wider range of clothing, on more elaborate furnishings for their home and a greater variety of leisure pursuits. For the first time, most people had a *choice* of how and where to spend their money [original emphasis].

W. HAMISH FRASER *The Coming of the Mass Market* (1981)

The final decades of the nineteenth century have been understood as a time of significant gain for the English working classes in which their living standards rose and quality of life improved, and most shared for the first time in the bounties of industrial capitalism, which included leisure.[1] But this view of an expanding, democratized leisure world, as several scholars have recently indicated, does not reflect the crucial role that gender played in it, or the experiences of women. Andrew Davies, for example, argues that in Manchester and Salford for much of the first half of the twentieth century, gender was a far weightier factor in determining—more precisely, limiting— the extent of people's leisure than was skill level, occupation, or notions of respectability. Nicky Hart goes even further and claims not simply that men had many more resources for leisure than women, but that they enjoyed them at the expense of their families' well-being. Hart castigates working-class men of the past for their selfishness and willful neglect of their families, and male scholars of the present for failing to acknowledge the centrality of gender in thus blighting working-class culture.[2]

This chapter focuses on what historians have seen as two of the most basic of leisure resources, free time and money, and their availability to working-class women in the late Victorian and Edwardian periods. As have others, I assume that leisure time and money can be read indirectly from work hours and earnings, but I look beyond formal employment to consider also the unpaid work that women performed in the home and the distribution of income within working-class family economies. In common with Davies and Hart, I see the gender politics of this era as affording working-class women few of the requisites for leisure. Women worked long, exhausting hours as wage laborers and as housewives—indeed, oftentimes as both. But unlike male workers, who could claim an undisputed right to leisure and to the resources necessary for it as a due reward for their labor, few women had the means or time that made much leisure possible. Chapter 4 considers what that leisure was like and what it meant.[3]

Chapter Three

LITTLE MEANS OR TIME:
MATERIAL CONTRAINTS ON
WORKING-CLASS WOMEN'S LEISURE

THE IDEA THAT THE CIRCUMSTANCES OF WORKING-CLASS
life improved sufficiently to allow people a great deal more leisure
is commonly expressed in writings of the period. Charles Booth observed in his massive survey of London's laboring classes in the
1880s that "to 'What shall we eat, what drink and wherewithall shall
we be clothed?' must now be added the question 'How shall we be
amused?' " Writing a decade or so later, Walter Besant was convinced that, as a consequence of the "remarkable expansion" of arti-
sans' leisure hours, the young working folk of London's East End
had a great deal too much time on their hands. According to Besant's
calculations, if one included the evening hours from seven to eleven
o'clock, Saturday half-holidays, and seasonal and state-mandated
holidays, fully one third of the young East-Ender's year was free for
leisure. "They seem to have nothing to do," he reflected, "and to
want nothing but to amuse themselves every evening."[1] The social
reformer Helen Bosanquet reported that old women from the slums
of London, crippled with rheumatism and racked with coughs
though they might be, were aggrieved if they did not "get at least

one outing from their mothers' meeting."[2] Indeed, a member of the 1894 National Council of Women believed that the leisure habit was so widespread and commonplace among working people that it had bred a distinctive type: the working-class "woman of leisure." At any hour of any day in the poorer districts of England's cities, such women could be seen "hanging with head and shoulders out of the windows, gazing idly down into the street, or gossiping in pairs by the hour together in the close or entry."[3]

Historians, too, agree that by the final decades of the nineteenth century, the working people of England had more leisure time, both more clearly defined and more regular. Most judge that living standards also generally improved after about 1850, when money wages and real (adjusted) wages both began to rise. The former increased significantly from 1850 to 1900, and by 1914, despite some short-term reversals, were double what they had been in 1850. During this same period, prices were, for the most part, either stable or falling, which meant that real wages began to rise in the early 1860s and continued to do so till 1900. The overall effect was that, except for certain parts of the country and certain trades, there was "a substantially improved standard of living for the mass of the population in the 1870s, 1880s, and 1890s."[4]

Set against this picture of evidently increasing prosperity was the widespread deprivation of the period, a deprivation that leisure historians have certainly noted. Hugh Cunningham points out that the new leisure experiences of the third quarter of the nineteenth century were limited to skilled, unionized workers, and James Walvin reminds us that "poverty and rising expectations of life . . . existed side by side in uncomfortable and ill-fitting partnership." Wray Vamplew also acknowledges the problems of generalizing about "the working class." "At any time," he notes, "the skilled artisan could probably afford a wider range of recreational activities than the unskilled labourer or factory hand." Yet, the scholarship has not gone much beyond generalized notions of "the working class"; nor has it disclosed which particular groups continued to face poverty while others enjoyed rising living standards and more leisure, or analyzed the circumstances that made such disparities possible. Among the most important of these circumstances was the availability of free time.[5]

Both common and scholarly wisdom associate free time with leisure, and while some have seen this association as problematic, understanding the former as a necessary resource for the latter does underscore the point that, typically, late Victorian and Edwardian working-class women had little of either. In charting the nineteenth-century increase in workers' leisure time, historians have given considerable attention to legislation that guaranteed set daily working hours and a Saturday half-holiday in certain industries. The most important measures are usually taken to be the 1847 and 1850 ten-hour acts, the factory extension and workshop acts of the 1860s, and the 1874 act that fixed textile workers' weekly hours at fifty-six and a half. This legislation was directed at women workers and its intent and impact are topics of intense debate among historians. My primary concern here is whether it meant much for women's leisure. In this regard, it is instructive to begin by noting that, from the third quarter of the nineteenth century, the standard working day for unionized male workers was nine hours, and that by the late 1890s the best-organized men's trades had secured eight hours as their "normal day." In contrast, by the turn of the twentieth century, the hours that women were legally permitted to work in occupations covered by the factory and workshop acts were: in textile factories, ten hours Monday through Friday, and five and a half hours on Saturdays; and in nontextile factories and workshops, ten and a half hours Monday through Friday, and seven and a half hours on Saturdays. That is, the average workday for women in even the most highly regulated occupations at the turn of the century was two hours longer than that of unionized male workers. Elizabeth Hutchins, who was inclined to believe that protective legislation had been beneficial, insisted that women's position in industry in 1915 was little better than that of their grandmothers. She pointed out that there had been no significant reductions in women's work hours since the 1874 Factory Act, while intensified production had increased the demands and strains upon workers. In her experience, the working woman in industry was "still liable to toil her ten hours daily . . . for five days in the week, though on Saturdays the hours have been somewhat curtailed." Excessive hours were a major contributing factor to the "mute sense of industrial inferiority" that Adelaide Mary Anderson, the principal women's factory inspector, found among women workers in the 1890s, and were one of the problems that she and her colleagues believed especially and uniquely confronted women.[6]

The Lady Factory Inspectors reported that, even in regulated trades, long hours placed an intolerable strain on employees and that excessive hours was the issue about which workers most frequently complained. As the popular press, parliamentary inquiries, women's organizations, and the factory inspectorate disclosed, laws governing hours of work were easily broken, ignored, or, for specific industries under certain circumstances, relaxed. The worst and most frequent offenses were in poorly unionized occupations, which is to say, most of the trades and industries employing women. The Factory Inspectors' Report for 1893, for example, showed that the top five offending trades in terms of excessive hours were all branches of needlework, which was historically a female occupation with low levels of organization. Laundry work was another occupation that figured often in reports of overwork. A Royal Commission of Labour found in London in 1893 that two-thirds of the steam laundries whose employees testified to the inquiry exceeded the maximum hours allowed by law, although no laundry that was actually inspected did so. When hours per day rather than per week were the measure, all the witnesses interviewed worked beyond the factory limit. Laundries prosecuted under the factory acts worked their labor force for periods as long as twenty-eight, thirty-seven, sixty-eight and a half, and seventy-three and a half hours at a time, when the prescribed maximum for laundry work was fourteen hours a day. In a range of other industries regulated by the factory and workshop acts, too, excessive hours were a common problem. Leaders in working women's clubs and other organizations reported that their members constantly worked beyond legal limits, and the factory acts made liberal allowances in certain nontextile industries (food processing, for example) for overtime of two additional hours a day. On application to the factory inspector, employers in these industries could use overtime on forty-eight occasions a year (this was reduced to thirty in 1901). Critics charged that what was initially conceived as an exceptional measure had thus come to be a general principle that effectively negated legislative controls on work hours in many women's industries. Workers seeking legal redress also faced intimidation from employers: the Women's Industrial Council found it necessary to organize a fund to assist women who had been fired for reporting factory act offenses.[7]

Even in employment governed by the factory and workshop acts, then, women's work hours were such as to hardly allow them much leisure time. And in those both long-established and newly emerging occupations that employed the greatest numbers of women, excessive hours were the norm.[8]

DOMESTIC SERVICE WAS ONE OF THE LARGEST OCCUPATIONAL sectors for women in this period, though it was contracting, particularly where alternative forms of work were available. The often long and irregular hours of work and lack of freedom and control of one's time were major reasons for women's antipathy to it. Ellen Darwin noted that, in manufacturing districts where factory work provided another option, women shunned domestic service. "[They] prefer the hard work and the long hours of factory life to the comparative ease and comfort, but, at the same time, dependence, of domestic work," she asserted.[9] Not everyone shared Darwin's upbeat view of life in domestic service. Female domestic servants, especially those who worked in schools, hotels, and lodging houses, constituted "the hardest worked class of women," insisted one supporter of their cause. "On Saturday the factory-hand works two hours less than usual. The house-maid, on the contrary, works harder. On Sunday, the factory-hand and the shopwoman rest completely, the house-maid only partially."[10]

Again, this characterization of other forms of women's work might bear critical examination, but there is little doubt that a lack of leisure was a source of considerable dissatisfaction among female domestic servants, and that employers policed their lives much more closely than did those in other occupations. The majority of women worked in single-servant households, constantly at their employers' beck and call, and very few had set schedules. At the end of the nineteenth century, they were still trying to win even minimal concessions with respect to hours, and this struggle was to continue well into the twentieth century. In the 1890s, many could expect to have only two or three hours of free time a week, taken on a Sunday, with maybe an additional hour or two for those in "easy" situations. In an attempt to improve women's terms of service, in 1897 the London Domestic Servants' Union proposed that their hours should be limited to seventy per week, but by the end of the First World War, most employers still gave only one afternoon a week and alternate Sundays off. As late as the interwar period, Ruth Redpath, who began her career as a fourteen-year-old general servant with a Yorkshire farming family, worked from before six in the morning until eight or nine at night, with one weekend a month free. A regime such as this left those subjected to it little energy or inclination for leisure, even had they had the time. "Worn out, tired out, ready for bed and same every morning." Redpath was evidently among those girls and women in service whose mistresses followed what Darwin believed was a common practice: "filling up what leisure the servant may have [had] with work designed to keep her out of mischief."[11]

Domestic service was but one of a number of female occupations that fell outside the scope of legislation and, in some of these, conditions and terms of work were so poor as to qualify as "sweating." This an 1888 Select Committee of the House of Lords defined as the payment of unduly low wage rates, excessively long hours, and unsanitary working conditions. Homework or outwork was the most notorious form of sweating and occupied, in the words of Edward Cadbury and George Shann, "hundreds of thousands of women and children." Often a last resort for women who otherwise could not provide for themselves and their families, most forms of outwork offered rates of pay so low that, despite long hours, earnings were barely enough to keep body and soul together. Depending on the particular trade and the skill and speed of the worker, a working day in the sweated home industries ranged from seven and a half to sixteen hours, but the average was around twelve hours. In some occupations, such as carding buttons or hooks and eyes, women reported working "all day" or "all the time" for average weekly earnings of just over three shillings. Employers whose businesses came under the factory and workshop acts might also, if inclined, benefit from sweated homework. The practice of sending work home at the end of the legal workday was so standard in some trades that factory inspectors despaired of ever enforcing the laws stipulating hours; examples of such transgressions abound in their annual reports.[12]

Sweating characterized many occupations in the retail trade and service industries, and these were employing increasing numbers of women toward the end of the nineteenth century. Shop assistants, waitresses, and barmaids often worked hours that critics asserted were "excessive, injurious to health, [and] destructive of spiritual and mental vigour."[13] Evidence presented to parliamentary inquiries between 1880 and the beginning of World War I certainly supported the first claim. An 1886 Select Committee of the House of Commons concluded that eighty-four to eighty-five hours a week were common for shop assistants and heard evidence from some witnesses of very long hours and very late closing times. A fifteen-hour day during the week and sixteen or seventeen hours on Saturday were standard for the retail trade in London and the larger provincial towns and cities. Milliners, dressmakers, and fancy drapers, who typically employed women rather than men, kept notoriously long hours. Harriett Barber and Charlotte Wilson, who between them had about twenty years' experience as drapers' assistants in various districts of London, testified that fourteen to fourteen and a half hours Monday to Friday and sixteen and a half to seventeen hours on Saturdays were the rule in most establishments. These hours included meal-times, which usually consisted of thirty minutes for dinner and twenty to thirty minutes for tea (but in some places, much less than that), and which were frequently interrupted by customers requiring service. The length of the workweek in retailing varied with the size of the establishment and its clientele, but neither hours nor the general conditions of employment were good. "On the whole," wrote one authority on the subject in 1897, the female shop assistant "is better fed and more bullied in the West End [of London], more starved and less interfered with in the east. She is always liable to arbitrary dismissal, and often to arbitrary fines, and her hours—especially in sales time—know no fixed limit." Smaller shops and businesses in poorer districts tended to stay open later into the night: 9:30 P.M. on most weekdays, 10:00 P.M. on Fridays, and until midnight on Saturdays. Doubtless, their hard-pressed workers welcomed even minimal gains, such as the half-day weekly holiday legislated by the 1908 Compulsory Half-Day Closing Act, as did Robert Roberts's mother: a "blessed relief."[14]

LONG HOURS WERE THE INEVITABLE COROLLARY OF MISERLY rates of pay and wages and, for many women, "the pitiful smallness" of their earnings was a powerful impetus to work excessive hours.[15] Cadbury, Matheson, and Shann summed up the situation they found in Birmingham in 1906: "Women's wages are determined by a customary standard, and [this] standard is the lowest possible, that of subsistence," they judged. "Already down as far as they will go [they] cannot go any further without the rapid deterioration of the woman as a worker." Even in forms of employment that could not be characterized as sweated, the remuneration for women's work was hardly equitable. Comparisons between the wages of women and men, where it is possible to make them, are one indicator of this. In Birmingham, "whenever women . . . replaced men the former always received a much lower wage, and . . . this wage was not proportionate to the skill or intelligence required, but approximated to a certain fixed level—about 10s. to 12s. per week."[16] A paper presented to the 1899 International Congress of Women concluded the same: "The general rate of remuneration for women's work is low—low in proportion to the intrinsic merit of the work, low in comparison with the remuneration obtained by men in the same or similar occupations."[17] On the whole, women's wages in Birmingham were one-half to two-thirds those of men, and while unskilled men could expect to earn between 18s. and 20s. a week, young women over the age of twenty-one earned only about 10s. and those below that age considerably less. Benjamin Seebohm Rowntree's 1899 study of York revealed that men earned on average 24s. a week compared to women's 10s. 9d. The pattern was a familiar one. An 1893 report on thirty-eight miscellaneous industries showed that for 355,838 male employees, the average wage was 24s. 7d. per week, with a range from 10s. to over 40s., while the average weekly wage of 151,263 women employed in twenty-three of these same industries was 12s. 8d. Of these women, 26 percent took home less than 10s. a week, 50 percent between 10s. and 15s., 18.5 percent between 15s. and 20s., 5.4 percent between 20s. and 25s., and 0.1 percent between 25s. and 30s.[18]

Occupations that predominately employed women—retail service, most forms of domestic service, food and drink industries, dressmaking, millinery, laundry work, outwork, and the like — typically paid low wages. The Royal Commission on Labour's inquiries into women's work in Bristol in 1893 revealed that, in seven traditionally female industries ranging from clothing to confectionery, by far the majority of female workers had wages between 8s. and 12s. a week. A significant number of these took home less than 8s. a week; in fact, in the confectionery industry, the earnings of over ninety-five percent of workers were below this level. With only a few exceptions, women's occupations outside the manufacturing sector paid very badly. In the university towns of Oxford and Cambridge just before the First World War, for example, female cleaners and chars, among the lowliest of service workers, were paid between 2s. and 2s. 6d. a day, and most managed to get such employment for only three to four days a week because of "the army of charwomen" that was always available for this kind of work. In Birmingham the average weekly wage for charring was 7s. 9d. Helen Bosanquet reported from London in the 1890s that those prepared to take on the much heavier work of cleaning institutions such as hospitals, asylums, and infirmaries earned from 7s. to 9s. a week, but the work was so exhausting that few could stand it for more than a year or two. Wages in domestic service were notoriously difficult to ascertain but, for general servants in London in the late 1890s, they were in the region of 3s. to 4s. a week (plus board and lodging), while in Yorkshire just after the First World War they ranged from 4s. 6d. to 10s. a week. In retail trade and clerical work, wages of 8s. a week "living out" were offered in reputable London shops in the 1890s; in Oxford in the second decade of the twentieth century, the highest wage female retail clerks and assistants could earn was 15s., while the average wage for those over eighteen was 10s.; in Birmingham the average wage for those over eighteen was 10s. 6d. Some women's retail and service work, entailing greater responsibility or managerial skills, was well-paid but it occupied only a tiny proportion of women workers. In Birmingham, for example, the most senior assistants in the larger, fashionable shops and experienced cooks and caterers commanded as much as 30s. a week; housekeeping paid on average 17s. a week; managers of public houses earned between 26s. 6d. and 27s. 3d.; more senior general clerks, 18s. At the opposite, most depressed end of the scale of women's work lay homework, in which earnings were rarely even at subsistence level. A sampling of those in a number of trades for the late 1890s includes the following: 6s. a week in brush-drawing; from 1s. to 1s. 6d. for a twelve-hour day making matchboxes; 11d. a day for eleven hours of buttonholing; 1s.

10d. a day for ten hours at paper-bag making; and about 1s. a day for fur-pulling.[19]

IT HAS TO BE SAID, THEN, THAT IF THE HOURS AND TERMS OF women's wage work improved during the later part of the nineteenth century, they still left a great deal to be desired. So much so that for one of the Lady Factory Inspectors, contemplating the life of the wage-earning woman was an uncomfortable experience; it was "such a grave reproach" to society. But contemplating the circumstances of the many other women who do not appear in the historical record as wage earners—nationally, only one of ten married women in this period was formally engaged in a paid occupation—is scarcely a more cheering exercise. On the front line in a constant battle against poverty, wives and mothers faced an unceasing round of labor in the home and in the service of their families that could be every bit as demanding and debilitating as any formal employment.[20]

Despite generally improving standards of living in the late Victorian period, the specter of poverty haunted most working-class people. According to Rowntree's study of York, every male outside the ranks of the skilled elite could expect to spend at least one, or more typically three, period of his life in poverty. Women, explained Rowntree, were in poverty throughout their childbearing years, as well as in childhood and old age, which hardly left much time in their lives when they were not indigent. This material deprivation and insecurity weighed especially heavily upon women because they played a critical role in managing the household. Their ingenuity in coping with meager, irregular resources, their unremitting labor, and their sheer dogged determination not to give up were sometimes the only things keeping families going. And this was so not simply for the poor. Just before the First World War, the Women's Co-operative Guild conducted a study of its members' experiences of maternity. The four hundred or so women who participated provided insights into lives that varied considerably, but Margaret Llewellyn

Davies found a common, dreary thread running through many of their letters: "The whole burden is placed upon the woman who has to bring up a family on thirty shillings." Llewellyn Davies is writing here about women who ranked among the more prosperous of the working classes or at least those whose husbands were in steady and reasonably well-paid employment. (Most trade unionists accepted thirty shillings a week as a fair wage.) By these women's own accounts, any exigency, such as the birth of another child, could seriously threaten their material well-being. Similar testimony comes from Magdalen Reeves's descriptions of life in Lambeth, London, on "round about a pound a week." These speak to the toll that the daily grind of domestic work and worry took on women—again, not simply poor women, but also those in families with a steady, decent income. Even young wives and mothers looked, to Reeves, "to be in the dull middle of middle age." "It comes as a shock when the mind grasps it," she mused.[21]

One of housework's most dulling, deadening features, as historians of the craft and as folk wisdom remind us, is that it is "never done." Tuned to the needs and tides of others, to satisfying their demands immediately and unstintingly, it is a form of labor that is not easily contained or regulated by the clock. It does not end with a factory whistle and there are no laws or union agreements ensuring that it does not unduly tax the strength of the workers. And it was labor that, in the late Victorian and Edwardian periods, women conducted under the most difficult conditions. Few working-class homes had amenities such as an indoor water supply, decent sanitary arrangements, or adequate facilities for storing, preparing, and cooking food, so even the most basic level of housework demanded a good deal of physical labor. Conscientious housewives scrubbed stone, tile, or wooden floors and black-leaded fire grates or, if they were lucky enough to have them, kitchen ranges. They painstakingly edged front doorsteps that proclaimed their respectability to the world with colored "donkeystone." A task such as laundering for a large family took two or three days of sheer hard slog when facilities were as simple as a wooden tub filled with water that had been heated in kettles on an open fire. Clementina Black believed that the technology and organization of domestic labor and the conditions under which it was performed were so primitive and oppressive that its reform was an even more urgent concern than reform in the industrial sphere. "It is true," she wrote in 1915, "that the underpaid wives of underpaid men bear upon their shoulders a burden of combined household and industrial toil far too heavy for any human creature. . . . But the portion of their toil which is most onerous, least productive and least in the line of modern development is not their industrial but their domestic work."[22]

As Black's comments make clear, and despite the impression conveyed by official statistics, married women added waged work to domestic labor. The ideal of the nonworking wife and the domestic ideologies invoked in support of the sexual division of labor masked the fact that many families only just managed to keep going under normal circumstances. Seasonal work, underemployment, unemployment, sickness, disability, and death threatened to reduce or remove the income of the primary wage-earner, and in too many instances, as Rowntree's study showed, a husband's wages were simply insufficient for his family's needs. In addition to demanding exhausting domestic labor from wives and mothers, these material circumstances pressured unknown numbers of them periodically to re-enter the wage labor market. Much of this sporadic wage work was of a type that fitted in with domestic duties, or was itself domestic. Taking in lodgers or laundry, for example, was a common strategy. One study of Irish immigrants in London shows that when the size of a family grew, causing the mother to give up wage labor outside the home, the household correspondingly increased the number of boarders it took in. Rowntree found that lodgers provided a regular, if modest (three percent) part of the average weekly income of working-class families in York. Domestic tasks performed for one's neighbors also had an exchange value. Just as the few extra shillings from a lodger might make all the difference in straitened circumstances, so the intermittent wages earned by a woman minding someone's children or doing their washing contributed a small but vital sum to household income.[23]

Those married women who bore the double burden of domestic and wage work endured lives of "pathetic drudgery," in the opinion of the authors of one contemporary study. "One sometimes even hears a woman boast of what is really her inferiority," they commented. "Where the man and woman both work during the day, the woman accepts it as right that she should do all the housework at night." But even wives and mothers who did not have to engage in wage labor found that free time was a resource beyond their means. The "incessant labour" that they put into keeping house, Margaret Llewellyn Davies believed, "inevitably [cut them off] from every higher human activity."[24]

Nor did women enjoy the leisure money that men could take as their right, and it is with this issue, the sharing of the family income, that the gender inequities of working-class leisure in late Victorian and Edwardian England appear in their starkest relief. Various kinds of sources paint a compelling picture of wives scrimping and saving while husbands spent scarce money on themselves and their pleasures. George Acorn recalls that his father gave eighteen shillings a week for housekeeping when first married and "never increased it." "When work fell slack my mother suffered the loss of wages," Acorn writes, "when work was plentiful and overtime the order of the day, he would have days off, spending the extra money on drink." Robert Roberts, author of two autobiographical accounts of life in a poor, working-class community in the northwest of England, shares similar memories. He tells of his mother's efforts to prevent her husband from draining the household's resources for drink, and of the general tendency of many male breadwinners in the community to settle in the pub at Saturday dinnertime and consume a fair measure of their wages in alcohol. Rowntree commented on similar customs in York and what he considered to be their hidden, unhappy consequences: "we *see* the man go to the public house and spend money on drink;

we do *not* see the children going supperless to bed in consequence [original emphasis]." Social investigators disagreed about the impact that drinking had on working-class living standards, but many documented that, in varying numbers and to a varying degree, men allocated only a certain proportion of their weekly wages to wives for housekeeping and kept the rest for personal spending. Helen Bosanquet found that among London's working classes it was not unusual for the amount a husband apportioned to housekeeping to remain fixed, notwithstanding fluctuations in the cost of food and other essentials. "There is a widespread opinion that 18s. or 20s. is the right amount for a husband to give his wife," she stated in her 1908 study, "and she is apt to accept it without further enquiries as to actual earnings." While the amount varied, both within and between individual families, the practice of men retaining some of their wages for personal consumption seems to have been common. Analyses of working-class family budgets conducted in 1899, and in the years 1910 and 1911, reveal that in approximately one-third of families, the husband routinely kept back for his own use a proportion of earnings ranging from about five to fourteen percent of the household's total weekly income. Reeves's study of working-class Lambeth indicated that the practice was widespread there. In every case, the sample budgets that women provided showed the male head of household retaining between roughly eight and thirteen percent of his wage for personal spending. This was in marked contrast to some northwestern textile districts where husbands handed over a complete wage packet to wives who then gave them their "spending brass." In Lambeth such behavior was the sign of "an extraordinarily good husband," not common custom. Until as late as the 1940s, some investigators believed that many women did not know what their husbands' wages were, and that men's profligacy placed an unfair burden on wives. "Of the wife's share of family income, the far greater part is spent on necessities, i.e., on things which the whole family consumes and uses, and which they cannot do without," concluded a researcher of family economies from the Second

World War era. "The greater part of the earner's pocket money, on the other hand, is spent for the individual benefit of the earner on things which are not essential for subsistence."[25]

WOMEN COULD NOT EASILY ASSERT SUCH RIGHTS, EITHER TO leisure money or to leisure time, and consequently it is not surprising to find that the very meager possibilities and narrow horizons of their lives are recurrent themes in many of the sources on working-class life in the period. Social reformers, for example, though often poles apart in their views of working people and their prescriptions for the problems confronting them, spoke with unanimity on the "unrelieved drabness, ill-health, toil"; the "suffering and . . . overwork, and poverty"; the "monotony and hopelessness" of many married women's lives.[26] Rowntree reported from York that a lady of his acquaintance who held a weekly meeting for wives and mothers frequently heard them remark that "the hour thus spent is the only one in the week when they can lay aside the perpetual burden of housekeeping." Reeves's investigation in Lambeth, which details the typical days of a number of young mothers, reinforces the impression of lives so full of work as to leave little latitude for anything else; as does Robert Dolling's account of his experiences as a parish priest in Portsmouth in the 1880s. The Reverend Dolling attempted to set up an "At Home" for wives and mothers but met with a number of difficulties, not the least of which was the fact that married women were so used to the domestic grind that they could not quite get the hang of not being usefully occupied. "At first it was difficult to make them understand that they need not bring a piece of work if they did not like, [that] they might talk to each other, indeed gossip, and move about the room when there was no singing or reading going on."[27] Annie Wilson's mother, similarly unpracticed in the ways of leisure, was such a stranger to the Edwardian music hall that, on a rare visit, she embarrassed the wage-earning daughter who treated her to a night out there by laughing "in all the wrong places."[28]

Unmarried wage earners like Annie typically could command some free time and other resources for leisure, but not universally so. Clara Collet's investigations of a range of female occupations in London in the 1890s for a royal commission on labor indicated that only a few working women had the free time or discretionary income to join recreational, educational, or trade organizations. A young milliner undoubtedly spoke for many others when she complained, in the mid-1880s, of the debilitating hours and conditions of her employment. "You have no idea how you feel at the end of the week when you have been sewing every minute of the day, as you might say," she wrote in a letter to the *Women's Union Journal*. "It is harder a great deal than most young men work, I am sure," she continued, contrasting her work and leisure circumstances with those of her brother. "[He] is a clerk in a warehouse in the City and he begins at nine and comes away at six; and then in the summer he goes off to play cricket or rides his bicycle." Cadbury, Matheson, and Shann's study of wage-earning women in Birmingham offers a telling insight into the vicissitudes that workers such as this faced. In the early part of 1904, a period in which trade and wages were particularly depressed, eleven young women, all unskilled, low-paid workers, recorded their expenses during one month. With earnings of between 5s. and 9s. a week, and averaging 7s. 6d. a week, they paid 5s. to their mothers for board and lodging. During that month most had to forgo at least some meals—two went without an evening meal on thirteen occasions each—and nearly all the balance of their income went on clothes and footwear, most of which they purchased through the club system. After this, only a few pennies were left for recreation and treats such as sweets and fruit. Beyond this, "there [were] a few tram fares, an occasional twopenny visit to the music hall, and one or two spent as much as 6d. in an Easter outing."[29]

But it is again in the family, when we consider women's resources and opportunities for leisure relative to those of men, that their meanness appears most acute, that the disparities between the leisure expectations of women and men yawn so widely. Men not only had the right to the lion's share of the family income and the right to retain a proportion of their earnings for personal expenditure, they could also expect that women would labor to provide domestic comfort and service their leisure in the home. In the words of Robert Roberts, men were used to "lording it" over their wives and children. The mechanism for this gendering of comfort and leisure was well established by the late Victorian period. It began to operate early in life and continued through young adulthood and into old age. "It is a [young girl's] inestimable privilege to be mother's help, which means that she shall assist in cleaning the place, run the errands . . . and nurse the inevitable baby," wrote a correspondent to the *Women's Union Journal* in 1884. Mother's "little helper" was almost a cliché of social reform literature in the period but one with which real women could readily identify. Hannah Mitchell, a working-class feminist and socialist, for instance, remembered her childhood experience of the familial sexual division of labor and leisure as one of the things that first aroused her feminist ire. After days of exhausting work on her family's farm, Mitchell was required to spend the evenings darning her brothers' stockings while they played games. It was a widespread custom for wage-earning daughters; in addition to contributing wages to the household economy, they were expected to help with the housework. Their brothers, meanwhile, enjoyed the same rights to repose and recreation as husbands.[30] "They used to sit back, wait for the meals to be done and then they were off out, out to the pub or the football match and so on. But they didn't think they were brought up to help in the house," recalled one woman of the Edwardian era.[31] Nor did they, even those whose political leanings should have made them acutely sensitive to such inequities. As a young wife in the decades spanning the turn of the century, Mitchell found it difficult to cope with the "domestic treadmill" and commented wryly on the fact that her male comrades' visions of social freedom clearly did not extend to women. "Even my Sunday leisure was gone for I soon found that a lot of the Socialist talk about freedom was only talk and these young

Socialist men expected Sunday dinners and huge teas with home-made cakes, potted meats and pies, exactly like their reactionary fellows," she recalled in her autobiography. "These same young men also expected that after marriage the girl who had shared their week-end cycling or rambling, summer games or winter dances would change all her ways with her marriage ring and begin where their mothers left off."[32] Once past the watershed event of marriage, working-class women were liable to slide into the drudgery with which contemporaries so often associated them—"blowsy, un-kempt, hair back to plaits, scrubbing a step, or in clogs and twisted stockings, shoving a loaded bassinet."[33] Yet husbands could choose to maintain the "same constant round of . . . recreations" to which they were accustomed as bachelors.[34] Roberts's father, for example, was a confirmed and often intemperate drinker who regularly spent his weekends (and, in the time-honored tradition of the skilled arti-san he was, Mondays and other weekdays, too) in a pub. His wife, meanwhile, "rarely went out, except for occasional visits to a fourth rate theatre at the end of the street or for an odd shopping foray." The Reverend Dolling had the same impression of his parishioners in Portsmouth in the 1880s: "Women are far more stay-at-home, and get far fewer treats than men," he noted. Rowntree, too, was struck by the dispiriting, monotonous, and unleisured lives of the wives of York's skilled workers. The mother of a young family, shut out from the exclusively male world of her husband's social life, rarely ven-tured far from home and, "even when able to get away for a day's holiday, or to go out for the evening [was] often obliged to take a baby with her."[35]

CLEARLY, WOMEN DID NOT UNEQUIVOCALLY AND UNIVERSALLY benefit from the general trend to fewer work hours and increased leisure time in the late Victorian and Edwardian periods. Wives and mothers, especially, had few resources for participating in the ebul-lient popular leisure culture with which the age is easily associated, and even those who were still unmarried and relatively carefree did not necessarily have the means for much leisure. But these general observations belie a more complex picture deriving from the particular and varied economic, ideological, and cultural circumstances of different women's lives, circumstances that played a significant part in shaping the nature and extent of their leisure. In the next chapter I look at both the broad patterns and forms of that leisure, and the factors that complicated these patterns and forms.

Chapter Four

LEISURE IN THE LIVES OF

WORKING-CLASS WOMEN

W ORKING GIRLS AND WOMEN FOUND VARIOUS MEANS AND used various resources, scant though these might be, to weave leisure through their day-to-day routines, work, and family responsibilities. They learned to snatch brief moments of respite within the round of work, to make work itself playful, to live for the moment, to take their pleasures when they were offered. Some simply enjoyed the years of relative freedom associated with youth; others, especially those not trammeled by cultural expectations of "respectable" womanhood or by material want or pressing care, made taking pleasure a lifelong habit.

Whatever the particular, enabling circumstances of their individual lives, working-class women made, experienced, and enjoyed their leisure in ways that were crucially influenced by the material and ideological factors stemming from the social and gender order in which they lived. This chapter focuses on some of the forms and locations of that leisure, examines the resources and strategies that women used to make it possible, and considers what their leisure signified for them and for others.

THE 1906 INQUIRY THAT EDWARD CADBURY, CECILE MATHE-
son, and George Shann conducted into women workers in Edwardian Birmingham revealed that for many, low earnings and
debilitating conditions of employment severely restricted their leisure horizons. Most of the working daughters of laborers, the authors
of *Women's Work and Wages* observed, raised on inadequate diets,
were "thin and undersized," some "suffered distinctly from partial
starvation," and few earned sufficient for even a minimal degree of
comfort.[1] Yet young women are among the most conspicuous figures
in descriptions of working-class amusements from the period, and
some of these evidently enjoyed circumstances far more favorable
to a vibrant and varied leisure lifestyle. Both Clara Collet and Cadbury et al. determined that there were wage-earning women whose
family situations were such that they did not have to work but who
chose to do so because they aspired to a higher standard of living,
one that included commercial amusements, stylish outfits, and the
like. "If the girl's parents are in very comfortable circumstances,"
Collet believed, "she frequently pays nothing towards the home expenses, and spends all she earns on dress and amusement." This
"pocket money" competition from the daughters of the more prosperous working classes depressed the wages of those girls and
women from the poorer reaches upon whose earnings many a family
economy crucially depended. "The match girl and the jam girl and
the rope girl," therefore, Collet wrote, "must either live on the sum
which their richer sisters use for dress, or they must work harder
than any of them."[2] Cadbury et al. concluded the same about the
wage-earning daughters of the more comfortably situated artisan
classes of Birmingham. Because of their higher standard of living,
these young women had higher expectations of life: "they have
more resources in themselves [and] on account of this they feel more
need for change and pleasure." Altogether better off than their low-
paid, impoverished counterparts from the ranks of the laboring
masses, the "better-class" of working women had more vitality,
which sought its release at the end of the workday and workweek in

a frantic pursuit of leisure. They were "thriftless" and "restless" and able to indulge their love of fun and fashion because thoughtless parents subsidized their necessary living expenses. Dispatching of their domestic duties on Friday evening—"that is 'candlestick night,' or the universal night for housecleaning"—they made sure that "the Saturday half-holiday [was left] free for marketing and outings with friends."[3]

Equally careless of pressing concerns, reformers asserted, were the many unskilled, low-paid factory and workshop hands whose cultural heritage predisposed them to living recklessly for the pleasures of today and putting up with the inevitable privations of tomorrow. These were quite distinct from the higher-grade, "pocketmoney" workers, Collet noted. The low-paid workers were the girls who had come to be "accepted as the type of . . . girl" to whom everyone referred when he or she spoke of the East End "factory girl." Though few in number in the more reputable box, brush, and cap factories, they were "in the majority in the jam factories, and [held] almost indisputable sway in the rope and match factories." Often the daughters of dock laborers and other irregularly employed workers, they were used to riding the rollercoaster that was life in the lowest strata of the working classes. "One week they have been on the verge of starvation, another they have shared in a 'blowout.' " They were inveterate and rowdy hedonists who had "learnt to hate monotony, to love drink, to use bad language as their mother tongue." They were thriftless and improvident, devout worshipers at the shrine of St. Monday who were happy to work only three days a week and spend their earnings and the rest of their time enjoying themselves. Wages of only eight to ten shillings a week gave these workers "as much as they care[d] to work for, and after that they like[d] holidays best," Collet judged, after studying the wage book of the Victoria Match Factory. This document showed that over half of the Victoria match girls who received the lowest earnings in a week did so because they absented themselves for at least one day and that their holiday was "nearly always taken on Monday." One young woman's history typified the devil-may-care take on life that Collet believed many shared. "She was not eighteen, had worked in two factories, been to service three times, had gone hop-picking and fruit picking and sold flowers and water-cresses in summer; she had set up for herself in lodgings with other factory girls and gone home again when the novelty had worn off." For women such as these, miserly earnings were no impediment to having a good time, and their high leisure preference ensured that they would never willingly be overworked. They would "work just as much as they need[ed] to" and no more.[4]

Running through these and many other contemporary accounts of the leisure of young working women are the same kinds of judgments and concerns with moral regulation that Mariana Valverde has analyzed in connection with fashion. What Valverde argues about upper- and middle-class interpretations of the working woman's love of finery, that it "signified or brought about moral ruin," can be argued equally about upper- and middle-class views of her leisure in general. Viewed through critics' lenses, license blurred into moral laxity and the young working-class woman out on a spree had either already fallen or was fast on her way to doing so. Distinguishable by the "freedom of her walk, the numbers of her friends, and the shrillness of her laugh," she was a stock character in pieces, more often hostile than sympathetic, that journalists, novelists, and social reformers penned on the lower classes at play. Among friends and family, sweethearts, casual acquaintances, and strangers, she is shown taking her pleasures, living carelessly and intemperately in the present, and courting the perils that her censorious observers were sure inhered in these habits.[5]

Recent studies of nineteenth-century consumer culture have indicated that for bourgeois women the public, and especially urban, domain could be a threatening, if exciting, place. Working women's presence there was much more assertive; indeed, it was the boldness with which they sallied forth that helped render streets and other public places no-go areas for respectable ladies. A woman abroad might well be a woman of disrepute. Working women risked the taint, too, but nonetheless streets, alleys, marketplaces, and parks were among their favorite playgrounds. On any given Saturday night (the "great night for amusement"), the main streets of working-class neighborhoods in London thrummed, "ablaze with light, and as busy as a fair," in journalist George Sims's account. "It is a fair, in fact . . . there are shooting-galleries, try-your-strength machines, weighing chairs, raffling boards . . . nothing is lacking but 'three shies a penny' and a Richardson's show to make a complete picture of an old-fashioned fair." When the Reverend Robert Dolling arrived to take up his pastoral duties in the district of Landport, Portsmouth, in the 1880s, he found, "from end to end" along Charlotte Street, "an open fair" full of "shrill gaiety." Dorothy Scannell's memories of the district of London in which she grew to womanhood in the decade before the First World War bear a strong impression of the many and varied delights of Chrisp Street, its central thoroughfare. Scannell depicts a bustling street culture in which business tumbled alongside pleasure. Besides grocers, butchers, drapers, and dry-goods shops, Chrisp Street boasted colorful traders and peddlers, and entertainers of all kinds: "the barrel organ playing outside the public house, the man playing the violin with his eyes closed, the Indian man with his head and legs all bound round with cloth . . . the noise, the smell, the music and, oh, the life!" Similar scenes were to be found throughout urban England; as Robert Roberts—not one to readily romanticize working-class life—observed, in even the poorest districts, "people laughed easily, whistled, sang on high days and jigged in the street—that great recreation room."[6]

In these not-so-mean streets, there was a rich and accessible culture of pleasure for the working woman: "they . . . afford her every kind of diversion," commented reformer Lilian Montagu in a 1902 essay on the leisure habits and haunts of the young wage earner. "In the evenings, on holidays, in the slack season," Beatrice Potter (later Webb) noted of the women of London's East End, "their thoughts rush out and gather in the multitudinous excitements of the . . . streets."[7] Portsmouth's Charlotte Street and Commercial Road were magnets for those looking for fun and excitement, the kind of places in which they "delighted to walk."[8] And not just walk: Punch and Judy shows, dancing bears, sellers of proprietary medicines and ointments, even craftsmen repairing housewares, all these were sources of entertainment.[9] Among the most ubiquitous and popular attractions were itinerant musicians, whose services could be secured for a penny. These were roving centers of lively street dances that figured girls and young women as the star "turns"; indeed, organ-grinders sometimes hired children to dance for them "in the hope of attracting a crowd."[10] Skegness, an east-coast seaside resort, for example, in its late Victorian and Edwardian heyday, rang to the music of "German Bands," one-man bands, hurdy-gurdies, and other barrel organs. Organ-grinders were regular favorites, playing as they did the latest music hall tunes and providing the accompaniment for the "spirited pavement ballets" and waltzes performed outside corner pubs.[11] For Jack London, a party of girls dancing to the tunes of the organ-grinder was the "one beautiful sight" to be found in the "abyss" of the East End.[12] It was in the city of London and other larger urban centers that this street culture was at its most developed, but there were versions of it in smaller communities, too.[13] Itinerant musicians and other entertainers traveled throughout the country, finding their way to rural, out-of-the-way communities. Grace Richardson, born in 1888, lived most of her life in a tiny Lincolnshire village that little of the "outside world" penetrated. Yet street pianos and hurdy-gurdies, "usually played by Italians," were regular visitors that gave good value for a penny. Occasionally, a "German Band" would also pass through the village, en route to resort towns such as Skegness and Mablethorpe. These, too, Richardson remembers as "a source of wonder."[14]

One of the perennial pleasures that streets and other thoroughfares offered was that of simply meeting up and walking along with friends; this, thought Charles Russell, was the "great outdoor

Romantic encounters were a much desired element of many young working-class women's social lives. But what might be nothing more than "a bit of a laugh," or even the beginning of a serious courtship, was to the censorious fraught with dangers. In this illustration by George Cruickshank, the hapless offspring of upper- and middle-class families suffer the consequences of their flighty nursemaids' neglect while "out for an airing" in the park. From Augustus Mayhew and Henry Mayhew, eds., The Greatest Plague of Life *(1859).*

amusement of the people.''[15] In manufacturing centers and industrial districts, young women workers took possession of public high-
ways and byways as soon as the factory whistle or bell sounded the
end of the workday, "walking arm in arm . . . singing and shouting
and pushing other wayfarers off the curbstone.''[16] The exodus from
factories and workshops was a kind of liminal rush from labor to
leisure, in which the young worker could shake off the one and ea-
gerly anticipate the other. William Baron, a dialect poet of the industrial northwest, described a tide of happy expectation pouring out
from the cotton mills in "Hawf Past Five at Neet":

> Yo'll see t'young lasses decked i' smiles,
> O rushin' fro' ther wark;
> To ged donned up to meet ther chaps,
> An' rumble reawnd bi t'park.
> It's t'thowts o' t'walk, un' t'pleasant talk,
> At meks ther faces breet;
> An' fills ther hearts wi' sweet content,
> At hawf past five at neet.[17] (ll. 25–32)

There were sundry attractions on the walk between workplace
and home: bookmakers waiting at the factory gate for those who
fancied a "flutter" (wager) on a horse race, corner shops selling
sweets and penny papers, friends to tease, groups of youths and men
with whom to flirt. Then, later in the evening, a hasty meal eaten
and household chores done, girls and young women took to the
streets again to saunter and gossip with their companions, window-
shop, and engage in banter and horseplay with lads and young men
likewise out in pursuit of recreation.[18] "They . . . like to loiter about
the streets, chatting to their particular friends," Montagu observed
benignly. "When she has done her work she must have her fling,"
Maude Stanley carped, less inclined to be indulgent about the leisure-time predilections of the young Manchester mill hand. "And
so she will saunter through the gas-lighted streets with some companion, male or female.''[19]

In certain discrete segments of time and at certain prominent locations, working women did not merely enjoy a casual, sociable walk
around; they promenaded. This ritualized display of self and view-
ing and encountering of others could be understood as the working-
class woman's equivalent of the London "Season."[20] On Saturday
evenings and Sunday afternoons, they put on their "Sunday
clothes" and formed up to parade along central streets and public
walks, through and around market squares and parks. "Footway and
roadway are alike taken up, and crowds, on the whole merry, pass
up and down for some two hours," Charles Russell recorded of the
custom as he observed it in northern cities and towns. "Both sexes
take part . . . usually in little knots of three or four or more boys or
girls."[21] Along the Bow Road and Petticoat Lane in the East End of
London, down Coney Street and up to Clifton's Mount in York,
through Fishergate in Preston, factory workers, shop assistants, and
domestic servants, dressed in the finest outfits their budgets would
allow, strolled along to admire and be admired. The crowded parade
street was one of the principal places in which to meet young men
and strike up with them the acquaintanceships that could lead to
"walking out," and ultimately to courtship and marriage.[22] By common consent, the "Monkey Run," the "Monkey Rack," "The
Drag" (the name given to the ritual varied from town to town), was
"for picking girls up." "We used to have a bit of a laugh and walk
down Coney Street . . . and the lads used to whistle at us," recalled
one York woman in domestic service, whose habit it was to sneak
out with her friend on Sundays on the pretext of attending church.
"If [their employers]'d . . . known we'd have been in trouble."[23]

Streets and other open, public spaces and the unrestrainedly free
and often raucous leisure culture that thrived in them did, indeed,
trouble upper- and middle-class commentators. The streets had a
"perilous fascination" for the working girls of London's East End,
who brought to their impromptu dances around the barrel organ
emotions that made a deep and disturbing impression on social reformer Helen Bosanquet. The whole setting of the dance, the drama

of which it was such a lively element, "the glare of the gaslamps, the busy thronging to and fro, the wild free intercourse among acquaintances and strangers alike [were] irresistible attractions to these excitable young creatures after the monotony of the day." "I have seen a letter from a girl describing the delights of the street dance and the meeting of friends, which, though perfectly simple in expression, was almost passionate in its intensity of feeling," Bosanquet wrote.[24] Such passions once aroused, she implied—especially in a young woman whose nature and environment disposed her to having little self-control—were dangerous. Similarly, the Commercial Road and Southsea Common in Portsmouth, though delightfully alluring places to young working women, were, in clergyman Dolling's view, "a perpetual menace . . . full not only of rollocking, good-natured, thoughtless soldiers and sailors, but of those most hateful of all living creatures, the older profligate." "Sin continually" stalked many of Dolling's parishioners in the streets of the neighborhoods in which they lived. There they saw "other girls who have no work to do—would to God they knew more plainly the awfulness of the work they do do!—able to dress well and go to places of amusement," he fretted, "while they themselves are unable to earn enough to keep themselves in the actual necessaries of life."[25] The passage from innocuous, youthful pleasure seeking to moral ruin could be effected frighteningly easily under such circumstances, according to journalist Hugh Shimmin. On Sunday evenings, the young folk of Liverpool customarily headed for the landing stages at the George's and Prince's Piers on the River Mersey to promenade and to meet up with one another. "Older heads, with more vicious intentions, then began to frequent the stage," Shimmin complained, until it was "almost impossible for a female to pass . . . without being subjected to the rudeness, vulgarity, obscenity, or profanity of the shameless hordes, of both sexes," who congregated there. The young women who assembled on the stages, with "their gaudy dress, rude speeches, and unseemly conduct," were not " 'social evils' proper," Shimmin judged, but were fast on their way to becoming outcasts from decent society, seduced by the "fast young men" attracted by " 'the game of the Landing Stage.' "[26]

The unashamed "indecency and immorality" that Shimmin saw in the Liverpool monkey run did not necessarily extend elsewhere—or, perhaps, simply was more discreetly conducted. In Preston there were specific parade venues where prostitutes solicited for business and prospective clients sized them up, but these were well-known to the local youth and the "respectable" avoided them.[27] Elsewhere, there might be some "coarseness" and a generally low "tone and character" to the custom, and rather too much "noise and distraction" to suit the taste of a social reformer such as Charles Russell, but those who took part insist that there was no "rowdiness or aught like that."[28] "It is not rough, nor is there anything which passes the bounds of decency or propriety," judged Charles Booth of the weekend promenading of the young people of Hackney, London.[29] This is not surprising, perhaps, as, in several towns, the whole proceeding was conducted under the watchful eye of a policeman or two who "kept you moving."[30] The diaries of Sydney Race, in which this young, middle-class man depicts himself as a self-consciously detached but fascinated participant in the rich, popular leisure culture of Nottingham in the 1890s, confirm these impressions. During Goose Fair, one of the streets in the town's central market district became the site of a seasonal monkey walk. "There has been the usual crush up Beastmarket Hill," Race notes for Friday, October 5, 1893. "Here all the young would be swells of each sex congregate & go up & down in long rows. At intervals rushes occur & a Great block is formed. The only drawback is that wicked policemen have a habit of throwing unruly persons out with violence." In the characteristically dualistic voice that Race uses in all his descriptions of Nottingham's "mass" leisure, he goes on to capture the invitingly promiscuous nature of the annual crush: "However it seems to be enjoyed by those in it & of course it gives an excellent opportunity to a fellow to help a young lady along & to catch her round the waist occasionally when in danger."[31]

From the perspective of the puritan that lurked not far below the surface of Race the young man about town, this sort of attitude and behavior flirted worryingly with moral laxity. But the promenading young women who so tempted him were not quite so ready to be victimized by sexual predators or as lacking in moral fiber as critics seemed to think. Even some upper- and middle-class reformers were aware that promenaders observed their own distinct codes of behavior and that these were by no means lax. As Lilian Montagu understood, "a self-respecting" young woman knew "exactly how far her intercourse" with any man with whom she took up could go "without [its] becoming dangerous." Hannah Mitchell was one, careful to establish and stay within clear parameters. She enjoyed the lighthearted flirtations of the monkey run and presented herself in it as a woman of some experience in romantic matters. "Sallie and I were both passionately fond of red roses, and whenever we could afford it we always wore them, pretending, like the silly girls we were, that they came from other admirers," she admitted. But Mitchell was not easy game for anyone; most assuredly, she would not be "picked up."[32] There must have been a fair few similarly resolute and discriminating lasses in Nottingham, too. Though the Beastmarket Hill crush drew Race time and again, and though he had "much fun" chatting and "chaffing" with the young working women at Goose Fair and other similar public festivities, he never records in his diary any amorous conquests as a consequence.[33]

Parades of a more elaborate, formalized, and ceremonial nature were also opportunities for young women to enjoy the dressing up, display, and social intercourse that made the monkey run so attractive. Religious and other groups marked the Whit and Easter holidays, holy days such as Corpus Christi, anniversaries, and parish wakes with ritual processions. These walks—carefully staged, orchestrated, and controlled—had largely replaced the more boisterous rough-and-tumble of earlier nineteenth-century popular festivals

Working-class women's delight in fashionable dress provoked great concern among their social betters, and the exuberant style that some boldly adopted increased those anxieties. Here the lady of the house surreptitiously looks on in horror and dismay as her maid sets off on a holiday "dressed out to the death." George Cruickshank, in Augustus Mayhew and Henry Mayhew, eds., The Greatest Plague of Life *(1859).*

and had become a major element in the commemorations and celebrations of a variety of voluntary associations. Clearly set off as special days in the annual calendar, and often tied to customary holidays with a deep, rich history, they were a source of intense, heightened pleasure, all the more so because of the extended period of anticipation and preparation that preceded them. Dresses and stockings of fine, delicate fabric and lisle thread, and shoes (not workaday boots or clogs) of the best make that one's means permitted, were de rigueur.[34] Lancashire cotton operatives were among those who could afford some enviable outfits for their Whit walks, wakes, and holiday processions. "Very pretty they were . . . with their slim waist lines and enormous 'bustle' bows of watered-silk ribbons," Hannah Mitchell recalled of one lot of Sunday school anniversary dresses that she, in a wryly ironic twist, had stayed up long nights helping to make.[35] In the annual Whit Monday processions in Preston, Lancashire, Elizabeth Roberts notes, tens of thousands of children and adults walked through the town, displaying both "social and religious solidarity" in their "conspicuous spending" on beautiful, impractical clothing.[36] Displays of religiosity upper- and middle-class observers found laudable; conspicuous spending on fashionable outfits came too close for comfort to the "sin of consumption" that Valverde discusses, the moral flaw of a love of finery.

In novels and parliamentary reports alike, Valverde discerns a discourse that identified working women's pursuit of fashion as a chief cause of the fall of many: "for the sake of a few ribbons" they were prepared to take to the streets.[37] The sacrifices that young wage-earning women were willing to make in order to be able to indulge "on a cheap scale" their desire for "*chic*" certainly impressed reformers, though they did not elicit approval.[38] "Almost without exception," Helen Bosanquet wrote in an 1898 study of wage-earning women's living standards, "they are only half-fed and half-clothed."[39] Yet during the "blossoming time" between the ages of "sixteen and eighteen or twenty," she wrote in another work in 1908, "no extreme of poverty will keep the flower or feather out of the hat, or the gay colour out of the dress."[40] Even the lowliest and meanest paid of London's young working women could afford the exuberant millinery "confections" that so often caught the eye of upper- and middle-class observers.[41] "Here are the factory girls," wrote Walter Besant in a sketch of Hampstead Heath on an August Bank Holiday Monday, "adorned with crimson and blue feathers."[42] "Very large numbers" of young girls fresh from school went into service as "generals," Bosanquet determined, and delighted in spending their hard-earned three or four shillings a week on the huge, gorgeously trimmed hats that seem to have been the primary identifying feature of London's East End factory workers. "Such hats! And such feathers in them!" she marveled.[43] The whimsical indulgences of the stereotypical factory girl were less troubling than the dire moral straits into which the equally stereotypical "better class" of working woman was likely to be carried by her elevated and inappropriate standards of dress. "The young lady who goes to a warehouse or a superior factory is singularly modest in this respect," Clara Collet judged. "The importance she attaches to outside things shows how much more keenly she is actuated by ideal than by material wants. She starves herself first . . . she stints herself in bed clothing and underclothing next," and finally, worn down by the drudgery and struggle, "she too often sacrifices maidenhood itself." These vain and misguided creatures "do not sell themselves for bread," Collet moralized, "they sin for the externals which they have learnt to regard as essentials."[44]

The strategies that working women employed in pursuit of a pleasing appearance might well have included exchanging sexual favors, but they had plenty of other tried and true economies that, in and of themselves, sullied no one's virtue. They frequently bought boots, clothes, hats, feathers, and, when they were preparing for marriage, household goods such as linens, by contributing small weekly sums into a "club" run by one woman who acted as an agent for a local shopkeeper. The club holder earned a discount on the goods purchased according to the amount of business that she managed to secure. Cadbury et al. described the system thus: "fifteen girls wanting boots will agree to pay 6d. each for fifteen weeks. Each pay-day they draw lots, and the fortunate one takes the 7s. 6d. and gets her boots." Popular as it was, the arrangement had its drawbacks. "The [shopkeeper] knows you're a club member," one woman explained, "and you have to buy from what he chooses to show you, and he puts away his best things; if you save your money you can look around elsewhere and get the clothes you like best." Clubs also incorporated an element of gambling that critics deemed "almost as risky in one way as the cup of tea with its spoonful of rum is in another; as the girls say, 'You may get your things before you've paid for them.' " And even such an innocuous form of credit betrayed the principles of thrift and self-denial that the upper- and middle-classes were fond of encouraging working people to embrace. Young women rarely saved, Cadbury et al. criticized, "except for some immediate object . . . through their clothing clubs."[45]

Yet constructing and maintaining a presentable appearance took time and ingenuity, and often entailed putting up with someone else's castoffs—the horror of which prospect struck reformer Maude Stanley on one occasion as she watched working-class women picking through the secondhand garments on sale in a street market. "What would it be to be doomed to be dressed in these cast-off garments?" she found herself reflecting in a moment of empathy that she all too infrequently reveals in her writings on those she determined to reform.[46] Ready-made or shop-bought clothing was a status symbol to which many lower-class women were rarely, if ever, able to aspire. Mary Kirby, for example, whose father brought home what was considered a "good" wage and was in constant, regular employment, "never [wore] many shop-made clothes." "I learned to make me own, and I've always made me own." Likewise, Margaret Hutchinson's mother made all her children's outfits from clothing that had been given to her. "She used to unpick everything and re-make them . . . and I had a grandmother who used to come some days and used to sit picking out all these clothes for us so that

mother could stitch them at night." Those who were skilled in tai-
loring or dressmaking could craft some beautiful outfits and through
occupational connections were able to buy high quality materials at
prices that put what was otherwise unattainable within their reach.[47]
Selina Cooper, a Lancashire working-class feminist and socialist, enjoyed the sobriquet of "Belle of Brierfield," thanks to the smart suits
that her mother tailored at home for her. In contrast, Kathleen
Dayus felt like "a proper charlie" when she first went out to full-
time employment in an older sister's dress that her mother had cut
down to fit and "cobbled together with black thread." Once she
was earning, Dayus had the means and the flair to assemble some
pleasingly attractive outfits from secondhand and hand-me-down
clothing, but to be able to buy new, good-quality clothes was a frustrating aspiration for her.[48] In the consumer culture that recent work
indicates was booming in this period, it was understandable that, as
soon as young wage earners could afford to do so, they satisfied their
yearning for something more. "You wanted better clothing. You
didn't want hand-downs and re-makes you know. You wanted something a little bit better," Margaret Hutchinson attested.[49] Individual
notions of what constituted "something a little bit better" ran the
gamut from what detractors saw as "shabby finery," and even sympathetic commentators judged "rather a tawdry smartness," to a
style of dress and appearance that allowed London prostitutes to
pass for ladies of quality.[50] The possibility of such a masquerade
succeeding was one source of the anxiety that working women's love
of style provoked among commentators. But even working women
who earned their fashionable attire through sheer "honest" labor
aroused censure for "aping" their social superiors or failing to put
their money to a more mundane, provident use. The perverse logic
makes sense only in the period of flux when the Victorian culture of
production (which lauded industry and thrift) met and clashed with
the emerging culture of indulgent consumption.[51]

THERE WERE NUMEROUS COMMERCIAL LEISURE ENTERPRISES
adding to the heady mix of pleasures. Journalists, clergymen, and

social reformers lamented that beer houses, gin palaces, coffee-houses, public houses, dancing saloons, singing saloons, theaters, "penny gaffs," "free and easies," and concert rooms represented the "darkest phase" of urban life.[52] But the moral clouds that some saw hanging over such popular leisure-time resorts couldn't darken the prospect of the heightened experience of *"life"*—"that subtle experience of passion"—that they held out for young working-class women with money to spare and the inclination for a "spree."[53]

Certain leisure resorts catered largely to men; certainly in the early to mid-nineteenth century, the women who visited public houses, drinking saloons, singing saloons, free and easies, and such were likely to be cast as disreputable at best and as prostitutes at worst. Parliamentary inquiries in the second half of the nineteenth century obsessed over the moral status of the young women who frequented public places of amusement. The concern at mid-century tended to be with the threat that prostitutes and other "low" women posed to the upper- and middle-class men consorting with them. Of dancing saloons in the metropolis in the early 1850s, Sir Richard Mayne admitted that he did "not know that they are directly immoral; but they are places where women of the town undoubtedly go, and where young men meet and dance with them." Coffee shops, public houses, beer shops, and theaters were similarly suspect as places where prostitutes plied their trade and "loose, idle young men about town" debauched the unwary or unthinking.[54] The reforming journalist Hugh Shimmin agreed. The female clientele of an entertainment lounge in Liverpool in the mid-1850s consisted of "women of a very low grade" whose "carriage . . . was very free" and whose "positions were very easy."[55] Such establishments were very popular with young working women, not all of whom were of easy virtue, but in associating there with "low" women and "loose" men, they risked their reputations—and more besides, by some accounts. The Reverend John Clay reported to the 1852–1853 Select Committee on Places of Public Entertainment that four-fifths of the beer houses in Blackburn, Lancashire, were brothels where innocent young girls were plied with drink and seduced, and thus fell into prostitution.[56] Witnesses to the 1854 Select Committee on Public Houses testified that there were numerous similar establishments in London, the worst of which, according to one, was the Eagle Tavern in the City Road. "As far as young females [were] concerned," the Eagle was "one of the most demoralising, if not the most demoralising place in London."[57]

Similar anxieties about actual and potential prostitutes attended the dancing halls and saloons to which young working women thronged. The *Women's Union Journal* commented prudishly on London's public dancing saloons, "we can only say that women who have any self-respect should not go to such places," and regretted that there were not more of these establishments conducted "under respectable conditions." Women workers "deserve and require such exercise and recreation as much as their richer sisters, many of whose lives are a constant round of amusement of various kinds," the periodical argued.[58] Shimmin found many young workers patronizing the dancing rooms of Liverpool that he explored in the mid-1850s on a foray into the "wilds" of that city.[59] At a twice-weekly public "assembly" that had originally opened as a dancing class, he watched as some "sixty-four persons, chiefly young people, the majority varying from sixteen to twenty years of age," took the floor to perform a quadrille "with becoming gravity." The girls appeared to be workers, mostly shop assistants and milliners, their partners, "youths, merchant's clerks, shop assistants, and a few mechanic apprentices." "There is no introduction necessary to gain admission [sixpence paid at the door was sufficient]," Shimmin noted portentously. "Young men or women [went] in some instances together, in others alone, and 'pick[ed] up,' with 'sweethearts,' or form[ed] associations and companionships." Between dances, couples "dawdled and chatted," or retired to the refreshment rooms and, at eleven o'clock, after dancing a final, lively galop, "in the majority of cases," the young men took their partners home. The rest of "the girls form[ed] little parties and ramble[d] home themselves." In another "very celebrated" Liverpool dancing saloon, some sixty to eighty young women and men gathered to dance under the direction of the proprietor. "[He] stands up in the centre of the room, having white kid gloves on, and in his right hand a baton, with which he beats time, and so directs the enjoyment of his visitors." "The girls here do not remove either bonnets or mantles, cloaks or veils, but just turn in from their walk," Shimmin observed. "Or in many cases, to judge from their appearance, from their work, to spend an hour or two in dancing with the male friends who may have brought them, or whom they meet here." All too readily, seduced by the music, the rhythms of the dance, the blandishments of the young men attending on them, Shimmin averred, respectable working women who disported in such places could slide into sin.[60]

The moral laxity and coarseness that reformers judged to prevail at other commercial amusements such as "penny gaffs" were equally disturbing. Penny gaffs were a cheap staple for young city- and town-dwellers and seasonal spectacles for rural audiences. At one in Whitechapel, London, in the 1870s, James Greenwood observed that the eager audience for a "new and original equestrian spectacle entitled 'Gentleman Jack, or the Game of High Toby,'" were mostly young costers (fruit mongers) of about fifteen to sixteen years of age, and "the female of [their] bosom." The only exceptions to these were "a few old men and a few children": all found—in Greenwood's judgment—the vulgarity and degraded humor of the sorry spectacle hugely entertaining.[61] In the 1890s, ragtag touring companies were still mounting the same kinds of performances for small-town and village audiences in the provinces. Sydney Race attended several that visited the Nottingham district in the 1890s, judging that, though some were decidedly "poor stuff" and appealed largely to the "rabble," others were of an unexpectedly high quality. At a Pavilion Theatre, temporarily erected from canvas and timber in Beeston on the outskirts of Nottingham in early December 1894, he and his friend enjoyed a typically melodramatic play, "Firematch the Trooper or the Striking of the Hour."

"The Company," Race approved, was "certainly far above the type
one would expect to find in such a place—all the performers seemed
refined, used no bad language, & spoke good English." On Boxing
Day at Sneinton Market, Race found "a very old Theatre with a
waggon in front to form a stage." "Royners" was "very down-at-
heel looking." The company was made up of "the master of the
affair, a woman, once good looking & still somewhat so now, in
tights, a girl of about 14, two children of say 10 & 6 & a boy of about
12 dressed as a clown." The scene that they acted out "was very
poor stuff," Race felt, all the more so because the woman had a
black eye "& so had always to stand with the other facing us wh:
[sic] upset things somewhat." "This was indeed a 'penny-gaff,' "
Race concluded, "& I felt quite sorry for the children. The man
looked decent and to have a heart but he was dressed poorly & I
heard him sware once or twice."[62]

The permanent music saloons and "amusement lounges" in provincial cities provided scarcely more elevated entertainment, Shimmin and others asseverated. In Liverpool and Manchester in the
second half of the nineteenth century, young women crowded such
places with friends, female and male, to take in vocalists and violin-
ists, jugglers and tumblers, clog dancers and ballet dancers, and *tab-
leaux vivants*. Average weekly audiences in each of the three largest
music saloons in Manchester in 1852 were estimated at twenty-five
thousand and consisted primarily of young mill hands, female and
male.[63] In the smaller, seedier "free concert rooms" and "song and
supper rooms" in Liverpool and elsewhere, semiprofessionals and
amateurs performed before "audiences . . . of various ages and
grades in life," "bare-necked, lightly-dressed girls" among them. In
one such establishment, Shimmin looked on, ever alert to signs of
the expected moral decay, while a violinist, a female vocalist, and a
minstrel singer—along with a young man from the audience who
performed an impromptu step dance—regaled some twenty-five
persons. "There were five females present," "evidently all from the
lowest" but not "the most degraded class," he determined.[64]

From mid-century, music halls were distinguished, in terms of audience, content, locale, and the like, from free and easies, singing saloons, and concert rooms, and distinct sectors of the licensed trade and commercial leisure industry clearly began to cater to young working women. By the 1870s, the increasingly capitalized, newly licensed music hall was shaking off its worst reputation and emerging as a widely popular entertainment venue attracting every gradation, stratum, and caste of the working and lower middle classes.

It became a distinctive and central part of the leisure culture of the young.[65] In the "row upon row and tier upon tier of solid humanity" of the music halls, cheap theaters, and "varieties" in London's working-class districts, for instance, Helen Bosanquet discerned "families, friends, and couples," while "youths in hundreds [took] their girls for an outing."[66] The crowds of young people in the cheaper seats of the East End hall impressed George Sims when he visited one night in 1889. "There wasn't room to cram another boy in the place," he observed. "The gallery and pit were full of boys and girls from eight to fifteen . . . and the bulk of the audience in the other parts were quite young people." The gallery, especially, was boys' territory: "Space . . . for a human foot to rest there was absolutely none."[67] The typical audience in one of the larger halls, the Canterbury in the 1890s, was rather more diverse and mature, largely comprising tradesmen, mechanics, and other working men, according to the reports of inspectors employed by the London County Council. Unescorted women risked being taken for prostitutes, but the badge of immorality could not be as readily pinned on them as it had been in earlier decades. Thus, observed one inspector, among the women at one hall were some identifiable as "wives," or as "girls" out with their "lads," and others belonging to a shadowy, unnamed further category, "whose *behaviour* [did not] mark them as prostitutes [original emphasis]."[68] To prejudiced minds, unaccompanied women were inevitably suspect, for they might indeed be prostitutes looking for customers, and some halls would not admit them, though others would if they were "respectably" and "decently" dressed. Owners and managers of the bigger halls, eager to deflect criticism about rowdy patrons and raunchy performers, pointed to the presence of "respectable" women (wives and sweethearts) as testimony of the wholesomeness of the leisure fare they offered. Laxness in controlling the kinds of women allowed in could cost a music hall its operating permit: the police opposed the granting of a license to the Oxford in London in 1874 because the management had admitted women "without men." In the 1890s, the Theatres and Music Halls Committee of the London County Council as a matter of course rejected applications from establishments that they suspected of being frequented by prostitutes.[69]

In the provinces, where the tamed, heavily capitalized music hall had its origins, the same process was at work, targeting women, especially, but not exclusively, those judged to be already outside the moral pale. Exercising the powers given to municipal and other public authorities by the 1888 Local Government Act, the Stage Plays Committee of the Borough of Sheffield established its licensing regulations in February 1892. Among the numerous proscriptions against riotous, indecent, and offensive behavior, both on the stage and in the house, the committee ruled "that no common prostitute . . . or other notoriously disorderly person shall be knowingly admitted into or permitted to remain in any theatre." In the first decade of the twentieth century, the Stage Plays Licensing Committee extended its policing of women's leisure practices by denying them the right to buy alcohol or even enter the bars in local variety theaters. In July 1901 the committee granted promoter Alan Young a twelve-month license for the Empire Palace Theatre of Varieties, but stipulated "that no women shall be served with intoxicating liquors in any of the Refreshment Bars, nor shall any women be allowed therein except the attendants." When Young applied for a similar license the following year, he was successful, despite being opposed by the Sheffield Citizens' Committee, the Sheffield Women's Christian Temperance Association, the Sheffield Free Church Council, and the Reverend J. Gilmore. Young's suit was strengthened by the chief constable, who assured the licensing committee that he had received no report of any breach of the regulations governing the Empire Palace in the previous year. The committee also removed the ban on selling alcohol to women; presumably the female patrons of the theater had proven themselves capable of self-control, or perhaps Young had managed to get the ear of a councillor sympathetic to a plea about loss of revenue.[70] Generally, it was a sound political strategy for theater and music hall promoters and managers to exert some control over the behavior of their patrons to the extent that it did not spoil the fun. And it was good business policy for them to play up, as they did, the presence of respectable family groups and chaste courting couples in the audience, to convey the impression of a largely unobjectionable—though still quite "vulgar"—program and a happily mixed—though still quite "rough"— clientele.

In the context of these changes, young working women out on the town were not quite so vulnerable to the charge of immorality or to being cast as victims of vice, and many took advantage of the pleasures that a growing leisure industry offered. Data on music hall audiences in the provinces suggest that women were a significant presence, and that it was neither wives with families in tow, nor single women in the company of their beaus, but young, unmarried wage earners who formed the largest single category of those attending. Analyzing the casualty and witness lists of official inquiries on disasters (fires and panics) in northern music halls from the mid- to late nineteenth century, Dagmar Hoher finds that young, female wage earners from a variety of trades and occupations made up the largest subset of women present. In halls in Sheffield, Manchester, and Liverpool (and in Dundee, Glasgow, and Aberdeen in Scotland), there were message girls, domestic servants, textile workers, scissors filers, and potters, "women . . . with money to spare."[71] Most typically, these attended in large groups, usually with their workmates but also with neighbors and family members in what one observer from the 1860s described as "monster convivial parties."

They lounged about, drank, smoked, ate, chattered, and laughed, as well as took in the entertainment provided on the stage.[72]

There were significant contrasts between different communities in this regard in Lancashire. The Manchester textile mills offered women relatively high wages and attractive terms of work, and there many more attended the halls than in Liverpool, where there was little female wage work and what there was tended to be casual, episodic, and poorly paid. Higher earnings and more precisely defined and generally shorter workdays provided these women with the kinds of resources for leisure that those in the more exacting, poorly regulated trades could only wish that they had. "We envied the cotton workers, who streamed out of the mill gates as soon as the 'buzzer' went at half past five," remembered Hannah Mitchell who, as a seamstress in the same region, often worked till ten o'clock or later.[73]

THE AIR OF COMMUNAL CONVIVIALITY SURROUNDING THE MUSIC hall experience also prevailed in the public house, where, again, young working women congregated with their workmates, friends, and neighbors and trysted with their lovers. Public houses, alehouses, and other drinking places had customarily tended to be largely masculine preserves (at least, with respect to those drinking in them) and there were proscriptions against "respectable" women frequenting them.[74] Rose Sturdy's father, for example, a publican who kept several licensed houses in York in the period before the First World War, refused to admit women. "We don't serve women. We don't have women in pubs, we don't have women in," she remembers him insisting. Sturdy herself took these injunctions to heart. "It would never occur to me to go in a pub," she commented.[75] But such sentiments were by no means universally held, varying from one town, district, and social grouping, indeed, from one establishment to another. A census conducted on one Saturday night in 1885 in the town of Nottingham numbered over one thousand "girls under twenty-one" among those entering seven public houses (how the census takers determined the age of the girls is not clear).[76] Benjamin Seebohm Rowntree assayed similar projects in York that yielded similar findings. His investigators observed a number of public houses in various neighborhoods of the city in July 1900, counting the numbers of women, men, and children entering and leaving, the length of time they stayed, and whether they drank on the premises. In one pub, watched for seventeen consecutive hours on Saturday, July 7, of 550 people entering, 179 were women and 113 were children. The busiest period was from eight until eleven in the evening, when "the house was simply packed with men and women shouting and singing." On Sunday, July 15, 211 adults visited the same establishment, and of those, 66 were women; on Wednesday, July 18, 81 of 253 adults were women. In two other houses, approximately one-third and one-quarter of the adults entering were women. Relatively few of these women drank on the premises and, of those who did, only a handful stayed for longer than about fifteen minutes. Most of the female customers, especially those in "the more respectable . . . districts," "carried out" their beer in jugs.[77]

Although men were in the majority, women had a definite presence. Again in York, Rowntree judged that "many girls spen[t] their evenings in public-houses."[78] Indeed, in terms of composition and certainly in terms of mood and behavior, the crowd in some pubs on a busy night seems to have been the music hall audience in all but name and locale. Noting that these two institutions were the pillars of working-class leisure in London, for instance, George Sims observed in one East End public house after the other, on barrels against the wall and on wooden forms, groups of young women and young men, sitting around talking. "And," he added, in the censorious tone that the upper and middle classes often adopted when commenting on working-class amusements, "spending an idle hour in putting the bulk of the week's wages down their throats." Rowntree, avowed temperance advocate that he was, was less judgmental of the assemblies of young women and men that made up the bulk of the custom of certain public houses in York, and obviously was aware of the pub's attractions. The rooms were "brilliantly lit" and "gaudily decorated," and in the winter were kept "temptingly warm." The clientele comprised almost entirely "young persons, youths and girls, sitting round the room and at small tables," and though everyone drank, no one did so heavily. "At intervals one of the company is called on for a song, and if there is a chorus, every one who can will join in it," Rowntree wrote. "Throughout the whole assembly there is an air of jollity and an absence of irksome restraint which must prove very attractive after a day's confinement in factory or shop."[79]

It seemed to Charles Booth and many of his informants that this kind of use of public houses by this kind of crowd was part of a changing pattern in working-class drinking and leisure habits. There was less drunkenness, most opined, but more drinking. The consensus was that "the increase in drinking is to be laid mainly to the account of the female sex," a development that Booth suggested was "one of the unexpected results of the emancipation of women." Because they were less dependent on men, women could afford to pay for their own drinks and so they were shaking off the long-standing association between drinking in a pub with a man and prostitution. Women felt less "shame at entering a public house," and even though when women and men drank together, the latter "[stood] treat," women often drank together and treated each other. Factory girls drank, stated one of Booth's informants, and sometimes "[took] too much," but were then "surprised at their own state. They do not drink for drinking's sake, and very little upsets them, especially on an empty stomach. That is why so many are noisy on Saturday, when they are paid and let out early, having had no lunch. They take a nip and become hilarious in no time."[80]

There were those who were quite adept at throwing off irksome restraint even in the confinement of the workplace. Drinking rituals had long been central to artisanal culture, and in some factories and workshops they continued to be important elements of women's work and leisure culture, despite employers' attempts at imposing stringent work discipline. Investigating the wages, working conditions, and standards of living of women in London in the 1890s, Clara Collet was dismayed at the extent of drinking that went on "in many factories, especially the day before Christmas." She surmised that the custom was linked to the relationships and hierarchies within the workplace and thought that it contributed to the corruption and abuse of female employees when their overseers were men.[81] Fuddled with drink, young female workers whose earnings could depend on whether they were in favor with the foreman were more vulnerable to the "grave moral danger" posed by "the indiscriminate mixing of men and women."[82] But specific customs varied widely and what was a long-established and carefully cherished practice in one establishment or trade might be unheard of in another. Edward Cadbury et al. described how, in some Birmingham manufactories, for example, "the custom prevails of treating the forewoman on pay day in the hope of propitiating her, and influencing her distribution of work in the coming week; for this purpose the party adjourns to a public-house." Party clubs organized to raise funds for celebrating Christmas and other seasonal holidays, or to mark someone's birthday, were another variant of women's workplace drinking in Birmingham. For several weeks in succession, individuals subscribed 1d. or 2d. into a common fund and, on the appointed day, the overseer stopped work half an hour early and the whole group enjoyed "cakes and tea, with which they mix[ed] rum or gin." To observe a particularly momentous event—an impending marriage, for instance—workers contributed a lump sum of 6d. or 7d. and a manager or employer sometimes supplemented the supply of alcohol with a "present of spirits." An enterprising local publican might also donate a bottle of gin or rum, anticipating that his generosity would be amply rewarded later when the drinking party decamped from workplace to pub.

"Gypsy" parties were a similar means of organizing and funding work outings. Anyone wishing to join the party paid an agreed-upon amount per week for a specified period in advance. If, once all the expenses incurred on the trip had been paid, any participants had contributed more than was needed, the money left over was returned to them.[83] "The working girl loves outings," Lilian Montagu commented on these events, "especially when they are on a big scale, for then they are thoroughly exciting." "To be completely delightful," the trip must "include a long drive in a brake, a protracted 'wash and brush up' immediately on arrival, followed by a lounge on the grass, with opportunities to 'catch the sun.' " A good feast, "plenty of songs and games, swings and merry-go-rounds," and to finish, "an orgie of photography," made for a perfectly pleasurable outing.[84] Sundays were favorite days for excursions, as were annual Bank Holidays. Charles Booth describes huge parties of day-trippers departing from London to Epping Forest, Greenwich, Epsom Downs, and Hampstead Heath. One "consisted of sixteen vehicles, containing all the girls from some large works with their young men, as to whom all that [one cynical observer] could say, was, 'Well, they dress better, but their manners are about the same.' " The manager of one factory that employed large numbers of young women told Booth that it was "useless to open the works on the day after Bank Holiday, or even for two days." Perfectly happy to forgo a day or two's earnings, the women liked to extend their spree and recovery from the same for as long as possible.[85]

THE EXCITEMENT AND GOOD TIMES THAT THE YOUNG WORKING woman pursued in pubs, music halls, and streets, in dancing, drinking, and dressing in the height of fashion, rendered her singularly open to censure. The more sympathetic appreciated that what some saw, at best, as a certain recklessness and, at worst, an expression of a dissolute nature might simply be a wish for "that . . . which the girls call *life*, and in which they revel." But it is very difficult to gain a sense of what this life felt like for the young women who sought it; the vast bulk of the sources so rarely offer any interior light on their emotions. There are little flashes, of course, and if they do nothing more than reflect the cultural and moral chasm that the upper and middle classes perceived to exist between them and working-class women, these are helpful. The story that one reformer recounted of her attempt to persuade a seventeen-year-old factory worker who was a confirmed drinker to give up the habit might be received in this way. "Ah Missus," the young woman is said to have responded when the lady urged her to try sobriety, "if once you knew the pleasure of getting jolly well drunk yourself, you wouldn't ask *me* to give it up!" Sources that attest to the layers and complexities of motivation, meaning, and implication hidden behind and within such a compact bon mot as this don't often come to hand. Those that do deserve close attention, and so I am quoting the following letter, written in 1917, at the very end of the period with which this study is concerned, in the fullness it warrants:

My Dearest Eric, I have received your letter and thanks ever so much, as I have been looking for one all the week & I was ever so pleased. Well dear I am glad you have arrived at Bridge all right & that you like the place. Sorry that you did not get your papers till late but I always post them on Friday night & always will do while you are away so please dont think I have forgotten you again for dear you know I shall never do that simply because *I love you* & no one else. I hope the weather will keep nice now you are under canvas for it will be quite a change especially from home life but never [mind?] dear old boy cheer up better days in store & also keep thinking of *one* who is waiting at home for you. (You know who that is I think)

I went to the Pictures last night, it was very nice. (Liberty gets more exciting than ever also there was a Film called Iris I dont know wether you have seen it. It was extra but it brought back painful memorys as in one part where the lovers had to part, but our case is quite different to that for the girl did not keep true till he came back, but I shall always be true to you for you are the only *boy I want*. I should have liked to have been with you when you marked our initials on the Bridge, but perhaps we may have the chance to go and find them together some day. Well Eric I thought you were going to give up cycling but it seems as if you have had to take it up again but never mind I am sure you enjoy it. I dont think I shall do much of it this summer. Well dear I think I have said all this time & as I hear baby has woke up I shall have to see to her while Mother finishes dinner wish you were here to have some with me. Hope so before long well Goodbye with My Best Love yr. Sweetheart for ever Hilda

PS Write as soon as pos. Won't you dear Love Hilda [emphases in original][86]

When Hilda wrote this letter, she had begun a transition from youthful romance and heady passion to a phase of her life in which she would have to work very hard to find much of either. But the memories lingered, brightening one young woman's way through one of the darkest periods of England's twentieth century and holding out the possibility of "better days in store" once the war was over. She alludes to the pastimes and pleasures that she and Eric had shared—cycling, regular visits to the pictures, their delight in one another's company. She has already begun to tend to his leisure needs, for she dutifully sends him his papers on "Friday night & always will" and offers this as an act of her devotion and fidelity. She offers, too, a fragile little prayer that he will return safely, that together they will be able to return to the bridge and find the initials—"our initials"—that he had marked there. We may wonder whether "baby" is their baby and, if so, whether they married as the maelstrom of the war swept them up. Hilda's casting of herself as Eric's "sweetheart" and of him as "the only *boy*" she "*want[s]*" would seem to suggest that they are not husband and wife. And if "Mother" is "granny-raising" their illegitimate child, then Hilda is exercising an inordinately powerful and not easily understandable will to disguise this, even from those most intimately and obviously in the know. Would the facts of either Hilda's married or maternal status make the letter any more poignant a testimony to the joy of life that she shared with Eric, a joy that, possibly, she would only ever be able to remember and never relive? I doubt it.

Iris, the film that Hilda fortuitously identifies in her letter and that so resonated with her, offers another starting point for wondering about the layers of meaning within and around a young working woman's leisure in this period. "Kinetoscopes," "living pictures," and "cinematographs" had made their first appearance in the 1890s as sideshows at fairgrounds, but by the First World War numerous cinema houses had been built in urban centers throughout the country, especially in the northwest.[87] Some young women, according to a conference of the members of the London-based National Organisation of Girls' Clubs held in September 1916, were self-confessed "great lover[s] of the pictures." Martha Drake, of the Marguerite Girls' Club in London, was one; she "thought that they made people ask themselves which was the correct way to travel through life." Lottie Poole of the St. John Club, Hackney, agreed. The pictures had helped her on several occasions "because they showed the folly of being wicked." Lilian Shoult, on the other hand, disapproved of picture palaces. Apart from the fact that they were "hot, stuffy, badly ventilated, and a great strain on the eyes," most of the pictures they showed "were neither instructive nor amusing—either horrible plots or murders or impossible adventures." Any beauty or other redeeming quality that films might have had, Dora Isaacs of the West Central Jewish Club argued, was "lost because they were preceded and followed by sordid tragedies or silly farces."[88]

Presumably, Dora would have placed *Iris* under the former heading, but not so Hilda. Like the papers faithfully dispatched to Eric and the initials carved on the bridge, *Iris* speaks to her about a wonderfully meaningful relationship—past, present, and in the hoped-for future. Iris's story is her story and it is not hard to imagine Hilda weeping as she watches, especially the "part where the lovers had to part." But at this crucial point, Hilda begins to mark out a different trajectory; she will remain true where Iris did not, her "dear old boy" will find her "waiting at home" for him, should he return. And it is on this cozy, domestic note that Hilda, having so seamlessly knit herself into the identity of the glamorous heroine on the screen, finishes, with the mundane, touching wish that "before long" Eric would be there "to have some [dinner]" with her.[89]

What Hilda views as a sweet romance in its original form was a serious drama, a "brutal" and "cynical" exposure of the rottenness at the heart of fashionable society.[90] The film was based on a play by one of the leading—according to one contemporary scholar of the theater, "the leading author among living English"—dramatists of the late Victorian and Edwardian stage, Arthur Wing Pinero.[91] Renowned for his impeccable stagecraft, and with a string of popular comedies and farces and several serious plays behind him, in *Iris* (1899–1901) and *Letty* (1903) Pinero took on the double standard of sexual morality that winked at men's adultery and promiscuity but insisted on absolute purity for women.[92] *Iris* tells the story of an indolent, beautiful, and rich widow, the play's eponymous heroine, whose combined love of luxury and lack of resolve condemn her to ruin. A clause in her husband's will forbids Iris from remarrying unless she gives up her inheritance, and so she must choose between penury with Laurence Trenwith, the play's young romantic hero, and luxury with Frederick Maldonado, his darkly villainous rival for Iris's affections. It is in Iris's separation from Trenwith that Hilda recognizes one thread of her own story, and Iris's lack of constancy— while Trenwith is away in Canada trying to make his fortune, Maldonado manipulates Iris into becoming his mistress—that she vows she will not mirror. The film ends with Iris, despite her failings, happily reunited with Trenwith after a violent confrontation with Maldonado, who threw her out of his flat upon learning that she planned to betray him by going off with our hero.

But this was not the ending that Pinero wrote for the play and which was acted out in the stage drama. In the stage version, Iris's fate is that which contemporary social mores decreed should be the fate of a fallen woman, and that which gave the play its dramatic, tragic force. When Maldonado learns of Iris's intention to leave him for Trenwith, even though he has offered her a veil of respectability with a proposal of marriage, he explodes with rage and condemns her to an ignoble end—prostitution or suicide—in the streets. That, Maldonado judges, is Iris's "punishment," her "reward," and the curtain falls as she walks out into the street to meet it. The play offers Iris no escape from her fate and critics and audiences alike felt its power and were stunned by its stark handling of the subject matter. To at least one eminent critic and fellow dramatist of Pinero, however, the sentimental ending tacked on in the film, the version of *Iris* that Hilda watched and that rang so true for her, was "perfectly crushing." In a letter to Pinero, George Bernard Shaw registered his dissatisfaction with the film's sentimental denouement. "Iris left the Maldonado flat; walked down a miserable alley-like approach to the graveyard in Bleak House; and found at the end of it the beached margent of the sea. She was walking into it—probably thinking it was a mirage—when Trenwith rushed to the rescue and the band played Tristan and Isolde. You might have knocked me down with a feather."[93]

The demands and expectations of the mass audience to whom cinema appealed undoubtedly permitted a woman of disrepute to evade what most Victorian and Edwardian sensibilities would have deemed just retribution for her immorality. And those sensibilities were among many things to which the war would give a severe jolt. But Pinero's original play, although it broached the double standard of sexual morality, did not question it; indeed, in meting out the standard punishment for a woman's fall from grace to Iris, Pinero clearly aligned himself with conventional mores.

We see a similarly conventional approach and set of assumptions about women—and a very familiar plot—in Pinero's next work, *Letty*, in which the dramatist moves away from the high society circles most familiar to him and into the world of the working classes. The play traces the fortunes of a beautiful and giddy working girl tempted to ruin by her longing for the good things in life. Letty has all the failings of her type. She loves expensive clothes and, in order to be able to afford them and make herself attractive for the aristocratic and appropriately named Letchmere, she has been practically starving herself. She wants nothing more than a life of ease and luxury and is torn between becoming Letchmere's mistress and marrying her loathsome but rich employer in order to achieve this. All the while, as she vacillates between them and then finally seems set on taking the low road to the high life with Letchmere, her two friends mark the point and counterpoint between glamorous, sinful abandonment and dull respectability. Hilda, a hedonistic and materialistic good-time girl, merely counsels Letty not to set her price too cheaply. Marion, a moralist who, in Hilda's opinion, "can afford to be prim . . . no gentleman is likely to glance in [her] direction," tries her best to keep Letty on the straight and narrow. In the end, Letty is saved from herself when Letchmere discovers—in a not-very-subtle, ironic twist—that his unhappily married sister is about to destroy herself by escaping into an adulterous relationship and goes off to her rescue.

This turn of events brings Letty to her senses, nudging her from the dangerous course upon which her desire for a life of ease and pleasure had set her. She finishes up "as it were, in harbour—through no desert of her own," married to a man from her "proper rank," sharing happiness with him and their child in a domestic snug, hoping for nothing more immoderate than a tolerably prosperous life and a shared drift into old age. In the play's epilogue, several years after Letty's fatefully interrupted assignation with Letchmere, she meets up with him again. While she is blooming with good health and happiness, he is a pathetic invalid, dying, we are led to assume, from an ailment brought on by his dissipation. Hilda and Marion reappear, too, the former as a demimondaine of the cheap theater whom the latter—still the same sensible working girl with the same stern sense of propriety—tries to persuade Letty to drop as even a casual acquaintance. Thus, as in *Iris*, Pinero maps out the unhappy destiny that awaits the woman—this time, the working-class woman—who risks her virtue in the careless pursuit of pleasure. Letchmere's fate is that which Letty would have shared had Pinero not effected her rescue. And Hilda's fate, to be placed beyond the pale of respectability—an exile that Pinero cannot permit her to avoid, that the integrity of the character and the structure and moral code of the plot demand that she suffers—would have been Letty's fate, too.[94]

RANKING ALONG WITH THE FALLEN WOMAN AS A CONDEMNED and cautionary figure in the Victorian and Edwardian moral discourse was the failed mother. Especially after what Ellen Ross calls the "discovery" of the mother in the late nineteenth century, reformers read the leisure habits of married women as explanations for all kinds of social ills—poverty, irresponsible husbands, unsanitary living conditions. More pointedly, they saw them as major factors in the general moral and physical decline that seemed to be afflicting the working classes.[95] In this way of seeing, the young, careless hedonist, even if she managed to avoid absolute moral ruin, was the drunken, feckless, and neglectful mother in the making. Her dissolute tendencies would be reborn in and visited upon her degenerate children, her debased tastes and habits and conduct would become theirs.[96]

Despite endemic poverty and the double burden of waged work and housekeeping that wives and mothers carried, there seemed to be a good deal too many of these idle and dissipated kinds of women among the working classes. "Women of leisure," M. B. Blackie labeled them. "You may see them any day, and at any hour, as you pass through the poorer districts of our cities," she complained. "There they are, . . . sitting about in groups on the doorsteps, passing remarks that are not *always* friendly on those who come in or go out [original emphasis]." There was no mystery to the circumstances that produced these women, Blackie informed the 1894 conference of the National Council of Women of Great Britain (NCWGB). "As early as possible when schooldays are over," she explained, "they have been hurried into a mill or factory." After "a few years of monotonous toil there, tending to dull the faculties rather than brighten them," they have rushed into marriages "imprudent on this ground, if on no other, that [they are] utterly ignorant of all household duties." Capable of only the most basic housekeeping, the young wife "soon gets through all the work that she thinks is absolutely necessary," and then the other deleterious effects of her factory employment reveal themselves. "Accustomed as she has been to constant employment, and to be surrounded with many companions, time soon begins to hang heavily on her hands, and, to while away the hours, she seeks the nearest companionship she can find, with the result [being] . . . bad companions who lead to bad ways."[97]

Gossiping and idling about—these and more registered on the moral measure of upper- and middle-class critics as failings in which working women could not afford to, and should not, indulge. Such leisure habits marked the married woman as a bad mother, the mother who perversely refused to give up the pleasures of her youth, and whose selfish indulgence and laziness caused her to neglect her home, husband, and children. Helen Bosanquet had sympathy for young wives who had learned to enjoy the pleasures of their single days and for whom the leisure they shared with their "young men" and husbands was a force that helped bind the couple together. "The young men and women meet at the theatre, the music hall, often at private parties; they become acquainted . . . and when they marry they keep up the same constant round of [evening] recreations," particularly in the early years of the marriage, during which a wife could continue to work outside the home and the couple enjoyed two incomes. But the birth of the first child confronted the wife with a choice that her husband was not compelled to make. She "has to choose," Bosanquet observed, "between husband and child . . . [and] to stay at home is to lose one of her strongest holds upon her husband—is to cease to share his leisure with him."[98] Those married women who chose not to give up this shared leisure, who chose not to give up the pleasures that they had come to enjoy as single, independent wage earners, faced opprobrium. Bosanquet, like Blackie, judged that there were too many who made the wrong choice. "By force of circumstance and disposition [these mothers] maintain the reckless jollity of their girlhood to the end; in others self-indulgence has so brutalised the face as to make it incapable of any expression at all."[99]

The most dangerous indulgence of all for the working woman, commentators judged, was drink. It was "their great enemy." "The love of it is the curse they have inherited," Clara Collet stated, "which later on, when they are no longer factory girls, but dock labourers' wives, will drag them down to the lowest level." Beatrice Potter believed the same. For the careworn and the careless workers alike among whom she toiled for a time in an East End sweatshop, she thought, "there [was] only one Fall possible . . . drink, leading slowly but inevitably to the drunkard's death." With the 1861 introduction of "grocers' licenses" that permitted shopkeepers as well as publicans to sell spirits and wine to be consumed off the premises, it seemed to many that the process was accelerated. More and more married women, and not simply among the lowest social ranks or the disreputable, were thought to be taking to drink. According to Blackie, "not unfrequently, even in otherwise respectable localities," married women's "drinking clubs" were to be found. "Several women club their money together, each subscribing so much, and one goes out to buy spirit. Then they sit down to drink it in company."[100] A Select Committee of the House of Lords, appointed in 1878 to inquire into the matter, heard from numerous witnesses— medical men, policemen, and clergymen—that grocers' licenses afforded "opportunities of obtaining drink to persons who would regard it as disreputable to resort to a public-house." Most worrying, they allowed women to "procure spirits unknown to . . . their husbands."[101] The Licensing Act of 1874, which granted retail licenses to wholesale beer dealers, was a similarly pernicious piece of legislation. Though few wholesale dealers had used the law, many small shopkeepers had done so, attested an 1882 memorial from the Manchester Justices of the Peace to the Secretary of State for the Home Department, and this had led to an increase in private drinking, "more particularly amongst women." "There is nothing to prevent any house or shop they go to for the purpose of procuring the necessaries of life from supplying them drink for consumption elsewhere."[102]

When pressed, witnesses to the 1878–1879 Select Committee could not adduce any firm evidence supporting their insistence that more women were drinking than before grocers' licenses were available, or that, if there had been such a change, it was a consequence of the 1861 and 1874 legislation. But the impression of an increase in drinking among women was widely shared by upper- and middle-class commentators and by working-class people. Charles Booth's informants and investigators reported that "many more women [were] seen in public-houses" in London. "You cannot but see it," an elderly resident of one district stated, "respectable women go into public houses without any compunction, a sort of thing never seen until late years." A member of an Anglican sisterhood concurred that "the time had long since gone by for regarding it as a scandal that a woman should drink at a public-house." Rowntree's observations of public houses in York confirmed that this was so, especially, he concluded, in poorer districts.[103] In a number of towns and neighborhoods, women claimed Monday as their drinking day. This was true, Robert Sherard observed, in Manchester where on "one day in the week the public-houses are [women's] domain. Monday is Woman's Day in the Manchester taverns." Booth noted a similar pattern of women's drinking in London. "They say," one of his middle-class informants told him, " 'we have our fling; we like to have a little fuddle on Monday.' "[104] For Kathleen Dayus's mother, who was a confirmed drinker (and a violent one), Monday was both a working day and a "fuddling" day; indeed, the one depended on the other. In a communal washhouse, together with a group of neighbors, Polly Dayus did her week's laundry. At day's end, she and her pals pledged the freshly washed and ironed clothes at the pawnshop and retired to the local pub with the proceeds of their labor to "wet their whistles."[105]

Although critics castigated the drinking habits of the working classes in general, married women's drinking provoked particular concern. Women's natures and social circumstances were understood to make them particularly susceptible to taking up the habit to begin with, to becoming inveterate drinkers, and to being more prone to drunkenness and disorderliness. "As the old song says," Blackie reminded the NCWGB, " 'idleness is the chief mistress of vices all,' " and the idling and gossiping to which married women were prone "quickly pave[d] the way towards drinking, just for the sake of sociability at first it may be, but soon an unconquerable habit is acquired." "Women treat each other as much [as], and even more than, is the case with men," Booth believed, and "thus the social side of the consumption of alcohol is emphasized." Because of women's neighborhood networking, drinking spread. "One drunken woman in a street will set all the women in it drinking," one of Booth's informants asserted. "A woman is so often talking with her neighbours; if she drinks they go with her."[106] In one rural community, whose inhabitants' drinking habits attracted the attention of an "improving" incoming squire, there was a veritable viper's nest of female drunkards and profligates, a mid-century select committee heard. Dispatched to inquire into "the moral and social condition of the people," the squire's agent reported that there were four public houses for a population of approximately six hundred to seven hundred villagers. He "found the females in a very demoralized state, and a large number had illegitimate children," and traced a direct line between both of these things and women's drinking habits. "I dated the demoralization and the frequency of chance children amongst the females, which occurred in mothers and daughters of one family at the same time, to their visiting public houses with the men," he testified to the select committee.[107]

In the common wisdom that reformers, medical men, and the

agents of law and order shared, older, married women were more likely than the young to become established inebriates. "The middle-aged are the drunkards, not the young," Booth heard from one source. Neither men nor women became "confirmed soakers before twenty-five or thirty," suggested another. "Or with women till after marriage. The drunkards are probably married women." Drunkenness "was never common before marriage," one policeman informed Booth. Young wage earners "drink, but it is more often the young married women and the middle-aged who indulge too much," another concurred.[108] In the experience of witnesses appearing before the 1854 Select Committee on public houses, it was well nigh impossible to reclaim a female inebriate. "It is no matter how bad a man is," one stated, "we, in many cases are successful in rescuing him." But "for every 50 reformed inveterate drunkards that I know (and my knowledge is rather extensive on that subject), I am grieved to say I do not know five reformed women." "It is more difficult to reform a woman than a man when she has once contracted these habits," affirmed a second. The 1878–1879 Select Committee on intemperance heard from witnesses that women became drunk sooner and on smaller amounts of alcohol than men and that, once drunk, they were more difficult to control. "There [was] no doubt," one member of the constabulary testified, that "men may be said to carry their liquor more quietly than women." Nor was there much doubt that it was "the fact of the greater excitability of temperament upon the part of women" that accounted for the high proportion of arrests of women that had been recorded in cities such as Liverpool, Manchester, and London.[109]

ALL OF THIS IS MOST SIGNIFICANT FOR WHAT IT REVEALS ABOUT attitudes to, and prejudices about, married women's drinking, and by inference, their leisure more generally. The maternal drinker, and even more so, the maternal "soaker," wreaked havoc in her family and community. By the final decades of the nineteenth century, she had begun to provoke "panic" among what Ross McKibbin calls "single-issue" moralists and reformers who attributed to her failings infant mortality, drunken husbands, dirty, destitute, and diseased children, hardened juvenile criminals, and woeful child prostitutes.[110] Testimony of these depredations abounded, implied clergymen, journalists, medical men, and reformers. It was there on the breath of mothers who accompanied their children to school. "Even quite respectable mothers," one schoolmaster told Booth, "when they come to see him in the morning, nearly always smell of drink." "Nearly all have a morning dram," another teacher believed. "The poorest and most destitute seem to look upon drink as the first necessity of life."[111] It was there in the "draggletail"[112] and frowsy dress, the "yawning and sottish state well known by tipplers as 'moreish' " into which mothers declined by the end of an evening out. It was there in the dirty, disordered, comfortless rooms bereft of furniture, bedding, even the most basic domestic utensils, "disposed of to supply her drink."[113] It was there in the empty housekeeping purse, stealthily plundered by housewives who procured drink "unknown to, and at the expense of, their husbands, by getting the liquor entered in the shopkeeper's bill as other articles of consumption for the family."[114] It was most pitifully there on the persons and in the condition and fate of the children of the drinking mother. There were the infant victims of smothering, a "plague" that Hugh Shimmin insisted could be traced to mothers' drinking. "Saturday night, when marketing; Monday, out shopping or at the theatre; Thursday night 'going to see the people come from the races' "—these were the black spots that marked the weekly pattern of maternal sotting in Liverpool.[115] There were the "ragged and runny-nosed" waifs,[116] the "coagulations of childhood" that waited patiently outside neighborhood pubs before "piloting homeward" their "forlorn and drink-sodden wreck[s]" of mothers.[117] There were the bassinettes of babies that blocked the gangways of Manchester's pubs on Woman's Day. There, "amidst the crowds of noisy women, under the fumes of tobacco smoke and alcohol," Robert Sherard wrote indignantly, "tiny fingers may be seen in convulsive agitation."[118] Thus exposed from their earliest days to the drinking habit, acquiring a taste for alcohol at their mother's breast or in sips stolen from the jugs of beer they carried home for her from the pub, commentators fretted, the children of drinkers would become drinkers themselves. The whole sorry cycle would continue.[119]

Not all married women drank, of course. According to the self-reports on leisure that Cadbury et al. had married women in Birmingham put together, only about one-tenth imbibed: 10.24 percent of those who were wage earners and 9.05 percent of those who were not. But given the hostility that maternal drinking engendered among inquiring bodies such as Cadbury and his colleagues, these figures quite likely underrepresented its extent. Not all working-class women's drinking was excessive or deleterious, either. Flora Thompson's description of a drinking party in her childhood hamlet in Oxfordshire presents it as a perfectly innocuous affair. Every now and then, one of the less sedate matrons of Lark Rise would invite a few neighbors in for a beer-drinking session. "They none of them got drunk, or even fuddled, for there was not very much each, even when the can went round to the inn a second or third time," Thompson writes. "But there was just enough to hearten them up and make them forget their troubles." Stephen Reynolds, an upper-middle-class man who happily made his home at times with a Devon fisherman's family, offers a similarly benign view of a "mothers' gossiping" that his landlady hosted. "On the table there was a jug of ale and stout and an hospitably torn-open bag of biscuits," and the women drank as they discussed their strategy for a boycott of local retailers who were charging excessively high prices. Wise as well as convivial consumers, indeed![120]

Whatever the actual "facts" of married women's drinking—its extent, whether it was excessive, its physical setting, its social context—the drinking wife and mother was a symbol of unregenerate, failed womanhood. She stood for the antithesis of the decent, good wife and mother whose central care and joy were supposed to be her family, her home. Drinking, or any other habit or amusement that made her unfit for those preoccupations, that undermined or damaged her integrity, was something that she must deny herself. A pressing question for reformers was how to ensure that this would be so. Mothers' meetings and settlement houses and missions seemed only to skim the surface of the problem and it was difficult to get women to attend at all, let alone regularly. And many of those who did attend seemed to be quite incorrigible, smuggling their gin bottles along on outings and embarrassing their chaperones with their behavior.[121] A more hopeful solution seemed to lie with the young, with girls and young women during the crucial years between leaving school and marriage, the years in which they were most vulnerable to acquiring a taste for the wrong kinds of leisure. Focusing on this segment of the working classes, reformers attempted to use rational forms of recreation to shape girls and young working women into good wives and mothers. The next two chapters examine this initiative.

PART THREE

RATIONAL RECREATION, C. 1880–1914

In the late Victorian period, the upper and middle classes began to supplement the close and often critical scrutiny to which they were wont to subject working-class women's leisure with schemes and programs for reforming it. The next two chapters examine two of these interventionist exercises, one undertaken largely in the community by female philanthropists, the other undertaken in the workplace by reform-minded industrialists. The former approached leisure as a preventive against immorality and delinquency among young women and offered rational, wholesome, and uplifting activities as counterattractions to what they considered to be the less wholesome, more sensational pleasures of the commercial realm. The latter instituted recreational programs for female employees out of a commitment to their belief in uniting industrial success with social progress and in the context of widely held concerns that factory work unfitted women for wifely and maternal duties. Both groups viewed leisure simultaneously as a sphere in which to shape working-class girls and women into good wives and mothers, and as a tool with which to do that shaping. And both groups found that the girls and women upon whom they worked were not always tractable, that, whether as a tool or a sphere of gender construction and social reformism, leisure could be somewhat less than perfect.

Chapter Five

WORKING GIRLS' CLUBS

*L*IKE THEIR COUNTERPARTS EARLIER IN THE NINETEENTH century, late Victorian and Edwardian rational recreationists were apprehensive about the deleterious consequences of wide-sweeping economic and social transformations. And, like other reformers and commentators of their time, they expressed considerable anxiety about the nation's putative physical and moral degeneration and about imperial decline. The working-class woman—and especially the young woman, the embodiment and hope of the next and all future generations—figured in their concerns as a central focus of attention. Two social institutions were charged with shaping working-class girls into the stuff from which wives and mothers of the empire were made: the family and, as a consequence of the post-1870 piece-meal introduction of compulsory elementary education, the school. Domestic service, which in 1891 employed almost a third of the female wage labor force, also was considered ideal training for marriage and motherhood. But to a nation that, according to Thomas E. Jordan, sensed it was in a social and cultural crisis, these mechanisms appeared all too fallible. While commentators applauded public education for inculcating such worthy habits as order, discipline, and cleanliness, they bemoaned the fact that it failed to teach anything really worthwhile and, besides, ended too soon, leaving girls "without any help or guidance at the most critical moment of their lives." In addition, by 1911, although domestic service was still one of the single largest forms of female employment, it was a declining occupation to which fewer and fewer young women were favorably disposed. Those with a zest for life and a reluctance to submit to the very immediate and sometimes oppressive authority of a master and mistress saw alternative employment in manufacturing, retail, and service industries as holding the promise of greater independence and a more interesting and lively work life. Finally, many reformers believed that lower-class families were incapable of raising young girls and women with the will or skills to be the mothers and makers of those healthy and happy homes that the nation and empire needed. This was a problem compounded by the changing patterns of employment, for factory and shop work were notorious for leaving women ignorant and careless of domestic duties.[1]

And there was the intoxicating, vibrant world of popular, commercial leisure. Full of worrying moral dangers, this also agitated upper- and middle-class reformers who set out to forewarn and forearm working-class women against its perils and to make available to them amusements that would ennoble rather than degrade.[2] This impetus for reform came within the compass of a broader female philanthropy mediated through churches, chapels, settlement houses, social missions, temperance and social purity organizations, and, the main focus of this chapter, working women's clubs.[3] Upper-class ladies playing out their customary bountiful roles, middle-class women aspiring to similar benevolence, clergymen's wives, sisters, and daughters, and numbers of earnest, college- and university-educated young women: these were among the main propagandists and providers of a consciously reformist model of leisure. They offered working-class girls and women alternative recreations to the public house and music hall, encouraged them to use leisure as a means of improvement, and attempted to imbue them "with a love for rational amusements indulged in a rational way."[4] They believed that they could reach over the social and cultural divide and, through personal influence and example, raise their laboring counterparts during workers' "precious hours of leisure."[5] They insisted that leisure could be made to transform recalcitrant girls and women into good wives and mothers. Drawing on—while at the same time constructing and fueling—what Jordan terms "the degeneracy crisis," they made working-class women's leisure important work, work that they claimed as their own, work for which they were singularly fitted.

Over and over again, in the language of their speeches, conference papers, and writings, reformers linked a condemnation of "low" culture and prejudices about working-class women's character and conduct with concerns about the present and future state of the nation and empire. "A vast work lies before us," Lady Albinia Hobart-Hampden announced in a typical call to arms, "who will rise up and do it?" Working women's recreation was "work of supreme importance both for the present and for the future welfare of [the] nation," she proclaimed enthusiastically.[6] Maude Stanley, fearing that "vice, disease, crime would sweep over this great Babylon as the waters of the Atlantic," urged, "we must raise barriers . . . we must stem the tide of evil," "[we must] establish in every locality clubs for working girls." Experience showed, Stanley asserted, that girls' clubs would do "a great work." "A work which raises, which ennobles, which brings out the best traits in a girl, which by its wholesome pleasures, by its varied interests, by its human sympathies between the ladies and the girls will make their lives happy and good ones."[7] In urban centers and rural districts, among "mothers, field and farm workers, [and] factory girls," leisure reformers felt that, through "garden-parties, out-door lantern exhibitions, girls' clubs, friendly teas,"[8] they were doing a "noble" and "very real work."[9] It was work that was "sorely needed," Hobart-Hampden assured them, work with issues stretching "far into the future, when these girls shall be wives and mothers," when they would wield "a mighty influence over the next generation." It was work that would make that influence "nobler and better because of the lessons learned long ago in some girls' club."[10]

Leisure, in fact, was much too serious to be left to lower-class women, who were liable to find "for themselves all sorts of amusement," some of which were "unworthy and unstimulating," and all of which were "unsatisfying." It was much "more than mere amusement."[11] In the view of many, the laboring classes were a "pleasure-loving race," often infuriatingly and irresponsibly so. They wallowed in a culture that was rooted in a past at ease with hedonism and sensual gratification and one that, despite a certain taming, still celebrated those values.[12] It was a culture whose appeal sympathetic reformers felt that they understood. Given the circumstances of working women's lives, they were not surprised that "the tired seamstress, the washerwoman after standing long hours at the tub, the wild factory girl after a day pent up within four walls" sought forms of leisure that tended to narcotize or excite. Was it any wonder that any one of these, as she made her weary "way back to comfort-less rooms, by courtesy called *home*, should linger at the swing door of the public house, with its glaring lights, its warmth and glow on winter nights? [original emphasis]" Was it any wonder that hard-working women found it difficult to resist yielding "to the seductions of strong drink which, for a time, brings a forgetfulness of sorrow, and drowns the gnawing sense of looking for something different?" Or that, to "the weary mother in some scattered country village, with her large family of children and scanty means . . . the visit of the grocer's cart, with its tempting bottles of cheap wines and spirits [is] an opportunity to which she flies to drown the cease-less aching of her limbs, and to revive the flagging energies which must be kept going if the home is to be kept going as well?"[13] Or that girls and women, confined for hours on end in dreary, miserably paid occupations, should seek, in "the garish lights and dresses, the impure atmosphere" of theaters and music halls, "the impossible passions" and "artificial emotions" of cheap literature, an exuberant release from the deadening "greyness" of their lives?[14]

CONSCIOUS THOUGH REFORMERS MIGHT HAVE BEEN OF THE appeal of the pub's cozy conviviality, alcohol's numbing, warming embrace, and the cheap passions and glitter of the music hall, they worried that working women were woefully ill-equipped for resisting the deeper, darker indulgences to which these things could lead. Young women, especially, were giddy and emotionally weak, "overflowing with animal spirits."[15] Too many had too little control over their sensual appetites or any discrimination when it came to satisfying them. They were "wild and careless," lacking in "purpose or perseverance," constantly craving change and variety.[16] They took their "silly and sensational"[17] pleasures recklessly and drifted through life with no higher object in view than "gaining [their] daily bread or getting as much amusement as possible."[18] Employing the "dark continent" convention of late-nineteenth-century imperialism, writers such as Walter Besant rendered the women of the laboring classes as an exotic and engaging fauna or a more earthy, primitive race of human. In Besant's description of "Liz," the stereotypical factory girl in his *East London*, she is infused with an animalism and exuberance that are not easily contained and that threaten the order and stability of civilized society. Liz has "quick and restless eyes" and "mobile" lips; she is full of fun and "quick to laugh," "ready-witted and prompt with repartee and retort." She cannot walk sedately, but must dance along the street. Like her workmates who, "adorned with crimson and blue feathers . . . run about laughing and shrieking," she is an "impudent, saucy bird, always hungry, always on the lookout for something more."[19] It was the kind of imagery that upper- and middle-class commentators and critics commonly employed in their accounts of working-class women at public play. "Ready with a saucy word, a sharp retort, a rude laugh, and often, alas! even foul words or swearing,"[20] female factory hands released from work and out for an evening of fun flowed "in shoals" and "swarms" along the crowded thoroughfares, "always on the look-out for a lark."[21] "With warm hearts, with overflowing good nature," these children of nature carelessly played in a "Garden of Eden of uncivilised life."[22]

Beatrice Potter judged that there was no "consciousness of sin" among the working girls and women she observed enjoying their larks in London's East End in the 1880s, and so concluded, "you cannot accuse them of immorality."[23] But for most rational recreationists, none of the working-class woman's "cheap amusements" were far removed from sin. Sin, in fact, was often the sorry consequence of those amusements. And though they might have differed as to the precise philosophical and moral underpinnings of their convictions, few reformers doubted that leisure was implicated in the condition of working-class women and, through them, the condition of their families, the nation, and the empire. In leisure they saw the dangerous possibility of a decline that, cascading through the lives of hundreds of thousands of women, threatened to bring all these to a parlous physical and moral state.

This anxiety ran through reformers' discourse on working women's leisure, a discourse in which they reworked the ancient tale of women's foolish, careless delight, temptation, and fall to construct and position themselves as agents of prevention and salvation. They rendered several versions of the story, some of which focused on adolescent, wage-earning workers, others on married women and mothers.[24] Some charted in detail the stages of a life course marked by a wretched beginning and a woeful end. Others telescoped the narrative around a first, fatal misstep—a drink taken at a workplace party that engendered "the taste for a dangerous indulgence," for example.[25] All warned of the dire consequences of what might first appear innocently in the guise of "harmless recreation." Maude Stanley's "Clubs for Working Girls" is an exemplar of these cautionary tales. Stanley's woman-child becomes a wage earner at fourteen and thus earns an exciting, frightening freedom and independence from her parents. Fearful that they might lose a contributor to the family exchequer, they "will not venture to draw the reins too tightly," but instead let her "have her fling." Seeking recreation in the street, the "main playground" of the people, she begins her moral descent by loitering with "some chosen companion" or indulging "in rough play with boys and lads." Eventually, the mere "walk around, the looking into the shop-windows, the passing by the glaring gaslit stalls in the evening markets" cease to be enough to entertain or divert. And so, if the means can be found, comes the first "visit to the music hall, the cheap theatres, the gin-palaces, the dancing saloons, and the wine shop." Then follows—finally, tragically, and inevitably, it seems—the "easy sliding into greater sin . . . [and] degradation . . . the downfall of all womanly virtue."[26]

In her narratives on the dangers of leisure, the reformer saw and framed herself as a moral and cultural superior whose duty it was to step in and prevent the unfolding of this calamitous course of events. She would save working girls and women, nation and empire, from the consequences of recklessness and profligacy. Moreover, she would act to make leisure a transformational experience that would uplift and enrich the lives of working women. Prepared for the task by birth and breeding, education and upbringing, she was a stalwart guide and teacher, a friend who would lead the working-class woman "forwards and upwards," who would provide the necessary instruction in the right kind of leisure.[27] Working-class women, caught up in a round of frantic and tawdry pleasures, mired in the debasing amusements of their native culture, needed help if ever they were to raise their thoughts to anything more elevated. And who better to give them that help than upper- and middle-class women? "We have had leisure and opportunities of culture and of entering into the elevating thoughts of our time," Lady Albinia Hobart-Hampden reminded her peers. "Have we not something we can give to our less favored sisters? Cannot we seek to show them the deeper meanings of life, and raise their thoughts above their surroundings?"[28] "There is . . . a real, a felt, and an unsatisfied need for social ministrations of a secular kind, such as our unoccupied

Working girls' clubs sponsored by upper- and middle-class women offered elevating and edifying forms of recreation as an alternative to the dangerous debasements that lurked in the world of mass amusements. Mandolin bands enjoyed a vogue in the late 1800s and early 1900s. The Mandolin Band, Victoria Working Girls' Club, n.d., courtesy of Vestry House Museum.

young ladies, and perhaps nobody else, could adequately meet," suggested Edith Simcox. "Any number of young ladies with a natural enthusiasm for the ordinary drawing-room accomplishments of singing and dancing, might be profitably employed as missionaries for the spread of such accomplishments."[29] This cultural missionary work the conscientious woman of privilege took as her special charge, for, if the working-class woman was society's Eve, she was its immaculate, Marian center. Consequently, it fell to her to educate and uplift her lower-class sisters. She could do this by raising the standards of their leisure, by enlightening them as to "the nature of true happiness," by making them conscious of "the capacity for *pure* enjoyment [that] exists in every human heart [original emphasis]," and by giving them opportunities for experiencing that pure enjoyment. "As women workers," Lilian Montagu argued, "we have to admit with Ruskin, that 'the object of true education is to make people not merely do the right thing, but enjoy the right thing,' and until we have courageously undertaken this educational work among our girls, we may well ask ourselves with shame 'Watchman, what of the night?' "[30]

REFORMERS PURSUED THEIR EDUCATIONAL VOCATION THROUGH voluntary associations, agencies, and other recreational enterprises that varied considerably in scale, permanence, and political and social tenor. All shared the common purpose of ameliorating the working classes. The Girls' Friendly Society (GFS), founded in 1874 by a group of Anglican women, was a very conservative and exclusive organization whose overarching aim was to bring together unmarried and "virtuous" young working-class women with one another and with lady "associates." By 1885, the GFS operated 821 branches in England and Wales and, in its peak years of 1913 and 1914, had 39,926 associates, 197,493 full members, and 81,374 "candidate" or probationary members.[31] Though the GFS's main sphere of action was the rural south, it was also influential in other parts of the country and in urban areas: by 1906, for example, it had 35 branches with 5,500 members and candidates in the industrial city of Birmingham.[32] "Snowdrop Bands" were a similar initiative established in the 1890s among (mostly northern) factory workers.[33] Closely allied with the GFS—indeed, expressly intended to serve as its extension—was the Mother's Union, set up in 1885 as a kindred association for married women. Within four years of its foundation, the Mother's Union numbered 157,688 members and associates in branches throughout Britain, and between 1902 and 1920 its branches and members doubled in number.[34] Feminist associations, such as the Women's Protective and Provident League (WPPL) and the Women's Industrial Council (WIC), also encompassed leisure in their efforts to improve the conditions of employment, status, and rights of women workers. Both organizations offered leisure activities, services, and facilities such as meeting rooms, pianos, circulating libraries, and holiday homes as well as recreational evenings and classes in history, reading, botany, arithmetic, grammar, French, German, Shakespearean literature, first aid, and drawing. And they regularly conducted business in the context of social, recreational gatherings, large and small, formal and informal.[35]

Important as organizational initiatives such as these were, they were neither the only contributions that upper- and middle-class women had to make toward improving working-class women's leisure, nor—according to more than one proponent—were they necessarily the most effective. "Vast numbers [of] . . . women and girls are not touched by such influences," Kathleen M. Townend informed the NCWGB at its 1894 conference. "These must be reached in humbler fashion, they must be brought into contact more with the individual." Privileged women certainly came up with some imaginative schemes in their individual attempts to touch laboring women's lives through recreation. "One lady . . . got up entertainments for poor people at her own house, and she called on those poor people from time to time. Then they gave out plants in the autumn, and in early March had a flower show." Others opened their gardens and grounds occasionally, for the "use and pleasure" of the less privileged, entertained female workhouse inmates "allowed out for a day," and organized concerts and "lantern exhibitions."[36] Recreational ministrations were among the duties that the sisters, daughters, and wives of some clergymen undertook. They invited female parishioners to tea, accompanied them on excursions to the country or seaside, and turned their dining rooms into makeshift dancing schools to give lessons to them and their "young men."[37]

BY THE 1880S, PERHAPS THE MOST FOCUSED FORM OF UPPER- and middle-class provision for working women's rational recreation was the "girls' club." Associations, large and small, national and local, and individual women organized fortnightly, weekly, or (usually) more frequent gatherings of this kind. Women's settlement houses in London, for instance, held girls' clubs four or five times a week, many of which were allied with the Federation of Working Girls' Clubs or the London Girls' Club Union.[38] There was a large and dynamic club movement in Birmingham. Cadbury, Matheson, and Shann indicated in their study of the city's female wage-earners that there were forty-five girls' clubs, with a total of four thousand members, run by Anglicans, Congregationalists, Wesleyans, the Society of Friends, and Unitarians. A number of Hebrew societies organized recreational classes as well, while a Sunday School Union ran fourteen Girls' Evening Homes with a combined membership of eight hundred. These figures, together with those numbered within the GFS, represented some eight percent of the city's wage-earning girls and women.[39] Beginning in the 1880s, an association of Nottingham Girls' Evening Homes and Clubs (NGEHC), which was still in existence in the late 1930s, coordinated the work of some half-dozen or so clubs throughout that city whose membership numbers ranged from twenty to fifty.[40] In 1902 in the northern city of York—to illustrate an individual project of this kind—seventeen-year-old Winifred Rowntree, daughter of the president of the York Cocoa Works, formed the "Honesty Girls' Club." This met one evening a week in the rooms of an adult evening school and, by the time of its founder's death in 1915, numbered two hundred members, ages five to over twenty-five, organized into five groups.[41] In teeming manufacturing towns and sleepy market towns, in sedate seaside resorts and rough, bustling ports, such as Loughborough, Mansfield, Retford, Bournemouth, Bristol, and Liverpool, like-minded upper- and middle-class ladies established similar associations and clubs for their laboring counterparts.[42]

The organizers and sponsors of these enterprises shared a common vision of their place and purpose in working women's leisure and of leisure's place and purpose in working women's lives. Their gatherings were counterattractions designed to bring young workers together with models of upper- and middle-class womanhood who would educate them in the right kinds of recreation and, through recreation, mold them into examples of lower-class womanhood. Their club rooms were alternatives to the streets, physical and moral havens from that dangerously free territory and from other disreputable leisure resorts, bulwarks against the corrupting influences of "low" amusements. In the recreational provisions that they made, working-class girls and women would have the opportunity to acquire the values, attributes, knowledge, and skills necessary for the self-improvement that reformers felt so many needed so badly.

The stated aim of the Loughborough Girls' Club, established in 1891, was to keep "the factory girls out of the streets and public houses, and away from the temptations and degradations to which they were exposed." Before the club started, its secretary noted in her 1905 report, hundreds of female factory workers had had nowhere to go in the evenings and nothing to do except "walk about the streets" or go to "places where even they themselves would rather not go, but having no alternative, went."[43] The girls' clubs in Birmingham performed similarly crucial work, social reformers judged. Providing "a counter-attraction to the streets, where many a girl [otherwise found] her sole relaxation," they exercised a "wonderful influence."[44] Kathleen Townend lauded the "splendid work" of the NGEHC in this regard. "In a town like Nottingham, thickly populated with women and girls employed in factories," she declared, " 'the devil's mission of amusement' forces its way with special temptations fostered by the public-house system." Fortunately, the NGEHC associations were there to "raise the tone" and act as "most blessed methods of counter-attraction," to "keep girls with a tendency to run wild" in "safe companionship."[45] The GFS self-assuredly claimed the title of the nation's "largest preventive society." Acting as a "fence between [working girls] and vice," the organization inveighed against any leisure behavior that might tempt its members astray, "whether it be drinking, extravagance, or the reading of light literature."[46] Likewise, the Mothers' Union warned about the hazards of wandering the streets at night and dangerous

companions and debasing amusements such as "impure" literature.[47] Both associations provided "safe" alternatives and spaces for
women's recreation—social clubs and meeting rooms—and counterattractions such as uplifting talks and garden parties hosted by clergymen's wives and titled ladies.[48] Reformers established circulating
libraries stocked with "pure" and "wholesome" books that were
meant to encourage working-class women to read and elevate their
reading tastes, to teach them to be dissatisfied with the "light literature," ranging from "blood and thunder to twaddle," that seemed
to have the most appeal.[49] There was, concluded one critic, "hardly
a magazine read by [working-class girls] which it would not be a
moral benefit to have swept off the face of the earth."[50] The hugely
popular "penny serials," "full of sensation and crime" and characters that spent "their lives in a continual state of melodrama," did
considerable "moral harm." Devoured week after week, they incited "a perpetual excitement and a longing that in their [readers']
poor little lives some great sensation should have a place." Even
worse were the translations of "French novels" that "low shops"
loaned out at a halfpenny a volume: "once such a taste is got,"
Maude Stanley gloomily prognosticated, "we know what it must
lead to."[51]

Despite all the worthy and high-flown intentions underlying
these elevating schemes, they had their opponents. Girls' clubs
drew criticism on a number of fronts. Some fretted about the dangers attending the ladies who ran them, from the risk of contracting
disease to exposure to other, unspeakable "evils."[52] Lilian Montagu's family was horrified to hear that she was planning to set up a
club in London's Soho district. "Informed relatives" had told her
mother that it was a part of the city that was "fraught with dangers
for young girls of good family." Montagu's response was matter-of-
fact: she didn't see why, with her better education and better breeding, she should be less likely than working women "to resist the
temptations that were vaguely talked about in hushed whispers in
[her] presence." Her family decided that she could visit the club on

certain, specified evenings, but never more than once in a week, and insisted that a chaperone accompany her on any forays that she made into the streets.[53] Another and common complaint was that clubs spoiled working girls for quiet, domestic amusements and, contrarily, kept them away from the one place in which they most belonged: home. "Many good people consider that our girls can and should find their best form of recreation after work hours in their own homes," Montagu acknowledged at the NCWGB 1902 conference.[54] The wife of a fellow clergyman took the Reverend Robert Dolling to task for setting up a girls' "Social" in his impoverished Portsmouth parish. Encouraging the girls from their homes and into the club, she scolded, "makes them for the present unmaidenly, and in the future, bad wives and mothers." Even supporters and sympathizers worried about such recreational projects, fearing that they might exacerbate the difficulties of keeping working girls and women at home and attentive to their domestic responsibilities. "They are too restless to stay indoors," the otherwise enthusiastic Cadbury, Matheson, and Shann grumbled of the "better-class" of young female wage earners in Birmingham. "Some . . . pay occasional visits to theatres and music halls, and a few join dancing classes. For others, the churches and chapels find the recreation [while] choir practices, Bible-classes, and missions fill all available time. An objection to this form of spending leisure is that the girls are seldom or never at home, except on Friday evening."[55] Miss Yeomans of the Finsbury Girls' Club in London, speaking to her Loughborough counterparts, granted that opponents often leveled this charge against her organization, but she insisted that neither she nor other reformers were bent on enticing girls from their homes. More to the point, they wished to provide amenities for those who, for whatever reason, did not spend their nonworking hours safely ensconced in the bosom of the family and, were it not for the clubs, "would be in the streets." Some of these "were not satisfied to spend their evenings at home after being out at work all day, but wanted some recreation of their own," she reasoned.[56] Many could not find satisfactory recreation in their homes even if they wished to do so. In families that boasted front parlors, mothers would not "give up the sanctified isolation"[57] of those architectural testaments to respectability, while in the more typical one, two, or three-room dwelling place, "all the available space [was] required for domestic or commercial purpose."[58] "They cannot stay at home," Lady Albinia Hobart-Hampden stated flatly. "The small rooms are full, the father having his tea, the little ones waiting to go to bed; and anyway the girls must have some vent for their energies after being pent up all day in a hot room." Besides, pointed out the duchess of Somerset, patroness of the Loughborough Girls' Club, most working-class homes were singularly unattractive places in which to spend one's time. "In so many cases [they] were uncomfortable and cheerless and it was little wonder that the girls should prefer to go elsewhere."[59] Better that the "elsewhere" should be a girls' club rather than the streets or a "low" amusement resort.

With reams being written in this period on the wretchedness of working-class homes, the physical freedom and independent spirit of young working women, and the hazards that awaited them in the wider world, it wasn't difficult to craft a compelling argument in favor of girls' clubs. Maude Stanley, for instance, convinced that the "startling" problems of the age, "the sufferings of the working people" and their "ugly and loveless" lives, lay chiefly in the overpopulation that resulted from early marriages, argued that there was no better remedy than "clubs for working girls and boys." "The girl who has her club will not need the idle companionship of lads," Stanley opined. "She will not want them, for she will have her girl friends, her interests, her occupations for her leisure hours in her club, and marriage when it comes will find her . . . better prepared for its duties in experience, in health, and in capacity at twenty-six than at sixteen."[60] In like vein, addressing the 1909 annual meeting of the Loughborough Girls' Club, the Reverend Canon Pitts deftly reworked the criticism that the institution took girls and women from their homes, kept them from their domestic duties, and unfitted them as wives and mothers. Club leaders "did not wish the girls to neglect their home life and go to the club every night during the week," Canon Pitts explained; they merely hoped that members would "pay an occasional visit . . . after their home work had to be done." Most significantly, the club was not a careless or willful exercise in undermining the family and domesticity. It was not meant to take the place of "home life." It served a far more positive purpose, a purpose of the greatest value: it was "a place where . . . girls could be taught what the ideal home life should be."[61] This domestic, uplifting mission constituted the core rationale for the establishment and support of working girls' clubs from the 1880s through the First World War era. In pursuit of this mission, upper- and middle-class women sought to model their working-class counterparts around a framework of womanhood that meshed with their own values and to reconstruct working-class homes along comfortably familiar lines.

BRICKS AND MORTAR, FURNITURE, FITTINGS, AND MATERIAL fabric may have been mundane, but they were nonetheless important considerations for those wishing to make clubs into academies for teaching working-class girls and women what the "ideal" home was like and how to make one. It was not always easy to secure suitable premises and, in attempting to do so and maintain them, upper- and middle-class women occasionally found themselves up against the kinds of material difficulties that continually confronted working-class women. In this, as in other encounters with the often stark and unpleasant conditions of lower-class life to which their club work brought them, they themselves received an education that they might not have anticipated or welcomed. A club's accommodation had to be close enough to the neighborhoods in which working girls lived to be convenient, but not in any area so insalubrious or threatening as to deter ladies from visiting. As many a respectable working-class family might find to its dismay, neighbors were not always of a type with which one would choose to associate. With the growth of the West Central Jewish Club (WCJC), Lilian Montagu sought larger rooms. Having found what seemed to be suitable facilities, she subsequently discovered, from "some knowledgeable people," that the rooms were "next door to, if not part of, a bad house." Unfazed, Montagu moved her organization in regardless and there it stood "for a short time" as a model of the ideal home, cheek by jowl with its wicked sister, the house of ill-repute.[62] Again, as working-class families knew only too well, rent was a major drain on resources, heating and lighting were additional, necessary expenses, and sanitary and other arrangements were sometimes less than perfect. Clubs relied on the philanthropic graces of landlords, as well as those of official patrons, and duly recorded in their annual reports and accounts the occasional gifts of coal and the like that helped to keep them functioning.[63]

The ideal accommodation comprised a number of rooms, each designated for a specific function or allocated to certain individuals, an ordered set of spaces partaking something of the middle-class home, something of the school—and as little as possible of the crowded chaos of the disreputable lower-class domicile.[64] Having sufficient rooms to segregate club members along various lines helped to keep things running smoothly and facilitated the promotion of peaceful, quiet, and controlled recreation.[65] Organizations that were able to realize such aspirations called attention to the fact, using ritual and ceremony to display and sanctify physical arrangements that were meant to conduce to orderly, peaceful domesticity and comfort. From 1891 to 1904, for example, the Loughborough Girls' Club was housed modestly and unsatisfactorily in one room. In November 1904 it began a campaign to canvass for funds toward new premises that boasted a large meeting room, a secretary's room, and a kitchen for cookery classes. In December, the new rooms were opened with dedication services conducted by no fewer than four reverend gentlemen (one a canon) and graced by the presence of numerous exalted patrons and benefactors, including Lady Percy St. Maur, the club's president.[66] In 1907 the club moved again to an even more expansive two-story building comprising a large hall for games, a sitting room for the younger members, and a secretary's room, all on the ground floor. On the upper level there were "two good rooms," one for the older girls and one for classes. Befittingly, the formal opening of these more commodious premises, this "pleasant, happy and instructive place of meeting," was conducted not by a mere canon, but by the bishop of Peterborough, and attended, again, by an influential company of ladies and gentlemen, titled, reverend, and otherwise. The municipal hierarchy, represented by the mayor of Loughborough, gave its sanction to the proceedings and to the club's work with a gesture of appropriately domestic and demure hospitality: it provided a tea for the occasion.[67] The Loughborough Girls' Club enjoyed the benefit of generous financial support from powerful and wealthy benefactors whose annual subscriptions and donations constituted its largest single source of income. Consequently, it could afford to rent rooms that were spacious, comfortable, and well furnished, lighted, and heated.

The NGEHC organizations had to eke out a much more precarious existence and work much harder at the physical construction of a semblance of home comfort for their members. The Ruddington Girls' Evening Home, for example, resorted to a "Ping Pong Room," loaned rent-free by a Mr. and Mrs. Parr, "friends" of the club, for one winter season because of the unacceptably "damp condition of the cottage in which it usually met."[68] The Hyson Green Girls' Club moved at least five times from 1889 to 1906 in search of satisfactory accommodation. Finishing up in the Court Street Mission Rooms, club leaders were already looking for new rooms by 1908; they were evidently unsuccessful, for in 1913, having determined that the mission was "not conducive to health," they were still trying to find another place in which to meet.[69] In January 1894, in anticipation of the club's third move in almost as many years, the executive committee met to plan an entertainment to raise funds for tables and curtains for its new rooms. At the end of the year, a sale of "small scrap books and other things made by the girls and other articles donated by the teachers" yielded 31s. 6d. "to be spent on

Spiritual and moral edification, if not the promotion of organized religion, was at the core of many working girls' clubs, and Bible classes were a common offering. Religious agencies reciprocated, adapting the customs of the popular recreation calendar to more sober and pious purposes. Ruth Stanley of Thurlstone, elected the Rose Queen of Netherfield Congregational Sunday School, is a sweetly earnest, plainly dressed echo of the Queen of the May in this undated photograph. Courtesy of Sheffield Archives, 696/Z1/11.

furniture." When the club opened for its 1895 season, it had relocated again. The new home, furnished in part with tables and chairs donated by friends and well-wishers, "presented a very comfortable appearance" and elicited "much admiration [from] the girls." The pride of the place was that key instrument of domestic accord and token of wholesome, rational entertainment, a new piano, which had been acquired through the consumer-friendly hire-purchase system.[70]

Much of the Hyson Green club's work in this twenty-or-so-year nomadism was directed to making its various abodes cozy, cheery, and comfortably appointed. This was not mere frippery or self-indulgence. Club leaders recognized the power—symbolic and material—of the physical environment and its centrality to their aim of providing members with a domestic ideal to which to aspire. Contemporary advice literature for middle-class newlyweds urged them to make homes "so bright and beautiful and pleasant that they . . . shed radiance on all in their immediate neighbourhood," homes that were "worth so very much precept," homes that, "like good deeds," shone " 'like a candle in this naughty world.' "[71] Club leaders wanted the same for the "evening homes" they instituted for working women. A welcoming hearth around which everyone could gather to share its comforting warmth was charged with meaning, as were "windows full of light and suggestion of entertainment." These were necessary amenities within and radiant tokens of the mission of spreading domestic enlightenment without. Proponents of clubs wanted "the stream borne outward of song [and music] to bring in those young wasters of their youth . . . those weird crowds of . . . wild, unkempt girls."[72]

The absence of these amenities signaled discord and desolation, a bleak house that was no home. This was so much so that, during several of the stormy periods that occasionally visited the Hyson Green club, among the first measures the executive committee took to restore peace were improving "the lighting of the room" and instructing the caretaker "to be particularly careful in making a good fire.''[73] Lilian Montagu learned early that such minor considerations could make a big difference. "We have always persuaded the girls to take off their hats and outer garments when they come into the Club," she noted of her own WCJC in London. "This apparently unimportant custom has a definite influence in . . . securing a home-like atmosphere." Maintaining that atmosphere would encourage members to feel that they had a vested interest in the club, would keep them coming back, and would impress upon them the desir-ability of weaving a similarly comforting cocoon for their own fami-lies in the future.[74]

CLUB SPONSORS FELT THAT IT WAS EQUALLY IMPORTANT TO build the personal intimacies, sense of belonging, and familial duties and responsibilities that they associated with a home, even to repli-cate idealized notions of familial roles and relationships between leaders and members. For Montagu, this meant establishing the kind of loving, nurturing, and accepting domestic bonds that had sustained her as a child. She took as a model for club leadership her mother, a woman she praised for having "throughout her life . . . no greater pleasure than that of sharing her children's interests." Montagu decried the fact that many working women felt that in their factories and workshops they counted "only as numbers." Through the good offices of the club's "loving relations"—Montagu as "Mother," her lifelong friend and companion Miss Lewis as "Father," sister Marian and other club workers as "aunties"—she hoped that its "family" would be a countervailing, rehumanizing force.[75]

In other clubs and organizations, leaders assumed sterner, more distant, and didactic roles and, when they used the language of the family to describe their relationships with members, it was with a strongly authoritarian tone. Thus, it was not so much tenderness and affection that was wanting in the home lives of working girls and women, as it was parental—especially maternal—guidance and con-trol, the likes of Maude Stanley and GFS officials believed. With "thousands of lower-class mothers . . . utterly and culpably careless about their daughters," clubs and similar organizations were essential means for delivering the "friendship, counsel, and instruction," the "protection" and "mothering" so sorely lacking among working girls and women. Bereft in their own homes of proper maternal models for training them to be "future generations of good wives and mothers," girls could turn to the ladies in charge of their clubs and find in them the "high standards" of womanhood to which reformers believed they should be aspiring.[76]

Club workers saw informal teaching through personal example as a particularly effective way of inculcating in working-class girls and women these more elevated notions of morals and manners. By getting to know "every woman, every girl, every child," by "having ideals for them" to which they soon lived up, the Reverend Dolling's sister felt able to claim the title of "ladies" for the members of the social club that she helped run in his Portsmouth parish.[77] It was "an education to [working] girls even to be with a refined woman, to watch her, talk to her," Lady Hobart-Hampden believed. So different and superior was her "whole standard of life" from theirs that "unconsciously they [were] learning by being with her." If laboring women's lives were to be made "purer, and freer from temptation," then individual, personal contact between them and ladies was essential, Kathleen Townend felt.[78] Clubs were places where that personal connection could be made, and club leaders welcomed those ladies who visited them for the "very beneficial effect [they had] on the girls, which [was] shown in their improved manner and high moral principles."[79] Ladies who ventured into factories to hold dinner-hour meetings with workers and to encourage them to join "temperance societies, evening clubs &c." likewise imparted "superior" standards of character and behavior. "Their visits have been found to make a distinct difference in the workrooms," Cadbury, Matheson, and Shann reported from Birmingham. "Several employers have noticed an increase of refinement among the girls since a lady took an interest in them."[80] Refinement, an eminently desirable quality in a woman, expressed itself in dress, personal grooming, and general comportment—clothing, hair, and body that were clean, neat, and tidy, not tawdry, tatty, and grimy, quiet self-control, moderation, and decency in every aspect of behavior. These were among the ideals that the promoters and sponsors of clubs hoped their members would emulate, sloughing off their former "rude, vulgar, untidy, disreputable" habits to emerge as models of respectable and demure womanhood.[81] Yet some patrons of working women's recreation evidently found it difficult to admit qualities such as decorum and restraint in laboring women. Describing a dinner provided by Lady Brassey and a speech by her husband to 250 members of the London Women's Union in September 1883, the *Women's Union Journal* recorded that "the tables . . . were tastefully laid out and decorated with flowers." His Lordship felt constrained to remark that the gathering of "what were justly termed 'respectable and well behaved workwomen' " was "a *novel* and pleasant sight [emphasis added]."[82]

FOR SOME CLUBS, AS FOR ORGANIZATIONS SUCH AS THE GFS, THE Mothers' Union, and Snowdrop Bands, nothing less than absolute moral purity and piety would do. Indeed, a girls' club was an ideal way to begin missionary forays among the godless.[83] From the beginning, the GFS was set on preserving working girls' and women's virtue and preparing them for "Christian marriage and . . . motherhood." As surrogate mothers—good, Christian mothers—associates were moral guides and exemplars committed to educating their charges in "religious principles" as well as "domestic duties," and to trying to keep them from sliding into sin. The organization essayed an almost continuous surveillance of members from the time they joined as candidates at the age of eight until they married and could step out from the GFS's maternal umbrella and under a husband's patriarchal "protection." Its architects thus attempted to provide the controlling influences and instruction about which they believed working-class mothers were indifferent. Into the moral breach left by these delinquents, "the Girls' Friendly Society steps," one aristocratic associate pronounced. "Modesty in behaviour at home and on the streets is enforced . . . instruction [is] given . . . in the first principles of purity and honour . . . the protection and refining influence surrounding the daughters of the upper classes [is] extended to the daughters even of the lowest!"[84]

The Mothers' Union likewise devoted itself to upholding the sanctity of marriage by organizing bands of mothers who were "united in prayer" and, through their own exemplary conduct and unimpeachable characters, able to steer their families out of the moral morass and toward the higher, safer ground of righteous living. At the union's meetings, the wives of high-ranking churchmen and those of humbler clergy shepherded working-class women together to be instructed upon the morals, religion, and education of their children. The wife of Bishop Hoskyns of Southwell, for instance, addressing the inaugural meeting of the Retford, Nottinghamshire, branch in May 1908, urged the town's matrons to take responsibility for their children's immortal souls. If they would give up stimulants and teach their sons and daughters the Church Catechism, they would be fit and ready to "lead the future fathers and mothers of the Empire . . . in purity and holiness of life."[85]

The professed principle aim of the NGEHC was to awaken in young workers a sense of "their moral and religious duties" and to give them "a fuller knowledge and love of our Lord Jesus Christ." The Bristol Association of Working Girls' Clubs (BAWGC), judging that there was a pressing "need for a higher moral tone" among the young workwomen of that city, set its face sternly against "impurity of any description" among its members. To this end, it encouraged the establishment of Snowdrop Bands among its affiliates. Some of the Nottingham clubs had similar organizational links: the Hyson Green club had a Snowdrop Band that met once a month outside the club's regular schedule.[86] Like the GFS, the Nottingham association was strictly preventive in intent, and both organizations' insistence on insulating their members from vice meant that they were not prepared to attempt any redemptive work among those that had already "fallen." "In consideration of the interests of the general body of members," the NGEHC could not bring itself to admit "girls who [were] openly leading immoral lives," lest they corrupt the virtuous. This kind of exactitude had split the GFS in 1879–1880, when a breakaway organization formed that was more accepting of the often variable and fluid moral codes of some working women, and similar tensions arose in other associations and clubs. One way of resolving them was to segregate members, as did the St. Margaret's House and Stratford settlements in Bethnal Green, London. "Many of the girls of the neighbourhood were too rough to be amalgamated" with the "more docile," and so settlement workers set up a "rough girls' club" for the former.[87] Elsewhere, club leaders hoped that the values and behavior of the more "respectable" members would rub off on the "rough" and, indeed, some refused to exclude the "hooligan" and "thoroughly bad" girls for that very reason.

Most clubs, even those that did not adhere to the morally exclusive tenets of the GFS or the NGEHC, or were not directly connected with institutionalized religion, offered a touch of spiritual or moral edification as leaven for whatever "fun and merriment" members found in them.[88] Many sponsors shared Maude Stanley's credo that because it was "through religion alone we obtain perfect happiness," religion was the foundation upon which clubs should be built.[89] And the Pauline injunction to think on only "whatsoever things are true, honourable, just, pure, lovely, of good report" was a favorite quotation in rational recreation circles. The more optimistic club leaders believed that the "quieting influence of a hymn," communal prayers, and brief addresses exemplifying "the eternal truths" could leave a transforming "trail of light behind" in the hearts and minds of even the wildest, least tractable club girl.[90] So Bible classes were among the regularly scheduled activities, meetings opened and closed with prayers and hymns, clubs held special church services, and local clergymen and their wives were prominent in organizational and honorary roles.[91] For ethnic and religious minorities, girls' clubs offered rare opportunities for maintaining at least the form and, for some, also the spirit of an embattled faith and way of life. Lilian Montagu devoted all her work with the WCJC to "keeping Judaism alive among . . . young people." The commercial amusements that London offered on Friday evenings and Saturdays were a powerful force that militated against Sabbath observation. To counter this, for many years the club's leaders persisted with a guild fellowship whose members pledged to remain at home on Friday nights. Montagu prepared a service that was "widely circulated" and had "pretty badges representing the Shield of David made" for them to wear. She also organized Sabbath services on Saturday afternoons to coincide with the end of the working week and services on Holy Days, and talks on religion and "united act[s] of prayer" were long-standing traditions in the club.[92]

Temperance was another manifestation of the moral purity tendencies in working women's clubs. Snowdrop Bands had their temperance parallel in the White Ribbon Bands that formed in association with several clubs, and temperance lectures and meetings were common, often featuring an invited speaker from a group such as the British Women's Temperance Association.[93] Some groups devised their own pledges, and printed cards and books to be distributed among and signed and carried by members, charms against "intemperance and impurity of any description." Club rooms and other facilities were designated no-go areas as far as alcohol was concerned.[94] The BAWGC flirted with the notion of taking the battle against intemperance, and the "growing moral deterioration" it associated with working-class women's drinking, right into the heart of the occupational culture in which these habits were rooted. In the pre-Christmas season of 1901, the organization's executive put together a Special Management Committee to discuss the "existence of drinking clubs among girls in factories" in the city. The committee circulated a letter "inviting [club leaders] to speak privately to proprietors of the factories involved and to speak strongly to girls in their clubs and distribute leaflets reminding members to be temperate in all things." Results must have been mixed at best, for a month later drinking clubs were the sole agenda item of the association's Executive Council meeting. Contradictory accounts of whether there was a problem and, if so, its extent came from Miss Champion and Mrs. Davies, who, having visited a local cotton factory, concluded that "such practices were quite impossible as the girls [were] constantly subject to being searched." Mr. Elijah Thomas disagreed. He, too, had made some inquiries, visiting the owner of a factory where such clubs were reputed to exist. Things were "far worse," he reported. The factory authorities "always dreaded Christmas time and the marriage of workers," for these frequently led to the "break down of many." They welcomed any suggestions that the BAWGC might have to help "prevent so sad an evil."[95]

Penetrating and influencing the workplace culture was an intimidating task to which not all club leaders were equal; the home and women's domestic responsibilities were comfortably within their "natural" sphere, and on these they primarily and most consistently focused. Temperance, purity, religiosity, and the like all came within the reach of this broader concern, elements of the moral branch of the domestic education that reformers instituted. There was a strongly practical thrust to this, manifested in the instruction clubs offered in the basics of housekeeping and domestic crafts, lectures and discussions on topics such as hygiene, home nursing, and nutrition, though the programs varied depending on sponsors' philosophies and the resources they had at hand. Most of the NGEHC organizations had to make do with a fairly narrow curriculum, focused on domestic skills and crafts: plain and fancy sewing, knitting, dressmaking, blouse making, basket making, first-aid, and Bible classes.[96] Some clubs admitted that the humdrum nature of much of what they did could be a problem. The Cross Street Evening Home in Nottingham noted in its report for 1906–1907 that leaders and members alike "very much felt the lack of an occasional address on

Temperance, Hygiene, or any other useful or interesting subject," and appealed for volunteers to assist in "that branch of [their] work." The only break that they had enjoyed in their "usual routine" over the winter had been "Miss Parker's most excellent recitation on October 8" and the New Year Party.[97] The Honesty Girls' Club in York had somewhat more varied fare, offering the standards—needlework (a compulsory subject), blouse making, millinery, part-singing, and a Sunday afternoon class—as well as Old English folk dancing and modern dancing, swimming, allotment gardening, and nature study.[98] The WCJC, able to draw teachers from the talents of the metropolitan cultural elite, had a very diverse program. There were, of course, "domestic science classes" for preparing club members for "satisfactory home keeping," but also public affairs, languages, art, music, drama, and literature to stimulate and satisfy creative and intellectual appetites. The Soho Girls' Club and Home, similarly situated, offered comparable diversity: from domestic skills to botany, English literature, and Greek mythology.[99]

THE EARNEST, IMPROVING TENOR OF THE RHETORIC OF THE ladies who sponsored these clubs and taught these classes, their representation of themselves as women with a mission, rescuing working girls and women from the clutches of a deleterious working-class culture—all this insinuates class condescension, social control, and heavy-handed didacticism. Yet, even in the sources that produce this impression, that muffle and filter the voices of working women, there are obvious signs that these women were more than equal to charting their own course, exercising their own agency, and making clubs accord with their interests, needs, and wishes.

This is apparent in the fundamental and perennially challenging issue of whether any would choose to join or attend a club. Where there was an identifiable constituency with which such a venture might readily fly, reformers had little difficulty in establishing clubs. Those that emerged as an extension of some previous enterprise such as a Sunday school, Bible class, or evening institute had a core

of leaders and members whose existing relationships and like interest in educational, moral, or spiritual development helped hold them
together. This, in Maude Stanley's experience, was the "best way
of starting a girls' club." There was already a "connection between
members and ladies, and . . . friendliness on one side and . . . confi-
dence on the other side engendered by the intercourse already carried on between them." It is important to note that the initiative
for such ventures did not always come from the ladies. The WCJC
originated as a proposal from some of the working girls, mostly employed in the sewing and millinery trades of Soho, who participated
in Lilian Montagu's Sabbath classes and "happy Sunday afternoons." They informed her that there was a large and keen constituency just wanting some financial and organizational support to be
able to transform itself into a club. With Montagu on board, within
a few years the WCJC membership numbered in the hundreds and,
by the mid-1920s, it stood between seven hundred and eight hundred. In clubs owing their origins to middle- and upper-class deter-
minations of a need to be met and sponsors' canvassing of potential
members, there were also ways of ensuring a core membership that
would help hold the enterprise together around a set of common
ideals. Winifred Rowntree formed the Honesty Girls' Club in York
from a nucleus of twenty-four daughters of the members of a local
Adult School, all likely to have been raised in sympathy to the principles of rational recreation. Six of these were still active and prominent in leadership roles fourteen years later, united and steadfast in
their loyalty to the "high ideal[s]" she had embodied suggested an
obituary for Rowntree. These were expressed in the club motto:

> She doeth little kindnesses
> Which most leave undone, or despise
> For naught that sets one's heart at ease
> And giveth happiness and peace
> Is low-esteemed in her eyes.[100]

Another strategy was to approach employers and seek permission
to visit workers during the dinner hour, engage the sympathies of

the forewoman or foreman, and have them bring forward those who were most likely to be interested in joining a club.[101] With foundations of members such as these, who had an inclination for and commitment to educational, improving, and wholesome leisure, who were in this sense kindred spirits with their upper- and middle-class sponsors, ready to respond as "echo[es] to the tender words and loving thoughts" of those "true friend[s]," clubs had a decent chance of getting off the ground to begin with and of thriving once established.[102] Where there was no existing connection or means of establishing sympathy between club sponsors and potential members, no matter how zealous the recreational reformer, the prospects of her mission's foundering—if it even began—were greater. Veteran campaigners such as Maude Stanley knew of what they spoke when they advised those who were fresh to the field to use established connections to build up club membership.[103] The anonymity of urban working-class life and the social and cultural distance separating the privileged from the masses made it well nigh impossible to connect with those determined to be most in need of reform. "How are they to be caught or brought under better influences?" Lady Albinia Hobart-Hampden worried. "How, indeed are we even to see their faces?" After spending several years as a settlement worker, Hobart-Hampden had had the magnitude of her task brought home to her. "The difficulty of reaching . . . young factory workers seems to me even greater than it did at first. They are never to be found at home, or if you are lucky enough to catch them on a Saturday afternoon they are busy dressing or sitting over the fire heating their curling tongs between the bars. With the rest of the family coming and going, tea on the table, and children all around you, conversation . . . is impossible."[104]

Once out in the streets, working girls and women were even more elusive and resistant to reformers' advances. "Repeatedly has the experiment been tried to give papers of clubs in the streets to workgirls," Stanley noted. "They have taken the papers, expressed a wish to come, but have never made their appearance."[105] And the fun to be had in the streets and elsewhere could tempt even the soberest, most rational of members away from the club on occasions—hence the policy in all but the largest clubs of opening only in the winter months or for only one or two nights a week in the summer. As Katie Cowper sympathetically commented, "one cannot wonder that [during the summer] they should prefer walking in the streets and getting what air they can, to spending the evening indoors."[106] Even during the winter, on certain nights attendance might be low and, where this was as a consequence of the rival attractions of that "low" leisure culture to which club leaders were supposed to be providing a rational alternative, they understandably found this disturbing. It was a problem at the Hyson Green club, especially during Nottingham's Goose Fair season. Terribly concerned about the threat that this annual carnival posed to the moral welfare of the town's working women, the club's executive took special care to be on duty at the end of September. Strategies for keeping "their girls" safely sheltered and occupied for the fair's duration included opening clubrooms before the official start of the winter program, hosting parties, and laying on special treats such as cocoa and buns. Sound as the scheme might have been in theory, in practice it was not a raging success. At the opening night of the 1897–1898 season, for example, twenty-six girls went to the club, "listened quietly" to an "interesting talk," and were "regaled with coffee and buns." A few nights later, on Goose Fair Thursday, ten attended, and on Saturday, the final, climactic night of the fair, only five judged the club's cocoa and buns the more attractive proposition.[107]

The problem was by no means unique to Hyson Green or to the Goose Fair season. All the NGEHC organizations painstakingly recorded the number of members on their registers and detailed in annual reports the average attendance on club nights, annotating the figures with comments expressing concern or pleasure—"good," "excellent," "very satisfactory," or "disappointingly small"—at the turnout.[108] In the large London clubs, there were sufficient interested members to allow for a fringe of "apathetic and indifferent" ones that could float in and out as the fancy took them.[109] Even so, if the club was to remain viable, leaders had to be sensitive to members' inclinations and arrive at some accommodation to them with respect to the activities offered, the organization's rules and policies, and the nature of personal interactions within it. In all these areas, the working-class membership had significant influence.

Getting the balance right between purely recreational and educational activities was a delicate affair. In some clubs, there was little or no interest in classes and lectures; members simply wanted a warm, comfortable retreat in which to meet and socialize with their friends. In the early years of the WCJC, its sitting room was often filled with a "large crowd of young people, chatting loudly, sitting on the table, or on the floor, on the sides of the chairs, and telling of their experiences and giving vent to their opinions." It was futile to try to establish classes where there was no interest in them; members simply voted with their feet and stayed out in the streets or congregated in the communal areas of the club chatting with their friends or, if so inclined, disrupting the formally scheduled activities. Unappealing as well were classes offered by inept or ignorant teachers, who, Lilian Montagu soon discovered, club members would not tolerate. The WCJC girls had had to make their own way in the workplace and were "very precocious" as a consequence. It was an effort for them to attend the club regularly, and they did not go "just to laze about" or to be fobbed off with "teaching [that was] only make-believe." Nor would they stand for condescension from club sponsors or scoldings from those in charge. "The girls said they would not be ordered about like children," Montagu noted, "and that they would much prefer to stay away from the Club than submit to constant interference with their liberty."[110] Even Maude Stanley, who insisted that club girls must never show undue familiarity or any disrespect to the ladies who supervised them, recognized that some lacked due sensitivity at times and she was quite prepared to jettison one of her peers rather than alienate the membership.[111]

Two issues in particular highlight the negotiating process that underlay club business and relationships: the questions of whether dancing was an acceptable activity and whether males should be admitted. On both, sponsors and members tended to break down into two fairly distinct camps. Members inclined to the opinion that both dancing and young men had to be part of a club's social life. Sponsors were uneasy at the prospect of either but recognized that obduracy was inimical to their intention of keeping members safe from the risks posed by pursuing these pleasures elsewhere. The compromise was for clubs to offer dancing and open their doors to the opposite sex occasionally rather than invariably, and only under carefully controlled circumstances.

Dancing's disrepute arose from the nature of the activity, from its association with insalubrious dance halls, because it incited "dangerous" passions, and because it might draw young women into a moral slough. Social dancing as widely practiced among the working classes, members of the Federation of Working Girls' Clubs agreed, had "a deteriorating influence on the character," which was why many would "not allow dancing in [their] clubs."[112] To permit it would be to promote an unhealthy appetite that would necessarily draw young women into seedy saloons and encourage them to "become habitual frequenters of dances." And so would begin the measured moral descent. "A whole week's wages [would] be spent in the ball dress," another week's wages would "go for shoes and gloves," debts would mount, and "thus not infrequently the temptation to provide for these pleasures by dishonest or by immoral ways [would be] yielded to."[113]

Yet working girls would dance, they loved to do so, and to repress this instinct was, even more surely, to court disaster. Club leaders who did so by forbidding the activity "under proper conditions to girls who [were] untrained to self-restraint" incurred a "grave responsibility," Lilian Montagu cautioned. "I have know[n] girls who, forbidden to dance in their clubs, have deliberately gone out to make, as they said 'blackguards of themselves round a street organ,'

and they have, of course, been conspicuously successful in their en-
deavours."[114] If they could not dance in their clubs under wholesome conditions, they would take even greater delight in satisfying
their natural, emotional needs in public dancing places where the
"cheapest and most deteriorating" forms of movement and music
prevailed.[115] And so dancing came to constitute one of the more popular activities in many clubs, though in some it was smuggled in
under the cover of "musical drill" or, even by outspoken opponents,
as a "physical exercise," a "game" that went by the name of "Sir
Roger de Coverley." ("The girls know differently," Maude Stanley
disclosed, "but are content to call it a game if by that means they
can get a dance.")[116] The approved forms were stately, graceful
dances such as the gavotte and pavane, or folk dances. These, with
their "noble and dignified," "pure," and sweetly stimulating movements and rhythms, performed to "good music," would "wake the
highest response and make a channel for the expression of lofty ideals and aspirations." "Vulgarizing," "suggestive," "cheapening," and
"enervating" dances, such as waltzes, "should not be allowed."[117]

Where men were admitted to club dances—and, as club members
generally agreed "that dances in which girls could only dance with
girls were as dull as sandwiches made of bread and bread," this
eventually happened—there were procedures in place to ensure that
propriety was observed. Carefully devised and conducted systems
of tickets and formal invitations, and prohibitions on "strangers" and
casual acquaintances screened out undesirables. Invitations to young
men from neighborhood choirs and Bible classes filtered in partners
with the right credentials. Squads of ladies and gentlemen were
drafted as chaperones, and starting and finishing times were scrupu-
lously observed. Similar policies governed other socials and entertainments and concerts that clubs put on. Some organizations used
the prospect of such events to maintain order more generally
through the club or as inducements for regular attendance, a practice
of which Maude Stanley heartily disapproved.[118]

In the Hyson Green club, and others where "rough girls" could be intractable, this seems to have been a necessary measure. Hyson Green closed its doors on a number of occasions because of the "bad behaviour" of some members, locks had to be put on cupboards to prevent the "mysterious disappearance" of sundry club equipment, and the ladies in charge regularly relied upon their gentlemen friends to "close" club evenings. The most serious disturbances occurred late in the club's season in 1897. One Saturday evening in March, when Miss Hazzeldine was in sole charge, a group of girls rioted and refused to leave the club at closing time. It was only with the assistance of a policeman that the hapless Miss Hazzeldine managed to induce the girls finally to leave. Club leaders sent letters to the four ringleaders, told the culprits' mothers about their behavior, and banned them for the rest of the season. Trouble persisted, however, and in April, the landlord complained about the "noise and disorder." The executive decided to close the club, withhold prizes that they usually gave out at season's end, and cancel the scheduled summer party, informing "the girls . . . that their behaviour had not warranted" these rewards. The club reopened the following September as usual. But the executive committee instituted a behavior register as well as an attendance register, refused admittance to anyone who did not pay her weekly penny, ruled the piano out of bounds, and tried desperately to get members to settle down to "needlework or work of some kind." By January, they had evidently had enough. Having suspended several girls who had been "very bad," the Hyson Green executive closed the club down. It remained shut until 1906, when a new group of sponsors bravely took the helm and managed to keep things afloat into the World War I era.[119]

The fate of Hyson Green gives pause for thought on the question of how successful such a venture could be among those who did not already share at least some of the common ground that Priscilla Murolo had found the club girls and women of New York inhabiting.[120] Some of the intended beneficiaries of English working girls' clubs evidently subscribed to the same kinds of values that their upper-

and middle-class sponsors held, no doubt some merely paid lip service to them, and some rejected them. Unquestionably, they knew their own minds and approached clubs in the same way that they approached other elements of the complex mesh of their lives, including other leisure opportunities and amenities. They were guided by their own senses of themselves as women and workers, they sought to pursue their own educational, intellectual, spiritual, social, and cultural interests, and they wished to satisfy the desire for companionship, relaxation, and amusement. There was a good deal over which they were prepared and able to contest and about which they negotiated in order to arrive at a workable compact. This was an ongoing, complex process entailing fluid and shifting within-class and between-class agreements and divergences over gender identities, women's desires and duties, the place of leisure in working women's lives, and the individual and social significance of that leisure. The dynamics of this began working even before a club's constitution—they were already operating within the broader social and cultural milieu, expressed in the concerns that reformers voiced over working women's leisure, and the interest or lack of interest that girls had in such an organization. When sponsors and potential members took their initial steps toward coming together in a club, they entered into the first of many exchanges that would fundamentally influence the shape it took, the activities it promoted, and whether it would get off the ground in the first place. The establishment of a club, its persistence, and the smoothness of the course that it ran signaled that this negotiating, accommodating, compromising, giving and taking were at work. In some clubs, such as the WCJC and the Honesty Girls' Club in York, it ran relatively smoothly. In others, such as Hyson Green, it shuddered and sputtered along in fits and starts, sometimes breaking down completely, unable to press on against differences that built up to crippling and eventually incapacitating tensions.

WHATEVER ELSE CAN BE SAID OF THESE AND OTHER UPPER- AND middle-class rational recreation initiatives, they were of benefit to others than just the working women for whom they were ostensibly intended. In the writings and pronouncements of leisure reformers, dominant though the motifs of solemn duty and sacro-secular mission are, the other strain that can be heard speaks to this: that rational recreation work could be an antidote to too much leisure.[121]

Philanthropic, charitable, and social reform movements were arenas in which upper- and middle-class women stretched the class and gender conventions that historical wisdom tells us frequently rendered their lives ones of "refined [and 'enforced'] idleness." By the turn of the century, charity work had been firmly established as a "respectable alternative" to genteel idleness, and many privileged women found in it a sense of purpose that was denied them elsewhere. Thousands established a presence in working-class neighborhoods and workplaces where, ministering to the poor and deprived, they sought and found self-fulfillment and excitement. (One contemporary estimated for the final decades of the nineteenth century that there were over five hundred thousand such women engaged in charity work in the United Kingdom.)[122] Some were inconsistent and half-hearted "workers" about whom the more diligent complained. These approached charity and philanthropy as they did shopping: in the words of Judith Walkowitz, as a "roughly equivalent recreational [activity] appropriate to their station."[123] But even the most idealistically minded experienced the foray into working-class culture as an adventure, a release, emancipation from dull respectability. As Martha Vicinus notes, the colonial and imperialist overtones of women's settlement work were in this regard much more than symbolic for middle-class women: "Emigration to Canada or Australia meant adventure, freedom, and space for their brothers. Tied more closely to their families, women could find freedom by 'emigrating' to the East End [of London]."[124]

Thus, the very features of working-class women's leisure, which rational recreationists bemoaned and determined to reform, paradoxically had a powerful appeal for them. While reformers exhorted working girls and women to avoid the dangerous, disorderly passions of popular culture and remain aloof from its cheap excitements, they themselves enjoyed rubbing up against that culture. Montagu, one of the keenest proponents of raising working women's recreational standards, nonetheless envied the "abandonment" with which they joined "the leisured classes" once the working day was over. Emily Kinnaird, in a 1900 presentation to the NCWGB conference on "The Right Use of Leisure," similarly admitted the contradictions inherent in the project in which she was engaged. "Leisure, to be leisure, must be spontaneous," she mused. "I have felt how easily leisure vanishes from our sight and eludes our grasp if we talk of it or try to organise it . . . leisure is abandonment to miscellaneous impulses."[125] Busily organizing and policing working women's leisure, women of privilege were able thus, in a qualified and guarded fashion, to partake of the abandonment and excitement of popular culture, to enjoy being "in" but not "of" its raucous world. Ellen Chase, a settlement worker in Deptford, London, loved the fact that "there was always something going on," that "there was always a spice about 'going into the street.' " Margaret Nevinson, who spent the early years of her married life in settlement work in Whitechapel, recalled that "life was always full of interest, change, and excitement. . . . I never remember one dull moment during the two years we lived there." At the beginning of her "apprenticeship" as a social investigator and reformer, Beatrice Webb, who experienced the "want of employment" in her comfortably upper-middle-class life as "almost torture, a silent misery," described her relationship with the East End and its lower-class inhabitants as a "weird romance." Though the squalor and coarseness of much of popular culture depressed her, Webb more often "[felt] envy than pity" for the East Enders. She relished the unprecedented freedoms that social missionary work brought her and her colleagues. "Ah! what would conventional West End acquaintance say to two young women smoking and talking in the bed, sitting, working, smoking and bath room of an East End School Board visitor?" she recorded in her diary of an afternoon she and a friend spent in the company of a former seaman employed by the local school board. "We have entertained freely and thoroughly enjoyed our life in working-class society."[126]

Few club sponsors acknowledged the paradox and tensions in such encounters with working-class culture, and in the nexus of class and gender relations that lay at the heart of women's rational recreation. Immured in a class system that was based on the assumption that "the lower classes labored to sustain the rich . . . in comfort,"[127] it was possible for most to avoid facing their own complicity in sustaining its inequities. Equally, they might never see or recognize the inequalities in the relationship between themselves and laboring women, between their own bounteous leisure and the latter's unremitting labor. Lilian Montagu did and the inconsistencies discomfited her. Noting how contradictory it was for social reformers to attempt to "improve" working women's lives through philanthropy when they were so often a cause of the hardships those women endured, she recalled asking a young female clerk of her acquaintance whether she was likely to get a desperately needed raise. " 'Oh no, I am afraid I cannot get one yet awhile,' " was the reply, " 'for we are owed at least £200.' She then gave me the names of one or two well-known social workers with whom her firm had contracted bad debts which were to be paid in the nebulous future." "The era must come," Montagu insisted, "when . . . life's opportunities [will be] better equalised, because on the other side of the scale [from the woman of leisure] there is the sweated, over-strained piece worker, whose charm is completely crushed by the excessive load of toil to which the over-leisured . . . contributes."[128] In the next chapter I examine one attempt to take rational recreation directly to that piece worker.

Chapter Six

"THE MAKING OF THE HEALTHY
AND HAPPY HOME": RATIONAL
RECREATION IN THE WORKPLACE

*I*T WAS FELT THAT . . . GIRLS WHO LEAVE SCHOOL FOR THE factory, and leave the factory to marry have little chance to become proficient in the domestic arts by helping at home."[1] Benjamin Seebohm Rowntree's reflections on the motivations underlying the opening of the Domestic School at his family's confectionery works in the northern city of York in 1907 said a great deal about dominant understandings of what it meant to be a working-class woman in late Victorian and Edwardian England. Bundled within his statement were a number of commonly held assumptions: that the state educational system was deficient in preparing girls for adult responsibilities, that their home life was supposed to give them an apprenticeship in marriage and domesticity, and that factory work was inimical to the same. The school also attested to the limitations of leisure as a sphere in which an ideal of working-class womanhood could be crafted or as a mechanism for shaping girls and women to fit that ideal.

The firm had initially put quite some store in this notion. From at least the 1890s, it had encouraged and sponsored recreational gatherings for female employees—informal work groups in domestic crafts such as knitting and crochet, formal instruction in dressmaking, and a number of societies. The directors viewed these leisure activities as valuable means for women workers to acquire the knowledge and learn and practice the skills that would prepare them for marriage and maternity when they left the Cocoa Works. Each club and class, no matter what its nominal focus, was an occasion for molding the characters of women workers, for nurturing "good" habits among them, and for promoting the tenet that "*the Home* [original emphasis]" was "the most important side of life."[2] Unfortunately, as far as the successful execution of these domestic designs went, too many of the girls and women at the Rowntree works simply could and did choose not to participate in the recreational programs. The Domestic School, which began life in 1905 as a small cookery school, was a tacit acknowledgment of this, of the fact that, when it came to the business of manufacturing wives and mothers, leisure alone was insufficient, that education and compulsion had to be conjoined with recreation and choice.[3]

The schools and recreational programs affirmed, in addition, the Rowntree firm's commitment to something higher than mere commercial enterprise; they were expressions of its fundamental belief that success in business should go hand in hand with social progress. This vision of enlightened capitalism derived from the family's Quaker faith, one that they shared with co-religionist confectionery manufacturers such as the Cadburys and Frys. These companies believed that the pursuit of their commercial interests was of a piece with their Christian charge of advancing the well-being of the workforce. Within their factories they nurtured a strong sense of family and belonging and a community of interest that they connected to the common weal beyond.[4] Everything that went on in the York Cocoa Works was meant to serve that end, was intended to ensure that Rowntree employees would be respectable and responsible members of a model working class—the bedrock of a model industrial, capitalist society. Male workers were to be formed into "good citizens," female employees were to be helped to be "good daughters and sisters . . . good wives and mothers," and the recreational programs were to help ensure that this would be so.[5]

Henry Isaac Rowntree, a respected member of the Society of Friends, established the Rowntree Cocoa Works in 1862, when he purchased a small manufactory in the center of the city of York. The business was a modest affair in its early years, employing only a dozen or so workers, but two major initiatives eventually helped turn around its fortunes and usher in an era of expansion. The first of these was the introduction in 1881 of a line of crystallized pastilles and gums that proved to be very successful. The second was the installation of equipment first developed in the Dutch chocolate industry that produced both a superior form of drinking cocoa and the cocoa butter that was an essential ingredient of eating chocolate. On the strength of these changes, over the next forty years or so the firm rose to become one of what Robert Fitzgerald terms the "chocolate triumvirate" of Cadbury, Fry, and Rowntree that dominated the industry.[6] The size of the workforce reflected its growth. In 1880 this stood at 100, by 1894 it had increased to 864, by 1904 it was 3,000, and by the outbreak of the First World War, it numbered 5,461.[7] Facilities in the center of York were inadequate for the rapidly expanding enterprise by the last decade of the nineteenth century. Consequently, in 1890 Joseph Rowntree, Henry Isaac's son, who had taken sole charge of the firm in 1883, purchased a large area of land a mile or so outside the city. There, he began constructing a modern, state-of-the-art factory covering some 220 acres, and in 1908 the company transferred all its operations to this new Haxby Road site.[8]

Although the turn of the twentieth century saw the firm transforming into a large-scale industrial concern employing thousands, the ethos of the family continued to infuse its culture. Members of the Rowntree family, from patriarch Joseph and his wife downward, played major roles in ensuring that this was so. They were involved in the day-to-day operation of the works, participated fully in its

Reformers feared that factory work was inimical to the formation of exemplary working-class wives and mothers. The educational and recreational programs that firms such as Rowntree organized were meant to address this problem and to promote a generally more enlightened industrial capitalism. At the York Cocoa Works amenities such as dining rooms, sports fields, and rose gardens constituted the transformative physical spaces for this social and cultural work. Courtesy of the Borthwick Institute of Historical Research, University of York.

social and cultural activities, and assumed leading roles as patrons, sponsors, and benefactors of workers' clubs and societies. The Social Department and the *Cocoa Works' Magazine* (*CWM*) supplemented and ultimately assumed the major burden of the work that family members did in this regard. In 1891 Miss Mary Wood was appointed as the first social worker responsible for overseeing the welfare and discipline of female workers, and in 1902 the *CWM* was launched. Joseph Rowntree welcomed the periodical as a way of making up for the "loss of personal intercourse" and "personal acquaintance" that had prevailed "in the earlier years of the business," as a way of animating all the workers with "a common aim." He concluded the first of the annual letters that he sent to the factory community via the *CWM* by linking it to those hundreds in the city of York that, each day, saw daughters, sons, and husbands off to earn their livings within the Cocoa Works' walls. Rowntree felt that the parents of his young employees valued the "healthful rooms" and "bright surroundings" in which their children worked, and that they valued even more "the tone of conversation and the influence of the place." He urged all at the works "to unite in keeping up a high standard in these respects." This concern with moral tone bespoke the disrepute that was readily attached to factory work, a prejudice that the Rowntree firm, as a major employer of women, worked hard to counter and one that gave further impetus and a distinct flavor to the recreational provisions that were made at the factory for female workers.[9]

The exact ratio of female to male employees at the Cocoa Works varied from year to year and seasonally, but girls and women constituted over half the waged labor force between 1880 and the beginning of World War I. In Joseph Rowntree's estimation, by 1913 he was employing one-third of York's fourteen- to seventeen-year-olds, and half the females in that age group.[10] As was typical of the economy as a whole, there was a rigid sexual division of labor in the factory. Female workers performed unskilled, labor-intensive tasks in the "dry" end of production—packaging, weighing, and wrapping. Male workers received apprenticeships in skilled trades and were employed as mechanics, joiners, and bricklayers, or worked in capital-intensive areas of production in the "wet" end—chocolate making and mixing and manufacturing units for coating. Employment and hiring policies reinforced these gender divisions and hierarchies. Female employees had to be less than eighteen years of age to be taken on and, until the 1940s, the firm was among many employers who enforced a marriage bar. These practices effectively segmented the labor force into permanent, male workers and female, mainly young workers who were dismissed when they married. As Chris Smith, John Child, and Michael Rowlinson note, for the confectionery industry at large this meant that the majority of its workers were girls and women who were only minimally integrated into the businesses that employed them and lacked any career prospects unless they remained unmarried.[11]

This was clearly the case at the Cocoa Works, where, among female workers, there was another hierarchy than that of gender, one that was based on age and marital status. Older and unmarried women held better-paid, supervisory, clerical, and low-level administrative positions, and the young worked on the production line. But all women's wages were on average lower than men's, and benefits such as pensions assumed that female employees were supplementary, temporary wage earners who would eventually marry and become dependent on a husband—as, indeed, most did. Customs such as the directors' gift of a tea service to long-serving female workers who left Rowntrees to marry and the publishing of wedding and birth announcements in the *CWM* all helped to imprint these dominant understandings and arrangements of gender on the Cocoa Works' culture.

THERE WAS A POWERFUL CONGRUENCE BETWEEN THE ROWNTREE history, guiding philosophy, productive and administrative structures, and the rhetoric and practices of recreation at the works. To begin with, most social clubs and classes were segregated according to gender and organized around gender-appropriate activities: metal and woodworking for young male employees and dressmaking, crochet, and knitting for the female workers, for example. Held during the dinner hour and after work, classes in domestic crafts started in the 1890s as informal gatherings—weekly sewing, knitting, and crochet bees. Gradually, the firm began to support and formalize these activities. From the first decades of the twentieth century, for a small weekly fee employees could receive instruction in dressmaking from the female staff of the Social Department, who also oversaw the purchasing and distribution of materials. Classes tended to be kept small to facilitate teaching, and the cost of materials was moderate. Miss Wetherill's class in the winter of 1904, for example, had about fifteen members who each paid one penny a week for a course of twelve lessons held on Friday evenings in one of the works' dining rooms. They ordered patterns and fabric at the beginning of the course and paid for them in small installments.[12] Cookery classes, "often talked about" and finally realized in 1903, were set up along similar lines: two shillings for a course of twelve lessons held one evening a week at a nearby elementary school.[13] Prior to the establishment of these classes, Emily Rowntree, until 1906 superintendent of the works' dining rooms and kitchen, wrote a series of "Cookery Notes" in the *CWM* offering "a few homely recipes" that she hoped would "be of use to the housewives among us." She also had a supply of cookery books for sale at a penny each, for which there was evidently a large demand.[14]

The firm employed a number of strategies to encourage workers to participate in these classes and to encourage diligence, industry, and excellence among those who joined them, such as rewarding those attending nine of the twelve dressmaking classes offered in the winter of 1906 by reimbursing the fees. Items of craftwork were on display in the corridors and communal spaces of the factory, too, and the names of anyone whose work was especially meritorious appeared in the *CWM*. Formal exhibitions added a competitive edge and offered opportunities for reinforcing habits that the works' authorities deemed worthy and discouraging ones of which they disapproved. Judges praised evidence of neatness, economy, and plain and simple tastes—admirable attributes in the working-class woman—and tut-tutted over grubby work and excessively decorative or frivolous items.[15] In the 1907 and 1908 Arts and Crafts Exhibitions, for example, Emily Rowntree and Mrs. D. S. Crichton adjudicated the merits of submissions to the "Girls' Work" section. "The plain sewing, skirts, and blouses showed very creditable work, and a decided tendency in the right direction towards usefulness and thrift," they observed approvingly of the 1907 entries. Making one's own underclothing was sound economy, "for the calico does not so readily come to grief in the 'wash.' " And, they added, "it need not be all 'plain' either: for those who are afraid of the monotony of sewing, there are always the crocheted and knitted edges, which make the garments look pretty, and the feather-stitching for the 'woollens,' and little children's garments."[16] The following year, the judges were evidently regretting their endorsement of these modest adornments. There was "so little [plain work and dressmaking] as to be hardly worth judging" and far too much crochet, lace, and "fancy work," some of which was submitted to the exhibition in a distressingly "soiled and crushed condition." Furthermore, having suggested that a mending competition would be a useful addition to the 1908 show—"darning, patching, turning up of skirts round the hem, etc., [are] all so necessary if we wish to be tidy with little expense"—they were rather miffed that no one chose to enter. "The practical value of the ability to make a nightdress thoroughly well is undoubtedly far greater than the ability to embroider a case for it," they admonished, advising that in future the prizes for mending and plain work should be of greater value than those offered for the fancy work.[17] Some words of wisdom on "finishing off" underscored the deeper lessons that they hoped competitors would take home with them: "don't be too 'slap-dash'; finish off the turnings of the seams, arm-holes, vents, etc., as neatly as you would on the right side. Not only is this taken into account in the judging, but it helps in the training of neat work of all kinds, and indeed, in the character of the worker.''[18]

No other recreational association at the Cocoa Works was so devoted to developing the character of its girls and women as were the Temperance Society and the Wednesday Class. The Girls' Temperance Society (GTS) originated in March 1902 with a dinner-hour meeting of some thirty workers who organized themselves, elected a committee, and secured the services of Miss Johnston of the Social Department as secretary. The group quickly attracted members (by April it numbered ninety) and gained the patronage of Mrs. Joseph Rowntree as one of its vice presidents and Miss Wood of the Social Department as the other. For a subscription of 3d. per quarter, members received a printed pledge card to sign and the benefit of monthly meetings at which distinguished members of the factory and larger community addressed them on the temperance issue and entertained them with recitations and songs. Speakers warned of the dangers of drink and the unhappiness and distress that trailed in its wake, and advised how to stand fast against its temptations and find enjoyment and pleasure without yielding to its dubious allure. At a March 1905 meeting, for instance, the GTS gathered to hear Alderman Agar give "some examples from real life of the results of indulging in strong drink, and [show] how young people, whose natural desire was to be happy, could be so quite as well, and better, without . . . it." The next month, members listened to Mr. W. Farrar of St. Luke's Church lecture on "the medical aspects of intemperance and the effect of alcohol on the different aspects of the body." In June the following year, Mrs. Hinchclife, the wife of the minister of York's Monk Bar Chapel, "spoke of the three reasons why girls should be teetotallers—for the sake of health, economy, and to help others who might be influenced by their example." And at a May 1908 meeting, Mr. Samuel H. Davies, the works' chief chemist, explained the proposed regulations and workings of the Licensing Bill that was then before parliament.[19]

The GTS encouraged Rowntrees' girls and women to adopt temperance because of the advantages that would accrue to them as individuals: a temperate life was a healthful, morally sound, and economically rational way of life. But in this, as in other aspects of reformist recreation at the Cocoa Works and beyond, the individual woman was never the sole or ultimate object of attention. She was the point of access, the conduit for delivering temperance to the working classes as a whole. So those who spoke at the society's meetings almost always considered those who listened in terms of their gendered, social roles, especially in the context of their relationships with men. Lecturers urged GTS members to enlist on the side of the angels, to see themselves as agents of sobriety and guardians of morality—their own, that of their friends, families, and menfolk. Miss Wood reminded the more senior workers of the great influence that they had on "those who come fresh into the factory" and charged them with accepting responsibility for seeing that they used this "on the side of all that [was] best." "[Invite] them to join one or other of the different clubs or societies," and to attend the GTS meetings, she suggested.[20] Doing so would be "a help both to themselves and to the other members, and very probably to some among their friends whom their action might influence more than they know."[21] "Even if there is no danger on your own account," the GTS committee advised the women of the Cocoa Works, "there is perhaps someone at home with whom the sight of your pledge card, and your example and influence, will carry more weight than any number of arguments."[22] Seebohm and Arnold Rowntree were among those whose "high and helpful words" the GTS hoped would have a "lasting effect" on members and assist in forming "a good public opinion in the Factory on this important matter."[23] Outside speakers included Sergeant Major Pincombe of the Depot Barracks in York, whose chief subject was "the influence of women and girls on others in their homes." The Reverend Mr. Ilvride of the Priory Street Presbyterian Church took a similar tack, but extended it to cast the darker image of woman the temptress in the shadow of her sister, woman the moral helpmeet of man. "Take care," he warned his GTS audience at a 1907 meeting, "that no fellow-creature's fall could ever be laid at [your] door."[24]

At certain times the power of the GTS women's influence for good seemed to be particularly needed. In the final weeks before Christmas, Bank Holidays, and the annual works' holiday, the organization went into high gear, holding series of special dinner-hour meetings to fortify its members against the heightened dangers of these occasions of festal release.[25] Arnold Rowntree offered "some hints about the forthcoming Bank Holiday," one year, advising "how to make the best use of it, and get the most enjoyment out of it"—the delights of nature if the weather was fine, books if it was not. Whatever the weather, he reminded workers, if they remained abstinent they could take pleasure in rational amusement that would allow them to return to work "with a contented mind," "not worse, but better both in mind and body," having made "a real holiday of it."[26] Likewise, the GTS rallied its members to the cause of sober, rational celebration of the 1902 winter holiday. "Shall we, the women and girls in this factory, each one determine that we will do all we can, and use all our influence, which is often greater than we know, to resist this evil[?]" the society appealed to its foot soldiers. If they would only do this, they would ensure that "the hundreds of homes represented here, however humble they may be," would know a happy Christmastime, one "with the real happiness which leaves no sting or shame behind."[27]

The aim of the Wednesday Class (initially "Miss Skirrow's Class"), too, was to inspire and elevate the character of its members and to arouse in them a sense of their moral and social responsibilities. Started in 1898 by Florence Skirrow at the invitation of her friend Emily Rowntree, the Wednesday Class's beginnings were even more modest than were those of the Cocoa Works—two workers formed the nucleus of an association that by 1911 could draw more than three hundred to its weekly dinner-hour meetings. First, at "cosy gatherings" in Emily Rowntree's office at the old Tanner's Moat factory, and later, in greater numbers in the Lecture Room at

the Haxby Road works, class members attended to lessons in submission to God's will, service to others, and self-denial.[28] Truthful-
ness, courage, perseverance, love for one another, and above all,
prayer, were the means; personal salvation and the welfare and
moral integrity of the larger community were the ends. "Let us take
[our Heavenly Friend] for our example day by day, and try to live
our life as He lived His," Skirrow urged the Wednesday Class members in 1905. "It was just to help us do this that our class was ever
started, and its purpose is the same now as it ever was then." She
taught her "family," her "children," her "Flock," to say their prayers "night and morning," to be ever more "truthful" so that they
could be "better and more steadfast friends," to "use the opportunities given . . . in the Factory of doing kindnesses for each other," to
love one another. By living their lives according to the "God-given
Law of Love," by training "bodies, souls, and spirits in good ways,"
by persevering and praying for "wills strong enough to say 'no' to
the evil," Wednesday Class members could make themselves ready
for "the Real Home."[29] Part of doing so was to make their earthly
home a better one, as Emily Rowntree's declaration to the works'
community on behalf of the class indicated. "As women and girls
working in a large Factory in a city of old England that is very dear
to us, we mean to use our influence, and make our force felt, on the
side of all that is good and strong and noble and self-respecting."[30]

It was in the home, of course, that women's deployment on the
side of the good, the noble, and the self-respecting mattered most,
and home and family, and women's duties therein and responsibilities thereto, were topics to which the Wednesday Class gave serious
and considered thought. During the spring and early summer of
1907, the class discussed two questions that spoke to "some . . .
important points of life": "what they would wish from the one they
accepted as their 'partner for life'; and what the wife ought to do to
keep the home happy and comfortable." Emily Rowntree summa-
rized what she felt were the main points raised in class discussions
and expressed in papers that several members wrote on the subject.

A husband should not gamble, or drink to excess (complete absten-
tion seemed to be considered an unrealistic expectation). He should
be industrious, energetic, a good saver and wise spender of money,
"and one whom you could trust and thoroughly respect." For her
part, a wife should keep the home clean and "have her husband's
meals comfortably prepared." She should "be cheerful and no
grumbler, not get into debt, and as far as possible have interests in
common with her husband." Both should be "religiously minded
people."[31]

This final consideration must have been especially pleasing to
one of the Wednesday Class's most enthusiastic and steadfast
sources of support—the archbishop of York and his family. A number
of times when Florence Skirrow and Emily Rowntree were unable
to lead the class, Mrs. Maclagan, the archbishop's wife, stepped into
the breach; she also regularly invited the class on outings to the
palace and grounds at Bishopthorpe.[32] The archbishop himself addressed the class on several occasions. One of the most notable of
these was at a meeting in November 1911, presided over by Seebohm Rowntree. His Grace said that he had come to ask for the
class's help in discharging his responsibilities, which were "to make
our country better and to try to help people to remember the Lord
their God." With all the influence and authority that his position as
one of the two leading prelates of the Church of England brought
him, he was turning to them, the Rowntree women, for help in carrying out his responsibilities. In an eloquent and stirring address, he
stated that "each one of them was a centre of power." They had
power over each other, "to lift their lives or to let them down."
"They could talk with their friends about things that they would be
ashamed of if anyone they really liked were to hear; they could talk
all kinds of silly gossip; or they could talk of those things that keep
. . . life pure, wholesome and true." They also had another power,
one that "often caused laughter and good-natured 'chaff,' " and that
was "power over men." This was "a great trust from God and could
be used by them to make men sober, steady, pure, hard-working

and God-fearing, if only they would care to use it so." And they had power over something "even greater," "over the home." It was the homes that made a nation, "and they were the makers of the homes—not the sticks and chairs, the food and clothing and the rest, but the character of the home—this came from them, and they could make it or mar it." "The true way" for them to do this was "to ask for the Father's grace and to have his power working in and through them." "A rope that was made of the hearts and power" of girls and women such as themselves would be strong enough to hold up "the life of [the] nation." Yet it could so easily snap if they gave way to what was "mean and base." The Wednesday Class was there to help them remain strong and true, to help them serve God, to remind them that they were channels for his beneficent power, and so it was to the Wednesday Class that the archbishop had come for assistance in fulfilling his duty. In response, Emily Rowntree spoke for the class, wishing "very strongly that as a result of [His Grace's visit]," its members would indeed resolve "to make better this corner of the world in which we are placed, to remember the Lord our God."[33]

WHILE MORAL EARNESTNESS MAY HAVE BEEN THE PRIMARY agenda that these two organizations pursued, promoting sociability among workers and providing opportunities for recreation—of appropriately judicious, moderate, and wholesome kinds—were clearly central objectives. GTS meetings always included a little diversion, a vocal or instrumental solo or a recitation by one of the members, organizers, or guests. Communal hymn singing was standard fare, too, as it was for the Wednesday Class. Florence Skirrow, writing to her class from Torquay after she had moved to its southern clime for reasons of health, said that she took with her fond memories of this. "I often see before me, your enthusiastic and interested faces and hear in my ears your voices singing lustily the much-loved hymns. I hope you still sometimes sing 'What a Friend we have in Jesus.' "[34] Earthly friends, including members of the Rowntree family and the archbishop of York and his wife, gave material assistance for socials, concerts, and outings into the countryside. The GTS began its entertaining with a flourish, holding three evening socials in its inaugural winter season, one of which was honored with an address from Vice President Mrs. Joseph Rowntree. Musical items, songs, and recitations formed the formal programs and, together with some "light refreshments," made for several "very enjoyable evening[s]."[35] The organization's socializing extended beyond the factory community to connect it with like groups in the city. It put on concerts for the York Adult School Temperance Society, for instance, and occasionally shared venues and combined meetings with the Independent Order of Rechabites (a temperance organization) and the York Women's Temperance Society.[36] Excursions to the many rural beauty spots and scenic villages that were in easy reach of the city were annual summer events for both the GTS and the Wednesday Class. On one occasion the latter was accompanied by the Cocoa Works' Drum and Fife Band, providing an opportunity for a little dallying between male and female workers that was rare in an ordinarily strictly gender-segregated workplace culture. Emily Rowntree commented on this foray into the unfamiliar waters of officially sanctioned heterosocial recreation in an appropriately coy tone. "It was not difficult to see that some of the younger members of the Band had friends and acquaintances among the members of the class," she communicated to the *CWM*, "and so we hope on that account the pleasure was not altogether one-sided!"[37]

One-sided the pleasures to which these associations gave workers access were not—none was dispensed without a measure or two of worthiness in the mix. Picnics, cricket and other games, dancing, singing, and moonlit excursions on the river or out into the countryside were passing delights, valuable for engendering goodwill and fellowship within the factory, occasional treats in the lives of its hard-worked employees. What were supposed to endure were the lessons in duty, faith, morality, honesty, goodness—lessons that were to teach Rowntree girls how to grow up to be "good and useful women."[38]

By the later decades of the nineteenth century, upper- and middle-class reformers were offering organized physical recreation—swimming, gymnastics, and team sports such as field hockey, among others—as ideal forms of leisure for young working women. Top photo courtesy of Sheffield Archives, 278/Z5/3; bottom photo courtesy of the Borthwick Institute of Historical Research, University of York.

Physical recreation was also enlisted in the cause of fitting Cocoa Works' girls and women for lives spent in the pursuit of this ideal. The notion that the education of muscles and morals was one and the same thing had gained broad currency by the beginning of the twentieth century. Meanwhile, an emerging women's physical education profession was successfully melding this belief with ideas about health, national progress, the advancement of women, and domesticity and motherhood to develop a persuasive argument for extending its mission to the working classes.[39] Unlike working-girls' clubs, many of which could not afford to fully develop this aspect of their work, Rowntrees was able to draw upon the expertise that this movement claimed for itself.[40] Within it, the firm found a sense of purpose, a conception of womanhood, a recreational philosophy, and a commitment to social reform that accorded wonderfully well with its own.

Martina Bergman Osterberg, the Swedish founder of England's first college for the training of female physical educators, for example, saw the progress of the nation and the Anglo-Saxon race as rooted in a healthy and strong womanhood. The Swedish system of gymnastics (for which she was a most eloquent and impassioned propagandist) provided the best possible preparation for marriage and maternity. "I try to train my girls to help raise their own sex, and so to accelerate the progress of the race," she asserted in 1892, "for, unless the women are strong, healthy, pure, and true, how can the race progress?"[41] Through the "splendid army of well-formed and well-trained women" that Bergman Osterberg began turning out from her college in 1885, the putative benefits of physical training in general and Swedish gymnastics in particular trickled out to the working classes.[42] Leading campaigners for the cause of national regeneration, such as the Earl of Meath, welcomed the development. With "more colleges like yours, and more thorough systematic training of physical exercises in all schools, a long step would [be] taken to solve the problem which puzzles our statesmen in the matter of the physical condition of the masses of the people," he wrote

to Bergman Osterberg in 1905.[43] And more colleges like Bergman
Osterberg's there soon were: Anstey (1897–1899), Chelsea (1898),
Bedford (1903), and I. M. Marsh in Liverpool (1904)—"a tight little
specialist empire" of institutions for training the women who were
the primary agents of disseminating "scientific" physical culture to
the masses.[44] Dorette Wilke and Rhoda Anstey, for instance, were
actively involved in this work. Speaking in 1910 to the Women's
Congress at the Japanese British Exhibition, Wilke, the founder of
the Chelsea College of Physical Education, bemoaned the low standard of physical education given to working-class children. "Good
educational gymnastics" were essential to the "success and future
prosperity of our country," Wilke insisted, and the state needed to
do a better job of providing expertly trained teachers for elementary
schools. Physical training was especially important for "the Working
Girls of England."[45] They "should have every opportunity given
them to keep [their bodies] in vigour and health in order to make
them efficient workers and give them a fair chance in the competition of life—to help them live a fuller life—to let them enjoy life
better." Personal benefits such as these aside, physical training
would increase a girl's "working capacity" and would certainly make
her "a better wife—a better mother of the future race."[46] Anstey,
who had trained with Bergman Osterberg before establishing her
own college, similarly espoused the cause of national and racial
motherhood and its extension beyond the upper and middle classes.
"Girls were to be the future mothers of the race," and the young
women who attended the Anstey Physical Training College were to
be missionaries thoroughly versed in "the laws of life" and inspired
"to go out and spread the knowledge among others."[47] For Anstey
and her students, an important constituency among these others was
the wage-earning girls and women of Birmingham with whom they
worked through the Birmingham Club Girls' Union, the Anstey
Physical Culture Union, and the educational programs of the Cadbury firm.[48] The "intelligent and well-educated" women of Anstey
thus carried the message of and the means for "fresh health and

vitality," for individual happiness and social progress, to the women of the working masses.[49]

The Rowntree factory, its physical recreation programs under way by 1902 in the form of weekly evening lessons in swimming and gymnastics, was another center for this cultural transmission. For a fee of 2d. a lesson, plus an additional penny for the hire of a costume and towel, enthusiasts could enjoy the health benefits and acquire proficiency in the "useful art" of swimming on Wednesday evenings at the municipal baths. With the opening of the New Yearsley Baths in 1909, a gift from the Rowntree firm to the citizens of York, the opportunities for women's swimming expanded, as on Tuesday and Friday evenings the new facility was reserved for their exclusive use. Admission to the open-air pool was free, but towel and costume rental were respectively a penny each, and the charge for the baths was 3d.[50] The Girls' Gymnastics Club also earned the firm's approbation. The club met weekly, in the evenings, and received instruction primarily in the Swedish system, but also used the apparatus, light and heavy, of the German system, and performed musical drill. For 1902, one of the instructors of the Gymnastics Club was Millicent Procter, who hailed from York and had had two years of training at Bergman Osterberg's Physical Training College to recommend her. With Miss Procter began Rowntrees' tradition of recruiting its physical education and Social Department staff from the nation's leading women's colleges. In September 1910, when the first full-time mistresses of gymnastics and hygiene arrived to join the teaching staff of the works' Domestic School, one was a graduate of the Anstey College and the other was from the Dunfermline Physical Training College in Scotland. E. A. Maunsell had a First Class diploma from Anstey and teaching experience gained at a school in Worthing, Sussex; E. M. Archibald had a First Class diploma from Dunfermline and experience in both educational and remedial gymnastics. The following year Brynhild Benson, the glamorous and dashing daughter of a Shakespearian actor and another product of Bergman Osterberg's college, came to join the Social Department staff. And in 1912, Josephine Joseph, another of Bergman Osterberg's elite band, spent one term as a substitute gymnastics mistress in the Domestic School.[51]

Swimming and gymnastics underlined the hegemonic cast of the firm's recreational philosophies and provisions. This was not the raucous sporting revel that earlier generations of working women had known; it was orderly and disciplined and directed to consciously utilitarian ends.[52] Swimming recommended itself to middle-class reformers as an appropriate recreation for the working classes because it combined utility, health, and hygiene. Gymnastics, especially of the Swedish kind, served similarly pragmatic ends and was imbued with a powerful ideology of social control, moral uplift, and motherhood. It is not surprising, then, that the Girls' Gymnastics Club drew enthusiastic responses from the Cocoa Works' administration.[53] "What grace of movement; what increased stores of health, giving added resistance to any disease and especially to lung troubles," one member of the Social Department exclaimed after watching a 1902 display that included dumbbell exercises, Swedish drill, Indian club swinging, ring exercises, and marching in unison. The club exercises called forth a little gentle criticism, "some of the wrist work being a little weak," but the precision with which the whole class worked elicited praise, particularly as "precision and good-timekeeping" were, lamentably, qualities that were "more difficult to secure with girls than with boys."[54] All the more praise, then, to the teachers of the class and all the more reason for encouraging gymnastics instruction among the workforce.

Swedish drill recommended itself for encouraging such attributes as precision, discipline, thoroughness, and efficiency, and the Rowntree management was happy to acknowledge its efficacy in this regard. The eighteen participants in the 1904 display of Swedish gymnastics "showed very careful training and excellent discipline," an outcome that undoubtedly reflected the "really hard work" of pupils and teacher alike, reported the *CWM*. Furthermore, and boding very well for the future of the gymnastics program at the works,

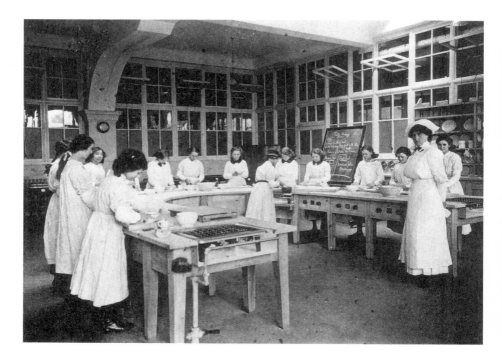

In 1905 the Rountree firm established a system of compulsory education in domesticity for female employees under the age of seventeen. By 1911 they received three hours of instruction a week in cookery, dressmaking, housewifery, health, hygiene, and gymnastics. Courtesy of the Borthwick Institute of Historical Research, University of York.

"in comparing the display with that of the two or three previous years," there was "a marked improvement in the discipline of the class. There was no whispering or fidgetting or self-consciousness." The physical and health benefits of the program were there for all to see, too, for "after two hours fairly continuous drill, the members of the class looked as fresh as ever, and showed how much their training had improved their breathing and staying powers."[55] As with workers' domestic crafts, the firm used a system of rewards and public recognition to encourage participation and excellence. From 1903, class members could earn prizes for their execution of various gymnastic feats and for such character-building exercises as regular attendance, and Joseph Rowntree and other members of his family took leading roles in the ceremonies at which these were presented.[56]

The arrival of the specialist-trained physical education mistress facilitated the development of another facet of women's recreation at the Cocoa Works: team sports. By the early years of the twentieth century, hockey, cricket, lacrosse, netball, and rounders had been popularized at Oxbridge colleges and many elite girls' schools, and it was generally accepted that such games should be an integral part of the upper- or middle-class schoolgirl's curriculum. Despite criticism from some quarters that girls and women who played too vigorously (or even at all) risked masculinization and nervous and physical enervation and damage, progressive educators argued persuasively that athletic sports were valuable complements to the training provided by gymnastics. Games were "splendid for improving general health, for cultivating deep-breathing and moreover for promoting unselfishness, self control, courage and public spirit."[57] And so, in 1911 and 1912, respectively, the first formal girls' hockey and cricket teams were founded at the Cocoa Works. By its second season, the Girls' Hockey Club had approximately thirty members who paid an annual subscription of two shillings. Practices and matches were held on Saturday afternoons on a pitch adjoining the works, and in its 1912–1913 season, the team's competitive schedule included both home and away games against ten other clubs in the York vicinity.[58]

RELATIVE BOTH TO THE MORE OBVIOUSLY UTILITARIAN ACTIVI-ties of swimming and gymnastics, however, and to boys' and men's sport at the Cocoa Works, the opportunity to play competitive athletic games came only latterly and to a limited extent to most of the Rowntree female employees. Formally constituted clubs and facilities for lawn tennis and croquet had been established by 1897, and for bowling, cycling, and boating and swimming by 1902. For the men's sports of cricket and association football (1897), there was an extensive system of interdepartmental competition, as well as several Cocoa Works' representative teams. There was no parallel interdepartmental competition in girls' team sports, and only one representative team in each sport until the interwar period. In addition, while there were no formal barriers to female employees' joining the Rowntree tennis and croquet or cycling clubs, the gender and occupational status hierarchies that structured work experiences and relationships in the factory operated as informal mechanisms of exclusion. Despite notices in the *CWM* encouraging any employee to join, the female membership of these clubs appears to have been limited to office staff and members of the Social Department. This de facto exclusion of the vast majority of Rowntrees' female workers reflected and reinforced the deep and systemic divisions of gender, class, and occupation that shaped the firm's culture.[59] Some sense of these divisions can be gained from the 1906 membership drive that the Bowling Club initiated. After beginning with the encouraging claim that "the members are anxious to welcome any employee," the club committee went on to reveal the limits of its inclusiveness and the perception that many workers had of the organization: "He may smoke while playing, and is not bound to dress in his best clothes. He may bring his wife or his sister to watch the game, and she can enjoy the fresh air with her sewing or knitting."[60]

Class and occupational divides also contoured the recreational experiences of the women employed at the factory, as Ruth Slate's experiences indicate. Slate was from a lower-middle-class home and had begun working at the age of fourteen. In 1915 Benjamin Seebohm Rowntree invited her to join the Cocoa Works as a social worker. Slate was conscious of the striking contrast between the female staff in the Social Department and the tired, faded-looking women working on the production line, and she felt a close affinity with the latter. Like them, she had been constrained by economic necessity to start work immediately after leaving school and felt keenly the toll that this experience had taken on her health. Slate's colleagues in the Social Department, on the other hand, had enjoyed

the benefits of an extended education and far less exacting life circumstances, and she envied them their carefree and fun-filled days
at secondary school and college, their buoyancy of spirits, their
wholesome and healthy looks. In a relatively privileged position in
the female occupational hierarchy at the Cocoa Works, she still felt
that her kinship was with those who were lowest on its ladder,
women who, like her, lacked the cultural, material, and physical resources for sport.[61] These women were vastly underrepresented in
Rowntrees' tennis, cricket, and hockey clubs.

In one case the exclusion of women was quite deliberate and
extended even to office and Social Department staff. The Boating
and Swimming Club refused to admit female members and, notwithstanding attempts by opponents to have this policy changed,
it remained in effect until the interwar period.[62] This organization
represented the more extreme wing of male conservatism at the
Cocoa Works, but every aspect of the factory's physical recreation
culture was shot through with gender. In activities in which the body
and physicality were central, the dynamics of power and control
were played out in a singularly heightened way. Each practice,
match, prize giving, and speech was an occasion for the representation and reproduction of dominant cultural understandings of womanhood and manhood. Women's gymnastic displays were "pretty
entertainments" that demonstrated not just the skill but also the
"grace" of the performers, and the "taste and industry" of those
who had made the "becoming costumes of dark blue and scarlet"
that the gymnasts wore.[63] In contrast, photographs of the "average
Cocoa Works' lad" in the *CWM*, along with details of the girth of his
chest, biceps, forearm, calves, and thighs before and after a course of
gymnastics affirmed that bulk, strength, and power were masculine
attributes. Similarly, the girls' events at the Annual Sports' Day were
characterized as a "picturesque" interlude, a "welcome touch of relief" in the "strenuous," serious program of competitions between
boys and men.[64]

The didactic, improving impulse behind the promotion of recreation at the Cocoa Works is unquestionable; whether it had the intended effect is another matter. As a number of historians have pointed out, the agendas of middle- and upper-class proponents of the kind of rational recreation that the Rowntree firm endorsed did not always accord with the agendas of those for whom such schemes were intended. This was clearly so at the Cocoa Works, where the range of employees' responses ran from enthusiasm through ambivalence and absolute lack of interest to hostility. On occasion, profoundly different value systems clashed—as when the management complained about the poor spirit in which some competitors at the 1903 Annual Sports' Day, aggrieved at the handicaps they'd been given, ran their races. Employees persisted in exercising whatever free choice they could with respect to their leisure, playing dinner-hour football in areas where football was prohibited, for example, despite notices proscribing the practice. Some engaged in minor acts of sabotage, such as damaging the fences and hedges surrounding the works' parks and playing fields. Frequent exhortations to employees to join clubs and classes and expressions of concern about low participation numbers reflected diverse and by no means universally positive responses to the recreational programs for girls and women.[65] The most vigorous organization, in terms of attendance numbers, was the Wednesday Class, which could attract large audiences to its meetings.

More typically, the participation rate in other activities was about five percent of the female workforce at best. Indeed, workers were decidedly particular when it came to their recreation. Lectures and classes, no matter how inspiring or useful, were not guaranteed to attract or hold the interest of large numbers, even when leavened with tea, music, and songs. Picnics and outings invariably did. The uneven fortunes of the GTS illuminate the fastidiousness of its members and, more generally, of the Cocoa Works' girls and women. Meetings were not always well attended and the committee struggled to maintain the level of subscription-paying members. When alternative attractions were available, the society found it difficult to compete. A dinner-hour meeting in May 1903, for example, suffered because "the fine weather attracted many of the members into the garden"—the *CWM*'s assurance that "those who stayed had an equally enjoyable quarter of an hour" probably did not convince too many.[66] A similar pattern prevailed with the Swimming Club. When the mercury was high, so was attendance; when it dropped, or when other delights beckoned, so did the number of swimmers. As the May-to-September swimming season progressed, there was always a tailing off in participation (at a rate of about 50 percent, according to the instructors' estimations), particularly among those who found it difficult to acquire proficiency. Significantly, however, even as the *CWM* lamented this fact, recreational swimmers from the Rowntree female workforce flooded the New Yearsley Baths both during the dinner hour and in the evening on "Ladies' Days."[67] For most, the recreational brand of swimming was apparently preferable to the educational.

In September 1905 much of the content of the female recreational programs at the Cocoa Works was taken up into the curriculum of the Cookery School. This undertaking, more than any other, declared the firm's determination that the girls and young women in its employment were going to have an education in domesticity. "The contention that factory life unfits a girl for home duties, by allowing her neither the time nor opportunity for learning what is necessary for the management of a home," Joseph Rowntree announced, "has decided the Directors to provide the school . . . as a means by which to remedy this defect."[68] The school was "exceedingly valuable," he believed. "A knowledge of cooking and the selection of economical foodstuffs and diets, of dressmaking . . . of the laws of health, including the management of young children, may be invaluable to those who in the future will be responsible for the management of homes."[69] In September 1907 the Cookery School became a fully fledged Domestic School. Some of the language used in the *CWM* to describe the purpose and manner of its operation implies that attendance was voluntary, but this was not so.

For two hours a week, all girls between the ages of fourteen and seventeen—approximately 650 in the school's first year—were required to attend classes in cookery, dressmaking, and health and hygiene.[70] A cookery school, comprising a kitchen equipped with gas and oven ranges and a lecture room, was built to accommodate the classes, and two teachers trained in domestic science were hired. Over the next seven years, the firm expended more and more resources on the domestic education of its female employees. In 1909 physical training was added to the curriculum, becoming the only subject that girls studied in each of the three years that they attended the school. By 1911 some 1,100 girls received three hours of instruction a week in dressmaking, cookery, housewifery, and gymnastics. Also in 1911, construction began on a large block of facilities opposite the main entrance to the factory on Haxby Road. Most of the ground floor of the New Block was taken up with classrooms, a lecture room, a concert room, club rooms, gymnasia, changing rooms, showers and baths, and offices for the teaching staff. Dining facilities and a large kitchen occupied the first and second floors of the building. The Domestic School now boasted a staff of a headmistress and eleven assistant mistresses, all fully trained in the subjects they taught. Its accommodation consisted of two cookery classrooms, two dressmaking classrooms, a forty-eight-foot square gymnasium, a large dressing room with bathing facilities, and two model cottages, designed and built for the purpose of teaching "practical housewifery."[71]

The new buildings were a powerful affirmation of the Rowntree firm's commitment to fitting the girls and women in their employment for their prescribed roles in a society ordered by gender. Civic, religious, and educational leaders viewed the Cocoa Works themselves as a model community, a center of family life, and a place in which there was a common life and spirit. Within that community, everything that was done—the organization of the work, the creation of wealth, and the recreational and educational activities—was directed to reinforcing and reproducing a stable social organism in which every individual had her or his place and role to play. Speaking on the occasion of the formal opening of the New Block in June 1913, the archbishop of York confirmed the place allotted to women in this scheme and the role that Rowntree played in molding them for it:

> I will venture to say . . . that whatever honour they may receive, or whatever positions of prominence they may gain in the Works here . . . the greatest honour that can possibly await them is to become a wife, and that there is an even greater honour that may in God's providence await them, and that is to become a mother. There is . . . nothing . . . that is more well worth doing than giving our girls the best possible training in the greatest of all arts, housecraft, in the making of that one article upon which everything else in the community depends, the making of the healthy and the happy home.[72]

THE SOURCES UPON WHICH THIS CHAPTER RELIES, OF COURSE, offer predominantly the official, hegemonic view of the Rowntree efforts to shape working-class womanhood through rational, educational recreation. Still, even they hint at the difficulties inherent in the enterprise. The firm's directors were very much aware that the majority of their employees chose not to involve themselves in the recreational programs—hence the move toward compulsory education for young female workers. That step was itself a source of resentment for some. "Among the younger employees," Joseph Rowntree commented in his 1911 annual address, "there may perhaps be a few who grudge the time we ask them to devote to educational work."[73] Writing in the 1920s, Benjamin Seebohm Rowntree concurred. He believed that a considerable number of the female workers enjoyed, appreciated, and benefited from the domestic classes, but admitted that "a few take little interest and it hardly seems to affect them." Furthermore, the pieceworkers would not be "persuaded that they [did] not lose money by attending," and some of these would have absented themselves "if attendance were not compulsory." Some pieceworkers, the fastest, did lose money as a consequence of their compulsory education. Day-wage workers were paid their standard rate while at class, but piece-rate workers did not receive their usual recompense based upon the amount of work they normally completed, only the minimum wage stipulated under the Industrial Agreement covering cocoa and chocolate manufacturers. Until they turned eighteen, that is, female employees had to submit their economic interests as workers to their employer's interest in advancing the cause of working-class domesticity and maintaining gender hegemony.[74]

As indicated above, however, workers' experiences of and responses to workplace recreation varied considerably. Some expressed appreciation and enthusiasm, some ambivalence, some hostility—and quite a few, probably the majority, had no interest or involvement. This was so not only at the York Cocoa Works but also at other companies that made similar provisions. The experiences of several women who worked for the Rowntrees in the interwar period, though strictly beyond the time frame of the present study, offer valuable insights into the question of the impact that the firm's recreational programs had on women's lives and what that meant to them.

Ethel Thompson had no involvement with any of the recreational or sports clubs and knew no one among her workmates who did. Her only recollection of the gymnastics classes was that there was not enough time to take the mandatory bath after the lesson. So, like many another reluctant student of compulsory physical education, Ethel and her pals subverted the hygienic regimen: "we just pretended to splash around in [the bath] . . . got back into our dresses and overalls and scampered . . . back to the cardboard box mill." What Ethel recalled most vividly of the factory was its discipline, enforced by stern and unsympathetic supervisors—"they were all 'company people' "—and the exhausting, unremitting work of the production line. Neither experience disposed her to spend any more time or energy at the works than she had to. "I was too whacked, poor little skinny thing, too whacked after my full day," she laughed when asked whether she'd joined any of the sports teams. At the end of the day, workers like Ethel who remained impervious to the firm's recreational rhetoric had simply had enough: "you didn't want anything more to do with Rowntrees, a lot of us."[75]

Ruby Pearson also recalled the strict discipline and hard work but appreciated the firm's attempt to provide for recreation. She spoke fondly of Greek dancing and music for the girls, and a large recreational room in which they gathered during their dinner hour for dancing or simply relaxing. The New Yearsley Baths were a real boon for Ruby, who, like many working people in the period, had no bathing facilities in her home. "It was super having that hot bath once a week, and a swim in hot weather," she recalled with enthusiasm.[76]

Joan Sadler appreciated the weekly gymnastics classes for much the same reason, but also because she valued what she learned. "We used to enjoy the keep-fit [her term] because they provided baths as well and lots of us didn't have a bathroom in the home . . . I remember what an extremely good . . . teacher we had . . . she really was a fine person and told you things that I've certainly remembered for the rest of my days." But Joan, too, had nothing to do with the Rowntree sports clubs—in fact, she had no memory of them at all. She did recall, however, that there were many sports teams and clubs for the male workers. For Joan, like Ethel and Ruby, and doubtless many other Rowntree workers, it was memories of "the discipline there" that endured. "I remember [that] more than anything," Joan reflected. It was "a continual grind . . . you were so pleased when it was half past five."[77]

At the Cadbury model factory in Bournville, near Birmingham, and the Boots Cash Chemists' works in Nottingham, female workers seem to have been rather more excited at the possibility of playing competitive team sports than were their Rowntree counterparts. The Cadbury firm established a Bournville Girls' Athletic Club

(BGAC) in 1899 that numbered 113 members in its first year. By 1903, a netball team was playing matches against teams from Anstey College and, by 1906, Bournville had three netball courts catering to five factory teams that played regularly during the dinner hour. Hockey was introduced in 1905, at which time there were sufficient interested players to form three teams; by 1911, there were five. On the eve of the First World War, the membership of the BGAC stood at 678, around sixteen percent of the female workforce at Bournville. For an annual fee of one shilling, the club offered hockey, cricket, netball, croquet, lawn tennis, swimming, gymnastics, morris dancing, an annual sports day, and a summer camp.[78]

At Boots, it took a reproachful letter to the *Boots' Athletic Club Journal* (*BACJ*) by "Vox Populi" to get women's sports off the ground. Male workers were "exceptionally well-catered for" in the matter of physical recreation but, "with the exception of an hour's swimming per week," there was nothing for women. Yet in one department of the works alone, there were "fifteen young ladies all ready and anxious to try their luck at hockey, and as this game seem[ed] to be very popular with the ladies," the writer felt that there was no reason why "their wishes should not be gratified."[79] To its credit, the Boots' Recreation Club responded quickly, forming a "Ladies' Committee" of seven by the end of the month and advancing cash loans to anyone wishing to buy a hockey stick. In January 1908 the ladies' hockey club, with some two hundred members, began practicing, playing interdepartmental matches, and organizing for a schedule of competition against external clubs for the following season.[80]

The disproportionately greater recreational privileges that Boots's male employees enjoyed provoked a fascinating response from one woman affected by the company's policies. In a rare expression of how some wives and families felt, "Peter Pan's Wife" wrote to the editor of the *BACJ*. Piqued by some previous correspondence from the Sheffield branch of the Boots' Recreation Club that had extolled the health benefits that male employees derived from participating in its Rifle Club, she fired off a stinging shot or two in response:

> Peter is not far wrong when he says "there are moments in our lives in which we live years, moments which pluck the roses from our cheeks and plant deep furrows on our brows." The wives of the crack shots waiting at home for the return of their lord and master, will quite agree with Peter as to the truth of that. We are quite ready to admit that "Peter needs fresh air." It seems to be a forgone conclusion that the wives and children can get along without.
>
> I say, and the wives of these great heroes (I beg pardon, members of the Boots Recreation Society) will agree with me that the society is a positive nuisance, and if there is a lady (married) who thinks otherwise, I should be happy to meet her.[81]

Epilogue

It is tempting to leave the final word of this study with Peter Pan's wife—she articulates so well, so sharply, most of its main themes. Working-class women's leisure was a contentious issue from the late eighteenth century to the early twentieth century. As patriarchal industrial capitalism emerged as the dominant mode of production in this period, it drew on and magnified sexual divisions of labor and gender inequities within the working classes. By the mid-nineteenth century, social and familial relations that accorded with particular understandings of gender were well established at an ideological level and had many extensive ramifications through working-class culture and leisure. Women, despite their continued engagement in productive and wage labor, were expected to take primary responsibility for the domestic sphere, for caring for homes and families, for tending to men's comfort. There, dependent and subservient, they were meant to provide the services necessary for maintaining their husbands as productive, contented workers, and producing and rearing children to serve as the next generation of workers. Men's status as heads of households and primary wage earners allowed them to arrogate certain rights and privileges, including the right to leisure and the means to enjoy it. Women, for whom wage labor was ideologically problematic, could not make the same claim to a right to resources for leisure.

By the second half of the nineteenth century, these forces had structured an ideological and material matrix that significantly constrained working-class women's leisure. Consequently, during the late nineteenth century, while some sectors of the working classes—most notably, skilled, male workers—enjoyed expanding leisure opportunities and resources, women had fewer means and less time to fully participate in what was a vibrant culture of popular leisure. However, even within a structural framework of constraint, women found the ways and means for leisure. Young, unmarried wage earners had the most time and resources—or simply the strongest will—for leisure; married women were much more constrained by the demands of domestic and other forms of labor and their pitifully small material resources.

Both unmarried wage earners and married, dependent women found that their desire for amusement came up against dominant understandings of working-class womanhood. There was also, by the mid-nineteenth century, a dominant vision of working-class leisure: that it should be rational, elevating, and "respectable," and not—as it had long been—hedonistic, rowdy, and "rough." It was the respectable model that most working-class men and the upper and middle classes saw as most appropriate for women. The second, which they saw as a threat to social and gender order, they had to continually work against, for it persisted as a powerful strain in popular culture. From the early Victorian period through the Edwardian, reformers attempted to involve working-class girls and women in rational forms of recreation, hoping that they would thus be able to mold them into exemplary wives and mothers.

"Peter Pan's Wife" (quoted at the end of chapter 6) provides a sadly ironic commentary on all of this. Despite the efforts and resources that reformers expended, and despite all their good intentions, many working-class women, certainly many wives, probably shared her sentiments. As long as gender and class relations were structured as they were, in the experience of very many working-class women, leisure—men's leisure—was a confounded nuisance. As for young, unmarried women, if the number of Rowntree workers who availed themselves of the opportunities provided for their pursuit of rational recreation is an indication, the best kind of leisure was that which one freely chose. Leisure that was made to serve some end, no matter how laudable, was not really leisure at all. And so, whether in the Rowntree Cocoa Works or any other sphere, leisure could not be anything but an imperfect means of ensuring that the working-class woman comported herself to gender prescriptions. If she was truly determined to make a "blackguard" of herself, rather than be made into a good wife and mother, then her leisure offered her a perfect means and time to do so.

Notes

NOTES TO THE INTRODUCTION

1. Carl Chinn, *They Worked All Their Lives: Women of the Urban Poor in England, 1880–1939* (Manchester, Eng.: Manchester University Press, 1988); Kathy Peiss, *Cheap Amusements: Working Women and Leisure in Turn-of-the-Century New York City* (Philadelphia: Temple University Press, 1986), 3. There is a rich literature on English working-class women that bears upon their leisure, though it does not examine it as a discrete topic. See Meg Gomersall, *Working-Class Girls in Nineteenth-Century England: Life, Work, and Schooling* (Basingstoke, Eng.: Macmillan, 1997); Sally Mitchell, *The New Girl: Girls' Culture in England, 1880–1915* (New York: Columbia University Press, 1995); Judy Giles, *Women, Identity, and Private Life in Britain, 1900–50* (New York: St. Martin's Press, 1995); Melanie Tebbutt, *Women's Talk? A Social History of "Gossip" in Working-Class Neighbourhoods, 1880–1960* (Aldershot, Eng.: Scolar Press, 1995); Sybil Oldfield, *This Working-Day World: Women's Lives and Culture(s) in Britain 1914–1945* (London: Taylor & Francis,1994); Dina M. Copelman, *London's Women Teachers: Gender, Class and Feminism 1870–1930* (London: Routledge, 1996); Carol Dyhouse, *Girls Growing Up in Late Victorian and Edwardian England* (London: Routledge & Kegan Paul, 1981); Ellen Ross, *Love and Toil: Motherhood in Outcast London 1870–1918* (New York: Oxford University Press, 1993); Judith R. Walkowitz, *City of Dreadful Delight: Narratives of Sexual Danger in Late-Victorian London* (Chicago: University of Chicago Press, 1992); Elizabeth Roberts, *A Woman's Place: An Oral History of Working-Class Women, 1890–1940* (Oxford: Blackwell, 1984).

2. Richard Hoggart, *The Uses of Literacy: Aspects of Working-Class Life* (London: Chatto & Windus, 1957); E. P. Thompson, *The Making of the English Working Class* (New York: Pantheon, 1964).

3. For useful reviews and critiques of the scholarship on English leisure, see Peter Bailey, "Leisure, Culture and the Historian: Reviewing the First

Generation of Leisure Historiography in Britain," *Leisure Studies* 8 (1989): 102–127; Jeffrey Hill, "British Sports History: A Post-Modern Future?" *Journal of Sport History* 23 (1996): 1–19.

4. Andrew Davies, *Leisure, Gender and Poverty: Working-Class Culture in Salford and Manchester, 1900–1939* (Milton Keynes, Eng.: Open University Press, 1992); Bettina Bradbury, "Women's History and Working-Class History," *Labour/Le Travail* 19 (1987): 23–43.

5. There is extensive sociological literature on women, gender, and leisure in Britain, Canada, and the United States. For a useful review and integration of this work into a conceptual model similar to the one I sketch out here, see Susan M. Shaw, "Gender, Leisure, and Constraint: Towards a Framework for the Analysis of Women's Leisure," *Journal of Leisure Research* 26 (1994): 8–22. For empirical studies of the material factors that limit women's leisure, see Jarmila L. Horna, "The Leisure Component of the Parental Role," *Journal of Leisure Research* 20 (1989): 228–241; Peter A. Witt and Thomas L. Goodall, "The Relationships Between Barriers to Leisure Enjoyment and Family Stages," *Leisure Sciences* 4 (1981): 29–49; John W. Shank, "An Exploration of Leisure in the Lives of Dual-Career Women," *Journal of Leisure Research* 18 (1986): 300–319; Susan M. Shaw, "Gender and Leisure: Inequality in the Distribution of Leisure Time," *Journal of Leisure Research* 17 (1985): 266–282; P. L. Hunter and D. J. Whitson, "Women's Leisure in a Resource Industry Town: Problems and Issues," *Loisir et Société* 15 (1992): 223–244; E. Green, S. Hebron, and D. Woodward, "Women, Leisure and Social Control," in J. Hanmer and M. Maynard, eds., *Women, Violence and Social Control* (Basingstoke, Eng.: Macmillan, 1987), 75–92; Jan M. Pahl, *Money and Marriage* (Basingstoke, Eng.: Macmillan, 1989); Rosemary Deem, "Women, Leisure and Inequality," *Leisure Studies* 1 (1982): 29–46.

6. Maureen Harrington and Don Dawson, "Who Has It Best? Women's Labor Force Participation, Perceptions of Leisure and Constraints to Enjoyment of Leisure," *Journal of Leisure Research* 27 (1995): 4–24, 20 (quote).

7. Karla A. Henderson and K. R. Allen, "The Ethic of Care: Leisure Possibilities and Constraints for Women," *Loisir et Société* 14 (1991): 97–114; Maureen Harrington, Don Dawson, and P. Bolla, "Objective and Subjective Constraints on Women's Enjoyment of Leisure," *Loisir et Société* 15 (1992): 203–222; Betsy Wearing and Stephen Wearing, " 'All in a Day's Leisure': Gender and the Concept of Leisure," *Leisure Studies* 7 (1988): 111–123; Karla A. Henderson and M. Deborah Bialeschki, "A Sense of Entitlement to Leisure as Constraint and Empowerment for Women," *Leisure Sciences* 13 (1991): 51–66; Susan M. Shaw, "Dereifying Family Leisure: An Examination of Women's and Men's Everyday Experiences and Perceptions of Family Time," *Leisure Sciences* 14 (1992): 271–286; Helen Lenskyj, "Measured Time: Women, Sport and Leisure," *Leisure Studies* 7 (1988): 233–240.

8. Karla A. Henderson, "The Contribution of Feminism to an Understanding of Leisure Constraints," *Journal of Leisure Research* 23 (1991): 363–377; C. Jody Frederick and Susan M. Shaw, "Body Image as a Leisure Constraint: Examining the Experience of Aerobic Exercise Classes for Young Women," *Leisure Sciences* 17 (1995): 57–73.

9. Nancy Theberge, "It's Part of the Game: Physicality and the Production of Gender in Women's Hockey," *Gender and Society* 11 (February 1997): 69–87; Steven Schacht, "Feminist Fieldwork in the Misogynist Setting of the Rugby Pitch: Temporarily Becoming a Sylph to Survive and Personally Grow," *Journal of Contemporary Ethnography* 26 (October 1997): 338–363; Elizabeth Wheatley, " 'Stylistic Ensembles' on a Different Pitch: A Comparative Analysis of Men's and Women's Rugby Songs," *Women and Language* 13 (1990): 21–26.

10. Elizabeth V. Spelman, "Woman as Body: Ancient and Contemporary Views," *Feminist Studies* 8 (1982): 108–131.

11. Hugh Cunningham, *Leisure in the Industrial Revolution, c. 1780–c. 1880* (London: St. Martin's Press, 1980), passim; Peter Bailey, *Leisure and Class in Victorian England: Rational Recreation and the Contest for Control, 1830–1885* (London: Routledge, 1978), passim; Eileen Yeo and Stephen Yeo, eds., *Popular Culture and Class Conflict 1590–1914; Explorations in the History of Labour and Leisure* (Brighton, Eng.: Harvester Press, 1981), 89–127, 187–208, 241–270; J. M. Golby and A. W. Purdue, *The Civilisation of the Crowd: Popular Culture in England, 1750–1900* (London: Batsford, 1984), 92–110; Richard Holt, *Sport and the British: A Modern History* (Oxford: Clarendon Press, 1989), 29–43.

12. On the association of unruliness with lower-class women see, for example, Carol Houlihan Flynn, "What Fanny Felt: The Pains of Compliance, in *Memoirs of a Woman of Pleasure,*" *Studies in the Novel* 19 (1987): 284–295; Susan S. Lanser, "Befriending the Body: Female Intimacies as Class Acts," *Eighteenth-Century Studies* 32 (1998–1999): 179–198; Christine Stansell, *City of Women: Sex and Class in New York 1789–1860* (Urbana: University of Illinois Press, 1987), 36–37. On gender and consumerism see, for example, Mary Louise Roberts, "Gender, Consumption, and Commodity Culture," *American Historical Review* (1998): 817–844; Victoria de Grazia, with Ellen Furlough, eds., *The Sex of Things: Gender and Consumption in Historical Perspective* (Berkeley: University of California Press, 1996); Beth Kowaleski-Wallace, "Women, China, and Consumer Culture in Eighteenth-Century England," *Eighteenth-Century Studies* 29 (1995–1996): 153–167; John Benson, *The Rise of Consumer Society in Britain 1880–1980* (London: Longman, 1994); Erika Diane Rappaport, *Shopping for Pleasure: Women in the Making of London's West End* (Princeton, N.J.: Princeton University Press, 2000).

13. Raymond Williams, *Marxism and Literature* (Oxford: Oxford University Press, 1977), 122–127.

14. Harriet Bradley, *Men's Work, Women's Work: A Sociological History of the Sexual Division of Labour in Employment* (Minneapolis: University of Minnesota Press, 1989), 41–42; Louise A. Tilly and Joan W. Scott, *Women, Work, and Family* (New York: Holt, Rinehart & Winston, 1978), 30–60, 41–42, 123–136; Ivy Pinchbeck, *Women Workers and the Industrial Revolution 1750–1850* (London: Routledge, 1930; reprint ed., Frank Cass, 1969), 53–65, 111–121, 282–284. On the intellectual roots and emergence of domestic and gender ideologies among the working classes, see Catherine Hall, "The Tale of Samuel and Jemima: Gender and Working-Class Culture in Nineteenth-Century England," in Harvey J. Kaye and Keith McClelland, eds., *E. P. Thompson, Critical Perspectives* (Philadelphia: Temple University Press, 1990), 86–99; Harold Bennenson, "The 'Family Wage' and Working Women's Consciousness in Britain, 1880–1914," *Politics and Society* 19 (1991): 71–72; Harold Bennenson, "Victorian Sexual Ideology and Marx's Theory of the Working Class," *International Labour and Working-Class History* 25 (1984): 1–23; Maxine Berg, "Women's Work, Mechanization and the Early Phases of Industrialisation in England," in Patrick Joyce, ed., *The Historical Meanings of Work* (Cambridge: Cambridge University Press, 1987), 73; Wally Seccombe, "Patriarchy Stabilized: The Construction of the Male Breadwinner Norm in Nineteenth-Century Britain," *Social History* 11 (1986): 53–76.

15. John Watkins, "Address to the Women of England," *The Chartist Circular* 1 (1841): 49.

16. See, for example, James Walvin, *Beside the Seaside: A Social History of the Popular Seaside Holiday* (London: Allen Lane, 1978), 11, 53–57, 63–64; James Walvin, *Leisure and Society, 1830–1950* (London: Longmans, 1978), 61–62; Bailey, *Leisure and Class in Victorian England,* 4–6; John Lowerson and John Myerscough, *Time to Spare in Victorian England* (Brighton, Eng.: Harvester Press, 1977), 19–20; Cunningham, *Leisure in the Industrial Revolution,* 140–191. Cunningham and others have questioned the idea of an unqualified expansion of working-class leisure in this period. See Hugh Cunningham, "Leisure," in John Benson, ed., *The Working Class in England, 1875–1914* (Bloomington: Indiana University Press, 1982), 166–264; Walvin, *Beside the Seaside,* 75; Stephen G. Jones, *Workers at Play: A Social and Economic History of Leisure 1918–1939* (London: Routledge & Kegan Paul, 1986), 4–5. Jones argues that a truly mass leisure culture did not emerge until after the First World War.

17. Nicky Hart, "Gender and the Rise and Fall of Class Politics," *New Left Review* 175 (1989): 19–47; Davies, *Leisure, Gender and Poverty;* Kathleen E. McCrone, "Class, Gender, and English Women's Sport, c. 1890–1914," *Journal of Sport History* 18 (1991): 159–182.

18. On similar concerns about young, female urbanites in Canada and the United States, see, for example, Carolyn Strange, *Toronto's Girl Problem:*

The Perils and Pleasures of the City, 1880–1930 (Toronto: University of Toronto Press, 1995); Joanne J. Meyerowitz, *Women Adrift: Independent Wage Earners in Chicago, 1880–1930* (Chicago: University of Chicago Press, 1988); Elizabeth Ewen, *Immigrant Women in the Land of Dollars: Life and Culture on the Lower East Side, 1890–1925* (New York: Monthly Review Press, 1985).

19. Wray Vamplew, *Pay Up and Play the Game: Professional Sport in Britain 1875–1914* (Cambridge: Cambridge University Press, 1988), 53.

20. On the cultural anxieties of the late Victorian and Edwardian periods, see, for example, Thomas E. Jordan, *The Degeneracy Crisis and Victorian Youth* (Albany: State University Press of New York, 1995); June Purvis, *Hard Lives: The Lives and Education of Working-Class Women in Nineteenth-Century England* (Cambridge, Eng.: Polity Press, 1981), 63–70; Anna Davin, "Imperialism and Motherhood," *History Workshop Journal* 5 (1978): 9–65. For the United States, see, for example, Ruth M. Alexander, *The "Girl Problem": Female Sexual Delinquency in New York, 1900–1930* (Ithaca: Cornell University Press, 1995); Priscilla Murolo, *The Common Ground of Womanhood: Class, Gender, and Working Girls' Clubs, 1884–1928* (Urbana: University of Illinois Press, 1997).

21. Peter Bailey, " 'Will the Real Bill Banks Please Stand Up?' Towards a Role Analysis of Mid-Victorian Respectability," *Journal of Social History* 12 (1979): 7–21.

NOTES TO PART ONE

1. Bailey, "Leisure, Culture and the Historian," 108, 112; Shirley M. Reekie, "A History of Sport and Recreation for Women in Great Britain, 1700–1850 (Ph.D. dissertation, Ohio State University, 1982), 33–95; Robert W. Malcolmson, *Popular Recreations in English Society, 1700–1850* (Cambridge: Cambridge University Press, 1973), 118–171; Cunningham, *Leisure in the Industrial Revolution*, 9–11, 15–75.

2. Amanda Vickery, "Golden Age to Separate Spheres? A Review of the Categories and Chronology of English Women's History," *Historical Journal* 36 (1993): 383–414; Alice Clark, *Working Life of Women in the Seventeenth Century* (London: Routledge & Kegan Paul, 1982); Pinchbeck, *Women Workers and the Industrial Revolution;* Bridget Hill, *Women, Work and Sexual Politics in Eighteenth-Century England* (Oxford: Basil Blackwell, 1989); Deborah Valenze, *The First Industrial Woman* (New York: Oxford University Press, 1995); Pamela Sharpe, *Adapting to Capitalism: Working Women in the English Economy, 1700–1850* (New York: St. Martin's Press, 1996); Jane Rendall, *Women in an Industrializing Society: England 1750–1880* (Oxford: Basil Blackwell, 1990).

3. Judith Bennett, "History That Stands Still: Women's Work in the European Past," *Feminist Studies* 14 (1988): 269–283; Olwen Hufton,

"Women in History," *Past and Present* 101 (1983): 125–141; Olwen Hufton, *The Prospect Before Her* (London: Harper Collins, 1995), 501–504; Lawrence E. Klein, "Gender and the Public/Private Distinction in the Eighteenth Century: Some Questions About Evidence and Analytic Procedure," *Eighteenth-Century Studies* 29 (1995): 97–109; Paul Langford, *A Polite and Commercial People: England, 1727–1783* (Oxford: Oxford University Press, 1989), 109; Linda Colley, *Britons: Forging the Nation, 1707–1837* (New Haven: Yale University Press, 1992), 241.

4. Cunningham, *Leisure in the Industrial Revolution*, 9–11, 15–75; Dennis Brailsford, "1787: A Sporting Year," *Research Quarterly* 52 (1981): 34–45.

NOTES TO CHAPTER ONE

1. Anna Clark, *The Struggle for the Breeches: Gender and the Making of the English Working Class* (Berkeley: University of California Press, 1995), 26–29; Peter Burke, *Popular Culture in Early Modern Europe* (n.p.: Maurice Temple Smith, 1978; reprint ed., Aldershot, Eng.: Scolar Press, 1994), 208.

2. Malcolmson, *Popular Recreations in English Society*, 20.

3. William Howitt, *The Rural Life of England*, 2 vols. (London: Orme, Brown, Green & Longmans, 1837; reprint ed., Philadelphia: Parry & M'Millan, 1854), 236, 239.

4. Malcolmson, *Popular Recreations in English Society*, 24–32.

5. Ibid., 23–24; William Hone, *The Every-Day Book: Or, Everlasting Calendar of Popular Amusements*, 2 vols. (London: Hunt & Clarke, 1826–1827), vol. 2, col. 224. Henry Mayhew describes a hiring market held in Bethnal Green, London, on the eve of the mid-Victorian period at which (according to one of his sources) females outnumbered males by three to one. Henry Mayhew, *The Morning Chronicle Survey of Labour and the Poor: The Metropolitan Districts*, 6 vols. (London, 1849–1850; reprint ed., Horsham, Eng.: Caliban Books, 1980–1982), vol. 3, 179.

6. Hone. *Every-Day Book*, vol. 2, cols. 436–437, 1206; Howitt, *Rural Life of England*, vol. 2, 284–285.

7. *The Great Diurnal of Nicholas Blundell of Little Crosby, Lancashire, 1712–1719*, ed. J. J. Bagley, 2 vols. (n.p.: Record Society of Lancashire and Cheshire, 1968–1970), vol 2., 141.

8. Hone, *Every-Day Book*, vol. 2., cols. 223–224, 1310 (quote); Thomas Hardy, *The Mayor of Casterbridge: The Story of a Man of Character* (1881; reprint ed., New York: Bantam Books, 1981), 1–21.

9. Howitt, *Rural Life of England*, vol. 2, 234–235; Hone, *Every-Day Book*, vol. 2, col. 1371; *The Diary of Sylas Neville, 1767–1788*, ed. Basil Cozens-Hardy (London: Oxford University Press, 1950), September 3, 1770, 80; John Brand, *Observations on Popular Antiquities*, 2 vols. (Newcastle-upon-

Tyne, 1777; revised ed., London: F. C. & J. Rivington, 1813), vol. 2, 316–317.

10. Hone, *Every-Day Book*, vol. 2, cols. 1309, 1195–1197.

11. Nottinghamshire Archives, Nottingham (hereafter NA), M 19804, Letter from A. L. S. to James Worth regarding Goose Fair, October 12, 1843.

12. Howitt, *Rural Life of England*, vol. 2, 239.

13. Hone, *Every-Day Book*, vol. 2, cols. 1307, 1310.

14. *Great Diurnal of Nicholas Blundell*, vol. 2, 132, 141; *The Diary of Thomas Turner, 1754–1765*, ed. David Vaisey (Oxford: Oxford University Press, 1984), 41, 113; *Diary of Sylas Neville*, 102, 170.

15. Henry Bourne, *Antiquitates Vulgares* (Newcastle, 1725; reprint ed., New York: Arno Press, 1977), 228; Howitt, *Rural Life of England*, vol. 2, 231 (quote); Joseph Strutt, *The Sports and Pastimes of the People of England* (London: Methuen, 1903; revised ed., Detroit: Singing Tree Press, 1968), 288–290; Brand, *Popular Antiquities*, vol. 1, 422–438.

16. Malcomson, *Popular Recreations in English Society*, 17–19; Strutt, *Sports and Pastimes of the People of England*, 287–288.

17. Hone, *Every-Day Book*, vol. 2, col. 1166; Howitt, *Rural Life of England*, vol. 2, 233. Women's visibility in food riots during the eighteenth century is another manifestation of their familial and communal nurturing roles. See Nicholas Rogers, *Crowds, Culture, and Politics in Georgian Britain* (Oxford: Clarendon Press, 1998), 220–222, 229–234; John Bohstedt, "The Myth of the Feminine Food Riot: Women as Proto-Citizens in English Community Politics, 1790–1810," in Harriet B. Applewaite and Darlene G. Levy, eds., *Women and Politics in the Age of the Democratic Revolution* (Ann Arbor: University of Michigan Press, 1993), 21–60.

18. Strutt, *Sports and Pastimes of the People of England*, 286 (quote).

19. *The Autobiography of Samuel Bamford: Early Days*, ed. W. H. Chaloner, 2 vols. (London: Simpkin, Marshal, 1848–1849; reprint ed., London: Frank Cass, 1967), vol. 1, 134 (quote), 136–138, 154, 159; Hone, *Every-Day Book*, vol. 1, cols. 402–406; *Mary Hardy's Diary* (Norwich, Eng.: Norfolk Record Society, 1968), 72, 91, 113 (quote), 121, 124.

20. Howitt, *Rural Life of England*, vol. 2, 231–234, 225–228; Bamford, *Early Days*, vol. 1, 136–138.

21. Bourne, *Antiquitates Vulgares*, 225.

22. Bamford, *Early Days*, vol. 1, 147, 154; Hone, *Every-Day Book*, vol. 2, col. 1260.

23. Hone, *Every-Day Book*, vol. 1, cols. 1153–1181, 1166 (quote).

24. Bamford, *Early Days*, vol. 1, 147–151; *Great Diurnal of Nicholas Blundell*, vol. 2, 261.

25. Howitt, *Rural Life of England*, vol. 2, 233 (quote); *Great Diurnal of Nicholas Blundell*, vol. 1, 145, 176, 261; vol. 2, 138.

26. Howitt, *Rural Life of England*, vol. 2, 232–233; Hone, *Every-Day Book*, vol. 2, cols. 638–639 (quotes).

27. Hone, *Every-Day Book*, vol. 2, cols. 1259–1260, 1262 (quote).

28. Ibid., vol. 1, cols. 541–598, 571–572 (quotes); vol. 2, cols. 574, 575, 579, 594, 615–616, 640, 648–651, 660; *Kalm's Account of His Visit to England*, trans. Joseph Lucas (Stockholm: Lars Salvii, 1753; London: Macmillan, 1892), 31.

29. Brand, *Popular Antiquities*, vol. 1, 179–212; Hone, *Every-Day Book*, vol. 1, cols. 537–598; Hone, *Every-Day Books*, vol. 2, cols. 595–598, 614.

30. Brand, *Popular Antiquities*, vol. 1, 211.

31. Hone, *Every-Day Book*, vol. 1, cols. 565–568, 583–585.

32. Ibid., vol. 2, cols. 1153–1156.

33. Ibid., 1161, 1162–1163 (quotes), 1158–1182.

34. Brand, *Popular Antiquities*, vol. 1, 230, 232 (quotes); Hone, *Every-Day Book*, vol. 2, col. 669.

35. Hone, *Every-Day Book*, vol. 1, col. 437, vol. 2, col. 112.

36. Howitt, *Rural Life of England*, vol. 2, 239.

37. Hone, *Every-Day Book*, vol. 2, col. 668; Bamford, *Early Days*, vol. 1, 153, 154, 158.

38. Hone, *Every-Day Book*, vol. 2, cols. 668–669. On the often raucous character of plebeian women's culture and leisure in New York in roughly the same period, see Christine Stansell, *City of Women: Sex and Class in New York City 1789–1860* (Urbana: University of Illinois Press, 1987), 14–15, 41–42, 58–62.

39. Unidentified newspaper, October 18, 1787, quoted in Brand, *Popular Antiquities*, vol. 1, 298.

40. Hone, *Every-Day Book*, vol. 1, cols. 422–425; Brand, *Popular Antiquities*, vol. 1, 154–156. Both women and men participated in the custom of lifting. In most places, women lifted men on Easter Tuesday and men lifted women on Easter Monday, though in Warrington, Bolton, and Manchester the reverse was true. In Ripon, Yorkshire, in the 1790s, and in Durham in the northeast, women and men seized one another's shoes or buckles and held them for ransom. By the 1820s adults had given up the Durham custom and only children continued with it. See Hone, *Every-Day Book*, vol. 2, cols. 448–449.

41. Brand, *Popular Antiquities*, vol. 1, 155–156.

42. Malcolmson, *Popular Recreations in English Society*, 96; Allen Guttmann, *Women's Sports: A History* (New York: Columbia University Press, 1991); Reekie, "A History of Sport and Recreation for Women," 33–95.

43. John Payne Collier, ed., *Illustrations of Old English Literature* (New York: B. Blom, 1966).

44. "Barley-brake" was a running and catching game played by two

teams of unspecified but usually large numbers. Strutt reports that the name was supposed to derive from the fact that it was originally played in a field among stacks of barley which served as the "goals" and "prisons." Strutt, *Sports and Pastimes of the People of England*, 68, 302.

45. S. A. J. Bradley, ed., *Wit and Mirth: Sixty Ribald Songs from Pills to Purge Melancholy* (New York: F. A. Praeger, 1967), 27.

46. Guttmann, *Women's Sports: A History*, 77; Robert W. Henderson, *Ball, Bat and Bishop: The Origin of Ball Games* (New York: Rockport Press, 1947), 70–78; Strutt, *Sports and Pastimes of the People of England*, 101. Guttman quotes the third edition (1838) of Strutt's work, viz., that stoolball was "more properly appropriated to the women than to the men, but occasionally it was played by young persons of both sexes indiscriminately." The editor of the 1903 version of Strutt's book expunged this association of the game with women, possibly because he judged it to be one of the "few obvious mistakes and rash conclusions" that he attributed to earlier editions of the work, of which there were at least four.

47. *Great Diurnal of Nicholas Blundell*, vol. 1, 134; Bourne, *Antiquitates Vulgares*, 198; Hone, *Every-Day Book*, vol. 2, col. 430; *Southey's Common-Place Book*, ed. John Wood Warter, 4 vols. (London: Longman, Brown, Green & Longman, 1850), vol. 4, 416–417. Even as recently as the late 1970s, women's stoolball was being played regularly in a number of parishes and villages in Kent and Sussex. See Shirley Prendergast, "Stoolball—the Pursuit of Vertigo?" *Women's Studies International Forum* 1 (1978): 15–26.

48. *Southey's Common-Place Book*, vol. 4, 416–417; NA, DD 105/2, Print of Women's Cricket Match on Selston Common, 1869.

49. *Reading Mercury* (1745), quoted in Nancy Joy, *Maiden Over: A Short History of Women's Cricket and a Diary of the 1948–49 Test-Tour to Australia* (London: Sporting Handbooks, 1950), 14.

50. Reekie, "A History of Sport and Recreation for Women," 35–53.

51. *The General Advertiser* (London), July 14, 1747, cited in Rachael Heyhoe Flint and Netta Rheinberg, *Fair Play: The Story of Women's Cricket* (London: Angus & Robertson, 1976), 14–15.

52. H. T. Waghorn, *Cricket Scores, Notes, Etc., from 1730–1773* (Edinburgh: William Blackwood, 1899), 64, cited in Reekie, "A History of Sport and Recreation for Women," 40, 41; E. P. Thompson, "Patrician Society, Plebeian Culture," *Journal of Social History* 7 (1974): 63–81.

53. Thomas Turner records in his diary numerous games of cricket in which he engaged as a player, spectator, and gambler in the period from 1754 to 1765. Usually, his wagers were modest, from as little as 1½ d. (pence) to a shilling. On one occasion he watched two local men play two games against each other for wagers of two guineas and half a guinea, and noted in his diary that there was no "greater stupidity in mankind than to

game for such large sums." *Diary of Thomas Turner*, 159, 275, 208 (quote), passim.

54. Joy, *Maiden Over*, 15–16.

55. A "century" is the cricketing term for scoring one hundred runs in an inning. Kathleen E. McCrone, *Playing the Game: Sport and the Physical Emancipation of English Women, 1870–1914* (Lexington: University of Kentucky Press, 1988), 141; Guttmann, *Women's Sports: A History*, 77–79; Reekie, "A History of Sport and Recreation for Women," 41; *Times* (London), June 20, 1793, 3, cited in ibid., 43; Strutt, *Sports and Pastimes of the People of England*, 97; Henderson, *Ball, Bat and Bishop*, 72; *Southey's Common-Place Book*, vol. 4, 416–417; Melvin L. Adelman, *A Sporting Time: New York City and the Rise of Modern Athletics, 1820–1870* (Urbana: University of Illinois Press, 1986).

56. Robert Chambers, ed., *The Book of Days* (London: W. & R. Chambers, 1866), vol. 1, 428; Reekie, "A History of Sport and Recreation for Women," 58.

57. Cunningham, *Leisure in the Industrial Revolution*, 23–24, 77–78; Malcolmson, *Popular Recreations in English Society*, 47, 56, 66–67.

58. Hone, *Every-Day Book*, vol. 2, cols. 1482–1486. Francis Place gives a vivid description of bullock hunting in the Smithfield Market area of London in the 1780s. Although the core action was similar to the Stamford bull-running, the sport Place describes differed in several important respects, most notably perhaps in that it was more of a twice-weekly raid on the cattle brought to market than an annual, communal festival. Place makes no mention of female bullock-hunters, either. See *The Autobiography of Francis Place*, ed. Mary Thale (Cambridge: Cambridge University Press, 1972), 68–70.

59. *The Diary of a Country Parson, 1758–1802: The Reverend James Woodforde*, ed. John Beresford, 5 vols. (London: Oxford University Press, 1924–1931), vol. 1, 90.

60. Hone, *Every-Day Book*, vol. 2, cols. 1399–1401.

61. *Great Diurnal of Nicholas Blundell*, vol. 1, 33, passim.

62. James Pellor Malcolm, *Anecdotes of the Manners and Customs of London during the Eighteenth Century*, 2d ed., 2 vols. (London: Longman, Hurst, Rees & Orme, 1810), vol. 2, 183.

63. *Morning Advertiser*, quoted in Reekie, "A History of Sport and Recreation for Women," 63.

64. Hone, *Every-Day Book*, vol. 1, col. 754; Henry Fielding, *Joseph Andrews* (London, 1742; reprint ed., London: Penguin Books, 1977), 159, 333; Holt, *Sport and the British*, 20.

65. *Southey's Common-Place Book*, vol. 4, 378.

66. Quoted in Guttmann, *Women's Sports: A History*, 75.

67. Bamford, *Early Days*, 102, 162; *Diary of Thomas Turner*, 198–199, 260, 294.

68. John Macdonald, *Memoirs of an Eighteenth-Century Footman: Travels (1745–1779)* (London, 1790; reprint ed., London: Harper & Bros., 1927), 59, 63, 91; *Diary of Sylas Neville*, 5, 22, 71, 73, 108; Carl Philip Moritz, *Journeys of a German in England in 1782*, trans. and ed. Reginald Nettel (1783; reprint ed., New York: Holt, Rinehart & Winston, 1965), 158.

69. *Diary of Sylas Neville*, 71.

70. *Diary of Thomas Turner*, 21, 167, 233, 234, 265; Thomas Wright, ed., *Autobiography of Thomas Wright, of Birkenshaw. In the County of York. 1736–1797* (London: John Russell Smith, 1864), 13–14, 35–36, 76–77; *Great Diurnal of Nicholas Blundell*, vol. 2, 62, 82; *Mary Hardy's Diary*, 31. See Amanda Vickery, *The Gentleman's Daughter: Women's Lives in Georgian England* (New Haven: Yale University Press, 1998), 135–147, for the concessions that some mistresses were prepared to grant servants in order to retain their services, and Patty Seleski, "Women, Work and Cultural Change in Eighteenth- and Early Nineteenth-Century London," in Tim Harris, ed., *Popular Culture in England, c. 1500–1850* (New York: St. Martin's Press, 1995), 143–167, on female servants' social freedoms and their employers' efforts to keep them in check.

71. *Great Diurnal of Nicholas Blundell*, vol. 2, 23, 83, 127, 136, 139, 141, 147, 264, 267; *Mary Hardy's Diary*, 33, 40, 69; *Diary of Thomas Turner*, 12, 22, 242; MacDonald, *Memoirs of an Eighteenth-Century Footman*, 182, 237; *Diary of Sylas Neville*, 105.

72. *Diary of Thomas Turner*, 64, 137–138, 141, 198–199, 260, 294, passim. See Lawrence Stone, "Money, Sex and Murder in Eighteenth-Century England," in Ian P. H. Duffy, *Women and Society in the Eighteenth Century* (Bethlehem, Pa.: The Lawrence Henry Gipson Institute, 1983), 15–28, for a fascinating look at the shared leisure of women and men from the gentry and lower ranks in eighteenth-century Herefordshire.

73. Rogers, *Crowds, Culture, and Politics*, 235.

74. "Stool-Ball, or the Easter Diversion," in Bradley, *Wit and Mirth*, 27; John Barrell, "Sportive Labour: The Farmworker in Eighteenth-Century Poetry and Painting," in Brian Short, ed., *The English Rural Community: Image and Analysis* (Cambridge: Cambridge University Press, 1992), 105–132.

75. Bourne, *Antiquitates Vulgares*, 198; Nicholas Rogers, "Carnal Knowledge: Illegitimacy in Eighteenth-Century Westminster," *Journal of Social History* 23 (1989): 363–364. On the sexual license associated with popular holidays and festivals, see also Malcolmson, *Popular Recreations in English Society*, 9–10, 76–79.

76. *Lichtenberg's Visits to England as Described in His Letter and Diaries,*

trans. Margaret L. Mare & W. H. Quarrell (Oxford: Clarendon Press, 1938), 118; *Autobiography of Francis Place*, 77–78. See also Clark, *Struggle for the Breeches*, 58–59.

77. Hone, *Every-Day Book*, vol. 2, cols. 1482–1486.

78. Unidentified newspaper, October 18, 1787, quoted in Brand, *Popular Antiquities*, vol. 1, 298.

79. *Gentleman's Magazine*, February 1784, 96, quoted in Brand, *Popular Antiquities*, 155.

80. Hone, *Every-Day Book*, vol. 1, cols. 1383–1389; Daniel Defoe, *A Tour Thro' the Whole Island of Great Britain, 1742*, ed. Samuel Richardson, 4 vols. (London: J. Osborn, 1742; reprint ed., New York: Garland, 1975), vol. 1, 125; Brand, *Popular Antiquities*, vol. 2, 112.

81. On the theme of a late-eighteenth-century "crisis" see, for example, Dror Wahrman, "Percy's Prologue: From Gender Play to Gender Panic in Eighteenth-Century England," *Past and Present* 159 (1998): 113–160; Londa Schiebinger, "Why Mammals Are Called Mammals: Gender Politics in Eighteenth-Century Natural History," *American Historical Review* 98 (1993): 382–411; Clark, *Struggle for the Breeches*, passim; Patricia Demers, *The World of Hannah More* (Lexington: University of Kentucky Press, 1996), 109.

82. Malcolmson, *Popular Recreations in English Society*, 89–171; Cunningham, *Leisure in the Industrial Revolution*, 20–22, 37–41, 38–47, 77–79, 84–92, 98–107; Alun Howkins, "The Taming of Whitsun: the Changing Face of a Nineteenth-Century Rural Holiday," in Yeo and Yeo, *Popular Culture and Class Conflict*, 187–208; Anthony Delves, "Popular Recreation and Social Conflict in Derby, 1800–1850," ibid., 89–127.

83. John Walsh, " 'Methodism' and the Origins of English-Speaking Evangelicalism," in Mark A. Noll, David W. Bebington, and George A. Rawlyk, eds., *Evangelicalism: Comparative Studies of Popular Protestantism in North America, the British Isles, and Beyond, 1700–1990* (Oxford: Oxford University Press, 1994), 20, 24, 27 (quote); Doreen M. Rosman, *Evangelicals and Culture* (London: Croom Helm, 1984), 43–67, 119–133.

84. Walsh, " 'Methodism,' " 30 (quotes); Malcolmson, *Popular Recreations in English Society*, 106–107; John Rule, "Methodism, Popular Beliefs and Village Culture in Cornwall, 1800–50," in Robert D. Storch, ed., *Popular Culture and Custom in Nineteenth-Century England* (London: Croom Helm, 1982), 48–70. Proscriptions against worldly amusements and indulging carnal desires, especially ones directed to women, abounded in the works of leading evangelists. See, for example, letters that John Wesley wrote to female Methodists on such matters in *The Letters of the Reverend John Wesley*, ed. John Telford, 8 vols. (London: Epworth Press, 1931), vol. 4, 279; vol. 5, 72, 140, 201, 233; vol. 6, 30, 208–209, 353. See also Wesley's *Journal*, in *The Works of the Reverend John Wesley*, ed. John Emory, 3d ed., 7 vols. (New York: Eaton & Mains, n.d.), passim.

85. Malcolmson, *Popular Recreations in English Society*, 89–171; Howkins, "The Taming of Whitsun," 187–208; Delves, "Popular Recreation and Social Conflict," 89–127.

86. Malcolmson, *Popular Recreations in English Society*, 104 (quote); Clark, *The Struggle for the Breeches*, 91–118; Deborah M. Valenze, *Prophetic Sons and Daughters: Female Preaching and Popular Religion in Industrial England* (Princeton, N.J.: Princeton University Press, 1985), 26, 35, 52; David Shorney, " 'Women May Preach but Men Must Govern': Gender Roles in the Growth and Development of the Bible Christian Denomination," in R. Swanson, ed., *Gender and Christian Religion: Papers Read at the 1996 Summer Meeting and 1997 Winter Meeting of the Ecclesiastical History Society* (Woodbridge, Eng.: Boydell Press, 1998), 309–322; David Hempton, *The Religion of the People: Methodism and Popular Religion c. 1850–1900* (New York: Routledge, 1996), 191–196.

87. See, for example, Susan Pedersen, "Hannah More Meets Simple Simon: Tracts, Chapbooks, and Popular Culture in Late Eighteenth-Century England," *Journal of British Studies* 25 (1986): 84–113; Demers, *The World of Hannah More*, 99–118.

88. Hannah More, ed., *Cheap Repository Tracts: Entertaining, Moral, and Religious*, 8 vols. (1795–1798; revised ed., New York: American Tract Society, 1825) (hereafter *CRT*). Subsequent references to specific tracts are all from this edition, unless noted otherwise. Arthur Roberts, *Mendip Annals: Or, A Narrative of the Charitable Labours of Hannah and Martha More* (New York: Robert Carter & Brothers, 1859), 26, 113, 150.

89. "The Two Shoemakers," *CRT*, vol. 5, 44; "Sorrowful Sam; Or, the Two Blacksmiths," ibid., 120, 137, 138; "The Good Mother's Legacy," ibid., vol. 8, 29–32.

90. "The Good Mother's Legacy," ibid., 31, 33, 34–35, 38, 41–42, 45–46; "The Two Shoemakers," ibid., vol. 5, 48–50. On similar themes, see also, "The Lancashire Collier Girl," ibid., vol. 5, 142–155; "Tawney Rachel; or, the Fortune-teller: with some account of Dreams, Omens, and Conjurers, Being Part III of Black Giles the Poacher," ibid., vol. 6, 47–67.

91. *Mendip Annals*, passim.

92. Pedersen, "Hannah More Meets Simple Simon," 108.

93. *Diary of Thomas Turner*, 274 (quote), passim; *Mary Hardy's Diary*, passim; *The Autobiography of Joseph Mayett of Quainton, 1783–1839*, ed. Ann Kussmaul (Aylesbury, Eng.: Buckinghamshire Record Office, 1986), 77, 81, 91 (quote); Valenze, *Prophetic Sons and Daughters*, 161–183, passim; Moritz, *Journeys of a German in England*, 129.

94. Clark, *Struggle for the Breeches*, 25–41; *Rules of Society*, meeting in Fore Street (London, 1787), quoted in ibid., 38; DD 67/1, *Rules, Orders etc., Observed by the Members of the Female Union Society*, held at the Sign of the Green

Dragon, Oxton, Nottinghamshire, England, founded June 30, 1824, NA; 4D 37, *Regulations of a Women's Friendly Society* meeting at the Bull's Head, Belgrave Street, Leicester, England, 1808, and 6D 57, *Records of Glenfield Female Friendly Society*, Leicestershire, founded 1839, Leicestershire Record Office, Wigston Magna, England (hereafter LRO).

NOTES TO CHAPTER TWO

1. On nineteenth-century rational recreation, see Cunningham, *Leisure in the Industrial Revolution*, 90–92, 99–107, 110–111, 155–156; Bailey, *Leisure and Class in Victorian England;* Yeo and Yeo, *Popular Culture and Class Conflict*, 89–127, 187–208, 241–270; Golby and Purdue, *The Civilisation of the Crowd*, 92–110; Holt, *Sport and the British*, 29–43.

2. For recent feminist works on Victorian England see, for example, Judy Lown, *Women and Industrialization: Gender at Work in Nineteenth-Century England* (Minneapolis: University of Minnesota Press, 1990); Mary Poovey, *Uneven Developments: The Ideological Work of Gender in Mid-Victorian England* (Chicago: University of Chicago Press, 1988); Sonya O. Rose, *Limited Livelihoods: Gender and Class in Nineteenth-Century England* (Berkeley: University of California Press, 1992); Walkowitz, *City of Dreadful Delight;* Clark, *Struggle for the Breeches.* For this chapter I am especially indebted to Clark's study.

3. William Cobbett, *Advice to Young Men, and (Incidentally) to Young Women, in the Middle and Higher Ranks of Life* (London, 1829), Letter III. See also Cobbett's *Cottage Economy* (London, 1822; reprint ed., New York: Augustus M. Kelley, 1970), 14–16, 19–22, 99, 120, and passim, for similar sentiments on women, amusements, and especially the effeminate indulgence of tea drinking.

4. Clark, *Struggle for the Breeches*, 25.

5. *The Pioneer; or Grand National Consolidated Trades' Union Magazine*, March 22, 1834, 262.

6. *Pioneer*, September 14, 1833, 11; March 1, 1834, 238; Barbara Taylor, *Eve and the New Jerusalem: Socialism and Feminism in the Nineteenth Century* (New York: Pantheon, 1983), 217–237.

7. *New Moral World*, July 20, 1839; November 9, 1839; *Northern Star*, January 13, 1840; August 22, 1840; all quoted in Eileen Yeo, "Culture and Constraint in Working-Class Movements, 1830–1855," in Yeo and Yeo, eds., *Popular Culture and Class Conflict*, 161–163 (quotes); Taylor, *Eve and the New Jerusalem*, 223–227.

8. *New Moral World*, June 6, 1840, quoted in Taylor, *Eve and the New Jerusalem*, 224.

9. Taylor, *Eve and the New Jerusalem*, 223–230; *Pioneer*, September 14, 1833, 13; September 21, 1833, 18.

10. *New Moral World*, May 15, 1841, quoted in Taylor, *Eve and the New Jerusalem*, 228. On Owenite temperance, see also the *Pioneer*, September 14, 1833, 13; September 21, 1833, 18; March 8, 1834, 238.

11. *Pioneer*, February 1, 1834, 181.

12. *Pioneer*, February 22, 1834, 212.

13. Clark, *Struggle for the Breeches*, 25–41; Margaret Hunt, "Wifebeating, Domesticity, and Women's Independence in 18th Century London," *Gender and History* 4 (1992): 23–34; Sonya O. Rose, "Gender Antagonism and Class Conflict: Exclusionary Strategies of Male Trade Unionists in Nineteenth-Century Britain," *Social History* 13 (1988): 191–208.

14. Jutta Schwarzkopf, *Women in the Chartist Movement* (New York: St. Martin's Press, 1991), 4. See also Dorothy Thompson, *The Chartists* (London: Temple Smith, 1984); Anna Clark, "The Rhetoric of Chartist Domesticity: Gender, Language, and Class in the 1830s and 1840s," *Journal of British Studies* 31 (1992): 62–88.

15. Schwarzkopf, *Women in the Chartist Movement*, 35–77; William Lovett, *The Life and Struggles of William Lovett* (London: Trubner, 1876), 266.

16. *Notes to the People*, vol. 2, May 1851–May 1852 (reprint ed., New York: Barnes & Noble, 1968), 629–632, 649–652, 670–672, 689–692, 710–712.

17. Ibid., 848.

18. On the Manifesto of the General Convention, see Thompson, *The Chartists*, 67, 69, 83. For the full text of the manifesto, see Lovett, *Life and Struggles*, 209–215.

19. Watkins, "Address to the Women of England," 49.

20. The quotation is from Sally Alexander, Anna Davin, and Eve Hostettler, "Labouring Women: A Reply to Eric Hobsbawm," *History Workshop*, no. 8 (1979): 179. For different perspectives on the family wage issue, see Jane Humphries, "Class Struggle and the Persistence of the Working-Class Family," *Cambridge Journal of Economics* 1 (1977): 241–258; Michelle Barrett and Maureen McIntosh, "The 'Family Wage': Some Problems for Socialists and Feminists," *Capital and Class* 11 (Summer 1980): 111–133.

21. For a particularly harsh criticism of working-class men's privileges, see Hart, "Gender and Class Politics," 19–47.

22. For "moral-force" and "physical-force" Chartism, see Clark, *Struggle for the Breeches*, 224–227.

23. William Lovett and John Collins, *Chartism: A New Organization of the People* (London: J. Watson, 1840; reprint ed., Leicester, Eng.: Leicester University Press, 1969), 21, 25, 57, 60; Lovett, *Life and Struggles*, 287.

24. Lovett, *Life and Struggles*, 96; Lovett and Collins, *Chartism*, 59–63.

25. Thomas Wright, *The Great Unwashed* (London: Tinsley Bros., 1868; reprint ed., New York: Augustus M. Kelley, 1970), 31, 37–41, 48, 190.

26. *The Working Man*, January 27, 1866, 57.

27. *The Working Man*, January 27, 1866, 57; May 26, 1866, 327; December 15, 1866, 238.

28. House of Commons, *First Report of the Royal Commission on the Employment of Children, Young Persons, and Women in Agriculture, Parliamentary Papers, 1867–1868*, vol. 17, No. 4068, Appendix Part I, xxiii, xxvi.

29. Susan Zlotnick, " 'A Thousand Times I'd Be a Factory Girl': Dialect, Domesticity, and Working-Class Women's Poetry in Victorian Britain," *Victorian Studies*, 35 (1991): 7–27; Hall, "The Tale of Samuel and Jemima," 78–102; Rose, "Gender Antagonism," 191–208; Bennenson, "The 'Family Wage,' " 71–108; Clark, "Chartist Domesticity," 62–98.

30. Patrick Joyce, *Visions of the People: Industrial England and the Question of Class 1848–1914* (Cambridge: Cambridge University Press, 1991), 279–304.

31. Martha Vicinus, *The Industrial Muse: A Study of Nineteenth Century British Working-Class Literature* (London: Croom Helm, 1974), 2; Brian Maidment, *The Poorhouse Fugitives: Self-Taught Poets and Poetry in Victorian England* (London: Carcanet, 1987), 13–14, 209, 211, 213, 227, 231, 243; Brian Maidment, "Prose and Artisan Discourse in Early Victorian Britain," *Prose Studies*, 10 (1987): 31; Zlotnick, " 'A Thousand Times I'd Be a Factory Girl,' " 10, 25 (quotes), 12–17, 20.

32. Edwin Waugh, *Poems and Lancashire Songs* (London: Whittaker, 1859), 6.

33. Brian Hollingworth, ed., *Songs of the People: Lancashire Dialect Poetry of the Industrial Revolution* (Manchester, Eng.: Manchester University Press, 1977), 139.

34. Clark, *Struggle for the Breeches*, passim.

35. "Rambles in Owdham, and Peep into the Workshops," in Hollingworth, *Songs of the People*, 84.

36. Joseph Ramsbottom, "Coaxin'," in Hollingworth, *Songs of the People*, 51–52.

37. Tilly and Scott, *Women, Work, and Family*, 126.

38. Hollingworth, *Songs of the People*, 137.

39. Burgess, "Neaw Aw'm a Married Mon," ibid., 54–55.

40. Burgess, "Ten Heawrs a Day," in Maidment, *The Poorhouse Fugitives*, 91–93; Barrett and McIntosh, "The 'Family Wage,' " 51–72; Robert Gray, "Factory Legislation and the Gendering of Jobs in the North of England, 1830–1860," *Gender and History* 5 (Spring 1993): 56–80; Rose, "Gender Antagonism and Class Conflict."

41. Waugh, *Poems and Songs*, 23–24, 55–58, 62–65, 93–94, 126–128, 135–137; Benjamin Brierley, "God Bless These Poor Wimmen That's Childer!" in John Harland, ed., *Ballads and Songs of Lancashire, Ancient and Modern* (London: George Routledge & Sons, 1875), 402–403; Sam Fitton, "Th'

Childer's Holiday," and James Standing, "Wimmen's Wark Es Niver Done (As if bi a womman hersel)," in Hollingworth, *Songs of the People*, 78–80, 75–78.

42. Standing, "Wimmen's Wark," in Hollingworth, *Songs of the People*, 77, 78.

43. Samuel Laycock, "Th' Courtin' Neet: Part Second," in *The Collected Writings of Samuel Laycock* (London: Simpkin, Marshall, Hamilton, Kent, 1900).

44. Ramsbottom, "Coaxin'," in Hollingworth, *Songs of the People*, 51.

45. Standing, "Wimmen's Wark," ibid., 77.

46. Fitton, "Th' Childer's Holiday," ibid., 78–80; Brierley, "God Bless These Poor Wimmen," in Harland, *Ballads and Songs of Lancashire*, 402.

47. Laycock, "Owd Fogey," "Eawr Jim," "Uncle Dick's Advoice to Wed Men," and "A Little Bit o' Boath Sides," in *Collected Writings*, 67–69, 176–177, 107–109, 170–175.

48. Laycock, "Eawr Jim," ibid., 176.

49. Zlotnick, " 'A Thousand Times I'd Be a Factory Girl,' " 15; Laycock, "Uncle Dick's Advoice to Sengle Men," "Uncle Dick's Advoice to Sengle Women," "Uncle Dick's Advoice to Wed Men," "Uncle Dick's Advoice to Wed Women," and "A Little Bit o' Boath Sides," in *Collected Writings*, 104–106, 101–103 (quote), 107–109, 98–99, 170–175.

50. Laycock, "Uncle Dick's Advoice to Sengle Men," in *Collected Writings*, 105.

51. Laycock, "Uncle Dick's Advoice to Wed Men," and "A Little Bit o' Boath Sides," ibid., 109 (quote), 170–175.

52. Maidment, *The Poorhouse Fugitives*, 227.

53. This paragraph is based on *The Working Man*, February 10, 1866, 91; March 31, 1866, 195–196; April 14, 1866, 227; May 5, 1866, 274–275; May 19, 1866, 315; June 2, 1866, 338–339; June 23, 1866, 387–388.

54. Geoffrey Mitchell, ed., *The Hard Way Up: The Autobiography of Hannah Mitchell, Suffragette and Rebel* (London: Faber & Faber, 1968), 43; Clark, *Struggle for the Breeches*, 264.

NOTES TO PART TWO

1. Historians have judged a decline in work hours and rise in real wages to be two of the most important factors in the creation of a laboring leisure class in the late Victorian period. Taken together with the development of cheaper and more efficient systems of transportation, the growth of a leisure entrepreneurship, a greater acceptance of the social value of recreation, and increased provision of facilities and services, these economic factors are viewed as major stimuli for the growth of a significant market for leisure

among the working classes. On this, see Bailey, *Leisure and Class in Victorian England*, 4–6, 80–91, 105; Cunningham, *Leisure in the Industrial Revolution*, 58–59, 64, 140–191; Walvin, *Beside the Seaside*, 11, 53–57, 62–64; Walvin, *Leisure and Society*, 61–63; John K. Walton, *The English Seaside Resort: A Social History 1750–1914* (New York: St. Martin's Press, 1983), 25–44; Vamplew, *Pay Up and Play the Game*, 52–53; Lowerson and Myerscough, *Time to Spare*, 19–20.

2. Davies, *Leisure, Gender and Poverty*, 55–81; Hart, "Gender and Class Politics," 19–20, 28, 29, 42, 47.

3. On the difficulties women faced in securing material resources and the strategies they used to overcome them, see Ellen Ross, "Survival Networks: Women's Neighbourhood Sharing in London Before World War I," *History Workshop Journal* 15 (1983): 4–27; Melanie Tebbutt, *Making Ends Meet: Pawnbroking and Working Class Credit* (Leicester: Leicester University Press, 1983). See also John Benson, *The Penny Capitalists: A Study of Nineteenth-Century Working Class Entrepreneurs* (New Brunswick, N.J.: Rutgers University Press, 1983).

NOTES TO CHAPTER THREE

1. Charles Booth, ed., *Life and Labour of the People in London*, 3 series, 17 vols. (New York: Macmillan, 1902–1903), ser. 3, vol. 8, 52; Walter Besant, *East London* (London: Chatto & Windus, 1901), 288–289.

2. Helen Bosanquet, *Rich and Poor* (London: Macmillan, 1908), 125. Helen Bosanquet (née Dendy) authored a number of studies on the working classes, both before and after her marriage to Bernard Bosanquet. She published these variously under the names Helen Dendy, Helen Dendy Bosanquet, Helen Bosanquet, and Mrs. Bernard Bosanquet.

3. M. B. Blackie, *National Council of Women of Great Britain Handbook: The Official Report of the Central Conference of Women Workers, 1894* (Ann Arbor, Mich.: University Microfilm 458 P-135, 1980), 142 (hereafter cited as *NCWGB: Report of Central Conference*).

4. W. Hamish Fraser, *The Coming of the Mass Market, 1850–1914* (Hamden, Conn.: Archon Books, 1981), 17 (quote), 66; Terence R. Gourvish, "The Standard of Living, 1890–1914," in Alan O'Day, ed., *The Edwardian Age: Conflict and Stability 1900–1914* (Hamden, Conn.: Archon Books, 1979), 14–15, 19–28, 31; Walvin, *Leisure and Society*, 26, 60–64; Walvin, *Beside the Seaside*, 55–57; George J. Barnsby, "The Standard of Living in the Black Country during the Nineteenth Century," *Economic History Review* 24 (1971), 22–39; Adrian Vinson, "The Edwardians and Poverty: Towards a Minimum Wage," in Donald Read, ed., *Edwardian England* (London: Croom Helm, 1982), 75; Paul Thompson, *The Edwardians: The Remaking of*

British Society (Bloomington: Indiana University Press, 1975), 292–296; Standish Meacham, *A Life Apart: The English Working Class, 1890–1914* (Cambridge, Mass.: Harvard University Press, 1977), 70–72; Vamplew, *Pay Up and Play the Game*, 51; Ross McKibbin, "Why There Was No Marxism in Great Britain," *English Historical Review* 99 (1984), 129.

    5. Cunningham, *Leisure in the Industrial Revolution*, 151; Walvin, *Leisure and Society*, 61; Vamplew, *Pay Up and Play the Game*, 53.

    6. Elizabeth L. Hutchins and Amy Harrison, *A History of Factory Legislation* (London: P. S. King & Son, 1926), passim; Elizabeth L. Hutchins, *Women in Modern Industry* (London: G. Bell & Sons, 1915), 183 (quote), 289–290; Sidney Webb and Beatrice Webb, *Industrial Democracy* (1897; reprint ed., New York: Augustus M. Kelley, 1965), 324, 335–341, 347–353; M. A. Bienefeld, *Working Hours in British Industry: An Economic History* (London: Weidenfeld & Nicolson, 1972), 14–144; Douglas Reid, "The Decline of St. Monday, 1766–1876," *Past and Present* 71 (1976), 76–101; Edward Cadbury, M. Cecile Matheson, and George Shann, *Women's Work and Wages: A Phase of Life in the Industrial City* (Chicago: University of Chicago Press, 1907), 19–43; Cunningham, *Leisure in the Industrial Revolution*, passim; Adelaide Mary Anderson, *Women in the Factory: An Administrative Adventure, 1893 to 1921* (New York: E. P. Dutton, 1922), 24 (quote), 25, 27–28. Rosemary Deem discusses the difficulties with and implications of accepting commonly held ideas about leisure when examining women's lives. See her *All Work and No Play? The Sociology of Women and Leisure* (Milton Keynes, Eng.: Open University Press, 1986). For progressive interpretations of protective legislation, see Hutchins and Harrison, *A History of Factory Legislation;* Cadbury, Matheson, and Shann, *Women's Work and Wages;* Jane Humphries, "Protective Legislation, the Capitalist State and Working-Class Men: The Case of the 1842 Mines Regulation Act," *Feminist Review* 7 (1981), 1–33. On the opposite side of the debate stand Jessie Boucherett, Helen Blackburn, et al., *The Condition of Working Women and the Factory Acts* (London: Elliot Stock, 1896); Bradley, *Men's Work, Women's Work;* Sylvia Walby, *Patriarchy at Work* (Cambridge, Eng.: Polity Press, 1986); Gail Braybon and Penny Summerfield, *Out of the Cage* (London: Pandora, 1987).

    7. Boucherett, Blackburn, et al., *The Condition of Working Women*, 67–68; Royal Commission on Labour, "Reports on Employment of Women," 1893–1894, vol. 37, C. 6894, 17; *Women's Industrial News*, n.s., December 1897, 8–9, 14–16; *Women's Union Journal*, May 1884, 46–47; Clementina Black, *Sweated Industry and the Minimum Wage* (London: Duckworth, 1907), 30; Anderson, *Women in the Factory*, 22, 24–25, 27–29; Webb and Webb, *Industrial Democracy*, 345, 348–351; Cadbury, Matheson, and Shann, *Women's Work and Wages*, 111–112.

    8. The 1911 census revealed that, of the roughly five and a half million

women workers enumerated, most were in occupations such as domestic service, food and retail service industries, and homework, which were not, or only imperfectly, regulated by legislation. Just over half (54 percent) of these were semi-skilled manual workers employed in domestic service, retail trades, and agriculture, 25 percent were skilled manual workers, 6 percent were low-level professionals such as teachers and nurses, 5 percent were unskilled manual workers, 4 percent were employers, and 2 percent were managers. Thompson, *The Edwardians*, 15; Tilley and Scott, *Women, Work, and Family*, 63–77, 123–136; Leonore Davidoff and Belinda Westover, eds., *Our Work, Our Lives, Our Words: Women's History and Women's Work* (Basingstoke, Eng.: Macmillan Education, 1986); Jane Lewis, *Women in England 1870–1950: Sexual Divisions and Social Change* (Brighton, Eng.: Wheatsheaf Books, 1984), 8–74.

9. Ellen W. Darwin, "Domestic Service," *Nineteenth Century*, August 1890, 287; C. Violet Butler, *Domestic Service: An Enquiry by the Women's Industrial Council* (London: G. Bell & Sons, 1916), 9–13.

10. Walvin, *Beside the Seaside*, 58.

11. *Women's Industrial News*, n.s., September 1897, 9; Thompson, *The Edwardians*, 77; *The Woman Worker*, July 1918, 12; *Women's Union Journal*, October 1884, 97; Darwin, "Domestic Service," 288; Butler, *Domestic Service*, 11–12; interview with Ruth Redpath, York Oral History Project (hereafter YOHP), November 1983 (transcript.)

12. Edward Cadbury and George M. Shann, *Sweating* (London: Headley Bros., 1907), 1–4, 8–18, 25–34; Black, *Sweated Industry*, 3, 16, 29, 187–189; Helen Dendy Bosanquet, *The Standard of Life and Other Studies* (London: Macmillan,1898), 159–161; *Women's Union Journal*, October 1884, 97; March 1886, 25; June 1886, 52; Lady Albinia Hobart-Hampden, "The Working Girl of To-Day," *Nineteenth Century*, May 1898, 725; Anderson, *Women in the Factory*, 30–39.

13. Reginald Brabazon, "The Early Closing Movement," *Nineteenth Century*, October 1882, 520.

14. Black, *Sweated Industry*, 48–74; House of Commons, Select Committee on Shop Hours Regulation Bill, *Parliamentary Papers, 1886*, vol. 12, *Minutes of Evidence*, 2, 228, 230, 234, 289, 293, 299, 300, 302–303; "Reports on Employment of Women," *1893–1894*, 3; *Women's Union Journal*, May 1884, 45; March 1887, 17; *Women's Industrial News*, September 1897, 11; Robert Roberts, *A Ragged Schooling: Growing Up in the Classic Slum* (Manchester, Eng.: Manchester University Press, 1976), 9; Cadbury, Matheson, and Shann, *Women's Work and Wages*, 107–110; Peter Bailey, "The Victorian Barmaid as Cultural Prototype," in his *Popular Culture and Performance in the Victorian City* (Cambridge: Cambridge University Press, 1998), 151–167.

15. Anderson, *Women in the Factory*, 60–62, 63 (quote), 64–67, 72, 73, 77.

16. Cadbury, Matheson, and Shann, *Women's Work and Wages*, 119, 135–136.

17. *The Englishwoman's Review*, n.s., January 15, 1900, 9–10.

18. Bosanquet, *The Standard of Life*, 157–158, 172, 176; Cadbury, Matheson, and Shann, *Women's Work and Wages*, 119, 120–121, 122; Benjamin Seebohm Rowntree, *Poverty: A Study of Town Life* (1901; reprint ed., London: Macmillan, 1908), 84. According to Rowntree, if the earnings of domestic servants were included in the calculation, women's average weekly wages in York were 12s.

19. "Reports on Employment of Women," 1893–1894, 34–36, 159; Cadbury, Matheson, and Shann, *Women's Work and Wages*, 329–330; Bosanquet, *The Standard of Life*, 159–161; *Women's Union Journal*, October 15, 1888, 78; March 15, 1886, 25; May 15, 1889, 35–36; C. Violet Butler, "Oxford," in Helen Dendy Bosanquet, ed., *Social Conditions in Provincial Towns* (London: Macmillan, 1912; reprint ed., New York: Garland, 1985); interview with Ruth Redpath, YOHP.

20. Hutchins, *Women in Modern Industry*, 289.

21. Thompson, *The Edwardians*, 15; Rowntree, *Poverty*, 136–138; Margaret Llewellyn Davies, ed., *Maternity: Letters From Working Women* (London: A. R. Mowbray, 1913), 6–7; Magdalen S. Reeves, *Round About a Pound a Week* (London: G. Bell & Sons, 1913; reprint ed., New York Garland, 1980), 3, 64 (quote); Webb and Webb, *Industrial Democracy*, 331; Ross, "Survival Networks," 4–27; Chinn, *They Worked All Their Lives*, passim; Tebbutt, *Making Ends Meet*, 36–67.

22. Caroline Davidson, *A Woman's Work Is Never Done: A History of Housework in the British Isles, 1650–1950* (London: Chatto & Windus, 1982); Susan Strasser, *Never Done: A History of American Housework* (New York: Pantheon, 1982); Thea Thompson, *Edwardian Childhoods* (London: Routledge & Kegan Paul, 1981), 76; Davies, *Maternity*, 153; Clementina Black, *Married Women's Work* (London: G. Bell & Sons, 1915; reprint ed., New York: Garland, 1980), 8; Anderson, *Women in the Factory*, 27.

23. Rowntree's study of York showed that just under 28 percent of the city's population lived in poverty. Almost 10 percent of these he characterized as living in "primary poverty," which he defined as having a total family income insufficient to maintain basic "physical efficiency." The rest were in "secondary poverty," which meant that they had sufficient income to maintain "physical efficiency," but expended some of it on nonessentials. Rowntree attributed over half the cases (51.96 percent) of primary poverty in York to low wages. The rest were caused by family size (22.16 percent), death of the primary wage earner (15.63 percent), illness or old age of primary wage earner (5.11 percent), irregularity of work (2.83 percent), or unemployment of primary wage earner (2.31 percent). Rowntree, *Poverty*,

117, 121; Lynne Lees, "Migration and the Irish Family Economy," unpublished paper, University of Pennsylvania, 1975, cited in Tilly and Scott, *Women, Work, and Family*, 125; Clara Dorothea Rackham, "Cambridge," in Bosanquet, ed., *Social Conditions in Provincial Towns*, 24; Butler, "Oxford," 63–64; Leonore Davidoff, "The Separation of Home and Work? Landladies and Lodgers in Nineteenth and Twentieth Century England," in Sandra Burman, ed., *Fit Work for Women* (New York: St. Martin's, 1979), 64–97; Ada Heather-Bigg, "The Cry Against Home Work," *Nineteenth Century*, December 1884, 985.

24. Cadbury, Matheson, and Shann, *Women's Work and Wages*, 137; Davies, *Maternity*, 6–7.

25. George Acorn, *One of the Multitude: An Autobiography of a Resident of Bethnal Green* (New York: Dodd, Mead, 1912), 5; Roberts, *A Ragged Schooling*, 9, 34; Bosanquet, *Rich and Poor*, 84; C. Madge, *Wartime Patterns of Saving and Spending* (London: National Institute of Economic and Social Research, 1943), quoted in Hart, "Gender and Class Politics," 29; Black, *Married Women's Work*, 10, 48, 257–269; Reeves, *Round About a Pound a Week*, 24, 80–87, 97, 133–142; Rowntree, *Poverty*, 135; Davies, *Maternity*, 159.

26. The quotations are from, respectively, Charles E. B. Russell, *The Social Problems of the North* (London: A. R. Mowbray, 1913), 17; Davies, *Maternity*, 3–5; Cadbury, Matheson, and Shann, *Women's Work and Wages*, 301.

27. Robert R. Dolling, *Ten Years in a Portsmouth Slum* (London: Swann Sonnenschein, 1898), 45; Rowntree, *Poverty*, 77; Reeves, *Round About a Pound a Week*, passim.

28. Thompson, *Edwardian Childhoods*, 79.

29. *Women's Union Journal*, May 1884, 46–47; "Reports on Employment of Women," 3; Cadbury, Matheson, and Shann, *Women's Work and Wages*, 232–233, 237–239.

30. *Women's Union Journal*, April 1884, 33; Mitchell, *The Hard Way Up*, 96; Roberts, *A Ragged Schooling*, 75–76; Rowntree, *Poverty*, 77–78.

31. Thompson, *Edwardian Childhoods*, 79.

32. Mitchell, *The Hard Way Up*, 96.

33. Roberts, *A Ragged Schooling*, 208.

34. Helen Dendy, "The Children of Working London," in Bernard Bosanquet, ed., *Aspects of the Social Problem* (London: Macmillan, 1895), 36.

35. Dolling, *Ten Years in a Portsmouth Slum*, 45; H. Bosanquet, *Rich and Poor*, 123; Rowntree, *Poverty*, 77–78; Mitchell, *The Hard Way Up*, 96.

NOTES TO CHAPTER FOUR

1. Cadbury, Matheson, and Shann, *Women's Work and Wages*, 231–241.

2. Booth, *Life and Labour*, ser. 1, vol. 4, 319, 322–323.

3. Cadbury, Matheson, and Shann, *Women's Work and Wages*, 233–34, 241–247.

4. Collet, "Women's Work," 311–326.

5. Ibid., 322; Mariana Valverde, "The Love of Finery: Fashion and the Fallen Woman in Nineteenth-Century Social Discourse," *Victorian Studies* 28 (1989): 169–170.

6. George Sims, *How the Poor Live* and *Horrible London* (London: Chatto & Windus, 1889; reprint ed., New York: Garland, 1984), 81; Dolling, *Ten Years in a Portsmouth Slum*, 39–40; Dorothy Scannell, *Mother Knew Best: Memoir of a London Girlhood* (New York: Pantheon Books, 1975), 40; Robert Roberts, *The Classic Slum: Salford Life in the First Quarter of the Century* (Manchester, Eng.: Manchester University Press, 1971), 124.

7. Lily H. Montagu, "Popular Amusements for Working Girls," *NCWGB: Report of Central Conference, 1894*, 147; Beatrice Potter, "Pages from a Work-Girl's Diary," *Nineteenth Century*, September 1888, 311.

8. Dolling, *Ten Years in a Portsmouth Slum*, 39–40.

9. Sims, *How the Poor Live*, 84; Lincolnshire Archives, Lincoln, Lindsey Old People's Welfare Committee (hereafter LOPWC), W. J. Burnham, unpublished MSS, 1963.

10. Booth, *Life and Labour*, ser. 2, vol. 8 (1896), 144.

11. Burnham, LOPWC (quote); Montagu, "Popular Amusements for Working Girls," 151; Edith Simcox, "Ideals of Feminine Usefulness," *Fortnightly Review*, January–June, 1880, 669.

12. Jack London, *The People of the Abyss* (New York: Macmillan, 1903; reprint ed., Joseph Simon, 1980), 174–175.

13. Freeman Wills, "Recreative Evening Schools," *Nineteenth Century*, July 1886, 130, 135–136.

14. LOPWC, G. M. Richardson, unpublished MSS, 1963.

15. Russell, *Social Problems of the North*, 102.

16. Montagu, "Popular Amusements for Working Girls," 148.

17. William Baron, "Hawf Past Five at Neet," in Hollingworth, *Songs of the People*, 92.

18. Maude Stanley, "Clubs for Working Girls," *Nineteenth Century*, January 1889, 75, 76; Katie Cowper, "Some Experiences of Work in an East-End District," *Nineteenth Century*, November 1885, 784; Montagu, "Popular Amusements for Working Girls," 147–148, 150, 152; Cadbury, Matheson, and Shann, *Women's Work and Wages*, 198, 232; interview with Ethel Thompson, York, July 1992.

19. Montagu, "Popular Amusements for Working Girls," 150; Stanley, "Clubs for Working Girls," 75.

20. Mitchell, *The Hard Way Up*, 84.

21. Russell, *Social Problems of the North*, 102.

22. Collet, "Women's Work," 322–333; Russell, *Social Problems of the North*, 102–103; Montagu, "Popular Amusements for Working Girls," 152; interview with M. Kendrew, YOHP, September 1983; Mitchell, *The Hard Way Up*, 81–84; Giles, *Women, Identity*, 104–105; Derek Thompson, "Courtship and Marriage in Preston between the Wars," *Oral History* 3 (1975): 39–44; Roberts, *A Woman's Place*, 71–72. On the ritual of bourgeois promenading in nineteenth-century New York City, see David Scobey, "Anatomy of the Promenade: The Politics of Bourgeois Sociability in Nineteenth-Century New York," *Social History* 17 (1992): 203–227.

23. Interview with Ruth Redpath, YOHP, November 1983.

24. Dendy, "The Children of Working London," 42–43.

25. Dolling, *Ten Years in a Portsmouth Slum*, 40.

26. Hugh Shimmin, "Sunday Night on the Landing Stage," in John K. Walton and Alastair Wilcox, eds., *Low Life and Moral Improvement in Mid-Victorian England: Liverpool through the Journalism of Hugh Shimmin* (Leicester, Eng.: Leicester University Press, 1991), 87–89.

27. Thompson, "Courtship and Marriage in Preston," 42.

28. Russell, *Social Problems of the North*, 102–103; interview with M. Kendrew, YOHP, n.d.

29. Booth, *Life and Labour*, ser. 3, vol. 1 (1903), 103.

30. Interview with M. Kendrew, YOHP.

31. NA, M24, 480/A/5 Papers of Sydney Race (c. 1876–1960), Diary, October 5, 1893.

32. Montagu, "Popular Amusements for Working Girls," 152; Mitchell, *The Hard Way Up*, 83–84.

33. NA, Diary of Sydney Race, July 6, 1893, August 23, 1893, October 5, 1893, October 7,1893, October 2, 1896, June 15, 1897.

34. Interviews with Ethel Smith and Gertrude Hutchinson, YOHP, December 1983; Roberts, *A Woman's Place*, 161.

35. Mitchell, *The Hard Way Up*, 70 (quote), 73.

36. Roberts, *A Woman's Place*, 161.

37. Valverde, "The Love of Finery," 170.

38. Montagu, "Popular Amusements for Working Girls," 150.

39. Bosanquet, *The Standard of Life*, 165.

40. Bosanquet, *Rich and Poor*, 104.

41. Montagu, "Popular Amusements for Working Girls," 150.

42. Besant, *East London*, 295.

43. Bosanquet, *The Standard of Life*, 176.

44. Collet, "Women's Work," 320–321.

45. Cadbury, Matheson, and Shann, *Women's Work and Wages*, 196–198.

46. Maude Stanley, *Clubs for Working Girls* (London: Macmillan, 1890), 263.

47. Lilian Montagu, *My Club and I: The Story of the West Central Jewish Club* (London: Herbert Joseph, 1943), 47; interview with Mary Kirby, YOHP, December 1985, January 1986; interview with Margaret Hutchinson, YOHP, July 1983.

48. Jill Liddington, *The Life and Times of a Respectable Rebel: Selina Cooper 1864–1946* (London: Virago, 1984), 24; Kathleen Dayus, *Where There's Life* (London: Virago, 1985), 108 (quote), 91–107, 109–113, 124–128.

49. Interview with Margaret Hutchinson, YOHP, July 1983.

50. *Women's Union Journal*, October 1883, 90; Cowper, "Work in an East-End District," 783 (quotes).

51. On the blurring of identities between prostitutes and other "public" women, see Walkowitz, *City of Dreadful Delight*, 50.

52. Hugh Shimmin, *Liverpool Life: Its Pleasures, Practices, and Pastimes* (Liverpool: Egerton Smith, 1856; reprint ed., New York: Garland, 1985), 10.

53. Montagu, "Popular Amusements for Working Girls," 151; Sims, *How the Poor Live*, 84. Emphasis in original.

54. House of Commons, Select Committee on Regulation of Public Houses, Hotels, Beer-Shops, Dancing Saloons, Coffee-Houses, Theatres and Places of Public Entertainment, *Parliamentary Papers, 1852–53*, vol. 37, *Minutes of Evidence*, 17, 20, 21, 60.

55. Shimmin, *Liverpool Life*, 25.

56. Select Committee on Public Houses, *1852–53*, 192.

57. House of Commons, Select Committee on Regulation of Public Houses, Hotels, Beer-Shops, Dancing Saloons, Coffee-Houses, Theatres and Places of Public Entertainment, *Parliamentary Papers, 1854*, vol. 14, *Minutes of Evidence*, 334.

58. *Women's Union Journal*, September 1884, 80.

59. Shimmin, *Liverpool Life*, 45–50.

60. Ibid., 15–17, 20–32, 38–44, 46–49 (quotes).

61. James Greenwood, *The Wilds of London* (London: Chatto & Windus, 1874; reprint ed., New York: Garland, 1985), 13 (quote), 12–20.

62. NA, Diary of Sydney Race, October 6, 1894, December 8, 1894, December 26, 1894.

63. Dagmar Kift, *The Victorian Music Hall: Culture, Class and Conflict*, trans. Roy Kift (Cambridge: Cambridge University Press, 1996), 1.

64. Shimmin, *Liverpool Life*, 26–38.

65. J. S. Bratton, ed., *Music Hall: Performance and Style* (Milton Keynes, Eng.: Open University Press, 1986), x–xii; Peter Bailey, ed., *Music Hall: The Business of Pleasure* (Milton Keynes, Eng.: Open University Press, 1986), vii–xxiii; John Earl, "Building the Halls," in Bailey, *Music Hall*, 1–32; Susan Pennybacker, " 'It Was Not What She Said, But the Way in Which She Said It': The London County Council and the Music Halls," in Bailey, *Music Hall*, 129.

66. Bosanquet, *Rich and Poor*, 123–124.

67. Sims, *How the Poor Live*, 82–83.

68. Theatres and Music Halls Committee of the London County Council, *Presented Papers*, Canterbury Music Hall, 1888–1904, February 23, 1891, August 9, 1891, quoted in Pennybacker, "It Was Not What She Said," 129; Cadbury, Matheson, and Shann, *Women's Work and Wages*, 242; Montagu, "Popular Amusements for Working Girls," 149, 151.

69. Pennybacker, "It Was Not What She Said," 118–120, 126–134; Dagmar Hoher, "The Composition of Music Hall Audiences," in Bailey, *Music Hall*, 74, 81, 84–85; Russell, *Social Problems of the North*, 95–96; Dendy, "The Children of Working London," 36.

70. Sheffield Archives (hereafter SA), CA 8–14, Borough of Sheffield, Minutes of Stage Plays Licensing Committee, February 2, 1892, July 31, 1901, June 2, 1902.

71. Hoher, "The Composition of Music Hall Audiences"; 75, 80–84; Kift, *The Victorian Music Hall*, 64, 72. On the varying employment opportunities for women in Liverpool and the cotton textile towns, see John K. Walton, *Lancashire: A Social History, 1558–1939* (Manchester, Eng.: Manchester University Press, 1987), 175–180, 286–290.

72. M. Brown, *Views and Opinions* (London, 1866), 255, quoted in Kift, *The Victorian Music Hall*, 72.

73. Mitchell, *The Hard Way Up*, 76.

74. Peter Clark, *The English Alehouse: A Social History, 1200–1830* (London: Longman, 1983), 282, 287–288, 311–312, 320–322; Brian Harrison, *Drink and the Victorians: The Temperance Question in England 1815–1872* (Pittsburgh: University of Pittsburgh Press, 1971), passim; Roberts, *A Woman's Place*, 72, 122–124.

75. Interview with Rose Sturdy, YOHP, November 1984, January 1985.

76. Kathleen M. Townend, "Methods of Recreation as They Affect the Causes of Intemperance amongst Women," *NCWGB, Report of Central Conference, 1894*, 141.

77. Rowntree, *Poverty*, 313.

78. Ibid., 370.

79. Sims, *How the Poor Live*, 82; Rowntree, *Poverty*, 310–311.

80. Booth, *Life and Labour*, ser. 3, vol. 8, 59, 61.

81. Collet, "Women's Work," 316–317; Helen Dendy Bosanquet, "The Position of Women in Industry," in Bosanquet, *Aspects of the Social Problem*, 66, 70; North East Lincolnshire Archives, Grimsby, Apprenticeship Indenture for Eliza Roberts, 1891.

82. Cadbury, Matheson, and Shann, *Women's Work and Wages*, 194.

83. Ibid., 195–197, 239.

84. Montagu, "Popular Amusements for Working Girls," 151–152.

85. Booth, *Life and Labour*, ser. 3, vol. 8, 48–50.

86. NA, DD 1895/4/1, Letter from Hilda to Eric, April 29, 1917.

87. NA, Diary of Sydney Race, February 1895; January 30, 1897; June 15, 1897; Leicestershire Record Office (hereafter LRO), DE 4691, letters of reference for May Greaves, picture pianist, Midland Electric Theatres, 1911, Provincial Cinematograph Theatres Ltd., May 8, 1911, The Lyric (Leicester) Ltd., February 6, 1915; MISC 139/3, Handbill for Silver Street Cinema, Leicester, 1896; DE 2768/4/2, program for picture entertainment and sacred concert at Evington Cinema, Leicester, February 18, 1917; *Retford, Gainsborough, and Worksop Times*, January 30, 1903, 6; December 25, 1908, 7.

88. *Girls' Club News*, November 1916, 5–7.

89. There were two film versions of *Iris*, one made in 1916, and the other, entitled *A Slave of Vanity*, made in 1920. John Dawick, *Pinero: A Theatrical Life* (Boulder: University Press of Colorado, 1993), 346, 348, 407.

90. *New York World*, September 24, 1902, 7, quoted ibid., 257.

91. William W. Massee, "Arthur Wing Pinero," in Oscar Herrmann, ed., *Living Dramatists: Pinero, Ibsen, D'Annunzio* (New York: Brentano's, 1905), 3.

92. Arthur Wing Pinero, *Iris: A Drama in Five Acts* (Boston: Walter H. Baker, 1905); Arthur Wing Pinero, *Letty: An Original Drama in Four Acts and an Epilogue*, in Clayton Hamilton, ed., *The Social Plays of Arthur Wing Pinero*, 4 vols. (New York: E. P. Dutton, 1919), vol. 3, 25–239.

93. George Bernard Shaw to Arthur Pinero, November 5, 1915, quoted in Dawick, *Pinero*, 348.

94. Hamilton, *The Social Plays of Pinero*, vol. 3, 190, 216–239.

95. Ross, *Love and Toil*, 5.

96. Collet, "Women's Work," 325; Potter, "Pages from a Work-Girl's Diary," 311.

97. Blackie, *NCWGB, Report of Central Conference, 1894*, 142–144.

98. Dendy, "The Children of Working London," 36.

99. Bosanquet, *Rich and Poor*, 102.

100. Collet, "Women's Work," 325–326; Potter, "Pages from a Work-Girl's Diary," 311; Blackie, *NCWGB, Report of Central Conference, 1894*, 142.

101. House of Lords, Select Committee for Inquiring into the Prevalence of Habits of Intemperance, and Effects of Recent Legislation, *Parliamentary Papers, 1878–79*, vol. 10, *Minutes of Evidence*, ix, xlvi.

102. House of Commons, Memorials from Manchester, Salford, Birmingham, and Bristol, Praying for the Alteration in Law of Granting of Licenses for Sale of Spirits, Wine and Beer for Consumption Off-Premises, *Parliamentary Papers, 1882*, vol. 64.

103. Rowntree, *Poverty*, 371–373; Booth, *Life and Labour*, ser. 3, vol. 8, 61–65.

104. Robert Harborough Sherard, *The Child-Slaves of Britain* (London: Hurst & Blackwell, 1905), 101; Booth, *Life and Labour*, ser. 3, vol. 8, 62.

105. Kathleen Dayus, *Her People* (London: Virago, 1982), 63.

106. Blackie, *NCWGB, Report of Central Conference, 1894*, 143; Booth, *Life and Labour*, ser. 3, vol. 8, 59–60.

107. Select Committee on Public Houses, *1854*, 331–332.

108. Booth, *Life and Labour*, ser. 3, vol. 8, 61–63.

109. Select Committee Report on Public Houses, *1854*, 337, 338, 382; Select Committee on Intemperance, *1878–79*, 124.

110. Ross, *Love and Toil*, 140; Ross McKibbin, *The Ideologies of Class: Social Relations in Britain, 1880–1950* (Oxford: Clarendon Press, 1990), 189; George R. Sims, *The Cry of the Children* (London: The Tribune, 1907), 14; Joseph Rowntree and Arthur Sherwell, *The Temperance Problem and Social Reform* (London, Hodder & Stoughton, 1889).

111. Booth, *Life and Labour*, ser. 3, vol. 8, 63.

112. Greenwood, *The Wilds of London*, 348–349.

113. Shimmin, *Liverpool Life*, 16; Walton and Wilcox, *Low Life and Moral Improvement*, 122–128.

114. Select Committee on Intemperance, *1878–79*, xlvi (quote); Memorials from Manchester, Salford, Birmingham, and Bristol, *1882*, 504, 506–507, 508.

115. Walton and Wilcox, *Low Life and Moral Improvement*, 144.

116. Dayus, *Where There's Life*, 130–131.

117. C. F. G. Masterman, *From the Abyss: Of Its Inhabitants by One of Them* (London: R. Brimley Johnson, 1902; reprint ed., New York: Garland, 1980), 85–86, 88.

118. Sherard, *Child-Slaves of Britain*, 101.

119. Booth, *Life and Labour*, ser. 3, vol. 8, 65–68; Shimmin, *Liverpool Life*, 16–17, 24, 85; Collet, "Women's Work," 324; Lady Laura Ridding, "The Relation of Amusements to Life," *NCWGB, Report of Central Conference, 1902*, 145.

120. Flora Thompson, *Lark Rise to Candleford: A Trilogy* (London: Oxford University Press, 1945; reprint ed., 1979), 102; Stephen Reynolds, *A Poor Man's House* (London: John Lane, 1902; reprint ed., Oxford: Oxford University Press, 1982), 127.

121. Dolling, *Ten Years in a Portsmouth Slum*, 46.

NOTES TO CHAPTER FIVE

1. Jordan, *The Degeneracy Crisis and Victorian Youth;* Dyhouse, *Girls Growing Up*, 79–114; Purvis, *Hard Lives*, 63–70; Davin, "Imperialism and Motherhood," 9–65; Catriona M. Parratt, " 'The Making of the Healthy and the

Happy Home': Recreation, Education, and the Production of Working-Class Womanhood at the Rowntree Cocoa Works, York, c. 1898–1914," in Jack Williams and Jeff Hill, eds., *Sport and Social Identity in the North of England* (Keele, Eng.: University of Keele Press, 1996), 53–83; Wright, *The Great Unwashed*, 37–41, 48; Dendy, "The Children of Working London," 33; Butler, *Domestic Service*, 9–12, 130; Darwin, "Domestic Service," 283–293; Clementina Black, "The Dislike to Domestic Service," *Nineteenth Century*, March 1893, 454–456; Hobart-Hampden, "The Working Girl of To-Day," 724 (quote).

2. Besant, *East London*, 124, 127–128.

3. On female philanthropy and reformism, see, for example, Barbara Leslie Epstein, *The Politics of Domesticity: Women, Evangelism, and Temperance in Nineteenth-Century America* (Middletown, Conn.: Wesleyan University Press, 1981); Frank K. Prochaska, *Women and Philanthropy in Nineteenth-Century England* (Oxford: Clarendon Press, 1980); Lori D. Ginzberg, *Women and the Work of Benevolence: Morality, Politics, and Class in the Nineteenth-Century United States* (New Haven: Yale University Press, 1990); Kathleen D. McCarthy, ed., *Lady Bountiful Revisited: Women, Philanthropy, and Power* (New Brunswick, N.J.: Rutgers University Press, 1990); Maria Luddy, *Women and Philanthropy in Nineteenth-Century Ireland* (Cambridge: Cambridge University Press, 1995). For similar concerns about young working women in the United States and Canada, see, for example, Meyerowitz, *Women Adrift*, 46–53; Peiss, *Cheap Amusements*, 164–171; Alexander, *The "Girl Problem,"* 11–66; Strange, *Toronto's Girl Problem*.

4. Townend, "Methods of Recreation," 139; Ridding, "The Relation of Amusements to Life," *1902*, 131 (quote); *Women's Union Journal*, December 1883, 112. On the widespread children's temperance organization, the Band of Hope, see Lilian Lewis Shiman, "The Band of Hope Movement: Respectable Recreation for Working-Class Children," *Victorian Studies* 17 (1973): 49–74.

5. Hobart-Hampden, "The Working Girl of To-Day," 726 (quote). Instructing and edifying the working classes through personal example was a primary impetus behind the settlement house movement that began in the 1880s. The first London settlement was Toynbee Hall, established in Whitechapel in 1884 and staffed by Oxbridge students. The first women's settlement was the Women's University Settlement, founded in 1887. Girls' clubs, mothers' meetings, and other social and educational classes were among the services that settlements provided to working-class communities. On the women's settlement movement, see Martha Vicinus, *Independent Women: Work and Community for Single Women 1850–1920* (Chicago: University of Chicago Press, 1985), 211–246.

6. Hobart-Hampden, "The Working Girl of To-Day," 724, 730.

7. Stanley, "Clubs for Working Girls," 74, 77.

8. Blackie, Discussion of Townend, "Methods of Recreation," *NCWGB, Report of Central Conference, 1894*, 142.

9. Townend, "Methods of Recreation," 139, 141 (quotes). See also *Englishwoman's Review*, January 15, 1900, 67–68; Cadbury, Matheson, and Shann, *Women's Work and Wages*, 270–271; Rackham, "Cambridge," 33.

10. Hobart-Hampden, "The Working Girl of To-Day," 724.

11. Montagu, "Popular Amusements for Working Girls," 153.

12. Dendy, "The Children of Working London," 33 (quote). On efforts to "tame" or "civilize" popular recreation, see, for example, Howkins, "The Taming of Whitsun," 187–208, and Golby and Purdue, *The Civilisation of the Crowd*, which challenges the interpretation of a traditional leisure culture in retreat as advanced in Malcolmson, *Popular Recreations in English Society*.

13. Townend, "Methods of Recreation," 141.

14. Montagu, "Popular Amusements for Working Girls," 151, 153.

15. Stanley, "Clubs for Working Girls", 82; Hobart-Hampden, "The Working Girl of To-Day," 727; Potter, "Pages from a Work-Girl's Diary," 311, (quote).

16. Hobart-Hampden, "The Working Girl of To-Day," 727, 729.

17. Russell, *Social Problems of the North*, 94.

18. Stanley, "Clubs for Working Girls," 74.

19. The term "dark continent" is from the journalist George Sims's *How the Poor Live*, 1. *How the Poor Live* was one of a number of journalistic exposés of the final decades of the nineteenth century in which the East and West ends of London, and their inhabitants, represented the divisions and cultural and racial hierarchies of England and its Empire. For more on Sims and other similar constructions of working-class London, see Walkowitz, *City of Dreadful Delight*, 21, 26–39; Vicinus, *Independent Women*, 219–221; Ellen Ross, "Good and Bad Mothers: Lady Philanthropists and London Housewives before the First World War," in McCarthy, *Lady Bountiful Revisited*, 174; Ross, *Love and Toil*, 11. See also Besant, *East London*, 128–129, 295. The sexually charged and voyeuristic tone of Besant's description of "Liz" was a convention employed by many upper- and middle-class male observers of working-class women. On this, see Leonore Davidoff, "Gender and Class in Victorian England: The Diaries of Arthur J. Munby and Hannah Cullwick," *Feminist Studies* 5 (1979): 87–141.

20. Stanley, "Clubs for Working Girls," 75.

21. Hobart-Hampden, "The Working Girl of To-Day," 726.

22. Potter, "Pages from a Work-Girl's Diary," 311.

23. Ibid.

24. More or less elaborate versions of this narrative of popular leisure

abound in the published sources. See, especially, Townend, "Methods of Recreation," 137–142; Stanley, "Clubs for Working Girls," 74–77, 82; Samuel Smith, "Social Reform," *Nineteenth Century*, January 1883, 910; Theresa Shrewsbury, "Prevention," *Nineteenth Century*, December 1885, 957–964; Hobart-Hampden, "The Working Girl of To-Day," 725–729; Montagu, "Popular Amusements for Working Girls," 147–154, 153; Ridding, "The Relation of Amusements to Life," 129–130; Dolling, *Ten Years in a Portsmouth Slum*, 38; *Women's Union Journal*, September 1884, 80; Bosanquet, *Rich and Poor*, 120; Blackie, *NCWGB, Report of Central Conference, 1894*, 142–145; Besant, *East London*, 119–129; Dendy, "The Children of Working London," 29–43.

25. Cadbury, Matheson, and Shann, *Women's Work and Wages*, 196.

26. Stanley, "Clubs for Working Girls," 74–77.

27. Ibid.

28. Hobart-Hampden, "The Working Girl of To-Day," 726, 728.

29. Simcox, "Ideals of Feminine Usefulness," 669.

30. Montagu, "Popular Amusements for Working Girls," 149, 153.

31. Brian Harrison, "For Church, Queen and Family: The Girls' Friendly Society 1874–1920," *Past and Present* 61 (1973): 107–138, 109 (quote); Shrewsbury, "Prevention," 957–964. On the GFS, see also Dyhouse, *Girls Growing Up*, 108–110.

32. NA, DD 716/51, Papers of Miss Marianne Harriet Mason, manuscript of autobiography, "A Pioneer Life"; Cadbury, Matheson, and Shann, *Women's Work and Wages*, 268–269, 275; LRO, Wigston Magna, England, 16 D58/1a, Minute Book and Records, Leicester Branch, National Council of Women, Minutes of Annual Meeting, March 18, 1919.

33. Bristol Record Office (hereafter BRO), Bristol, England, 32132, Bristol Association of Working Girls' Clubs, Minutes of Council Meetings and of Management Committee Meetings, 1896–1901, June 10, 1898, November 1, 1900; NA, DD 765/17, Hyson Green Home, Girls' Evening Home, Minute Book, September 22, 1894, September 28, 1909, November 17, 1909; Dyhouse, *Girls Growing Up*, 109–110.

34. Harrison, "For Church, Queen and Family," 109–111.

35. *Women's Union Journal*, June 1883, 49; July 1883, 58; August 1883, 66; December 1883, 112; September 1884, 80; February 1885, 10; April 1885, 26; June 1886, 50; March 1887, 19; December 1888, 91; February 1889, 9; July 1890, 56; *Women's Industrial News*, September 1897, 14, 28; March 1898, 28–29.

36. Townend, "Methods of Recreation," 139, 142, 145.

37. Dolling, *Ten Years in a Portsmouth Slum*, 24, 41, 46 (quote); Stanley, *Clubs for Working Girls*, 184.

38. Booth, *Life and Labour*, ser. 3, vol. 7, 40, 264, 277, 315, 355; Vicinus, *Independent Women*, 212, 232–234, 241.

39. Cadbury, Matheson, and Shann, *Women's Work and Wages*, 268–279.

40. NA, DD 76, Reports, Etc., of Nottingham Girls' Evening Homes and Clubs, c. 1889–1939; DD 765/2, "Report for the Year 1906–1907 of the Girls' Evening Homes, Talbot Street, Cross Street, Chelsea Street (Mr. Jardine's), Ruddington and Hyson Green, Nottingham," 8, 19.

41. *Cocoa Works' Magazine: A Journal in the Interests of the Employees of Rowntree & Co., Ltd.*, York (hereafter *CWM*), May 1915, 1757–1759; interview with Ethel Smith, YOHP, November 1983, transcript, 4.

42. *Retford, Gainsborough, and Worksop Times*, January 7, 1910, 7; LRO, DE2106/59, Newspaper Extracts Regarding Loughborough Girls' Club and Evening Home, 1891–1913; LRO, DE2032/3, "Programme of Sacred Concert in Aid of Funds of the Leicester Poor Boys' and Girls' Summer Camp and Institute," January 18, 1914; Dartford College Archives (hereafter DCA), University of Greenwich, England, "Madame Bergman Osterberg's Physical Training College, Report for 1895," 26, 29, 30–31, 32, 33; Anstey College Archives (hereafter ACA), *Anstey Physical Training College Magazine*, Autumn 1905, 17–28, Summer 1906, 6–8, courtesy of Mrs. Frankie Calland, Secretary of the Anstey Association; Chelsea College Archives (hereafter CCA), University of Brighton, England, Dorette Wilke, "Physical Training in Girls' Clubs," *Girls' Club News*, November 1916, 3–5; and "Physical Training for Girls," manuscript draft of paper presented to the Japan British Exhibition, Women's Congress, July 9, 1910. See also Colin Crunden, *A History of Anstey College of Physical Education* (Sutton Coldfield, Eng.: Anstey College of Physical Education, 1974), 10, 11, 14, 16, 18–21; Ida M. Webb, "The History of Chelsea College of Physical Education with Special Reference to Curriculum Development, 1898–1973" (Ph.D. dissertation, University of Leicester, Eng., 1977), 41, 48–50, 51, 52, 58, 139, 153.

43. LRO, *Loughborough Evening Herald*, November 9, 1905.

44. Cadbury, Matheson, and Shann, *Women's Work and Wages*, 271–272.

45. Townend, "Methods of Recreation," 141.

46. Harrison, "For Church, Queen and Family," 116.

47. Ibid., 111.

48. Shrewsbury, "Prevention," 961; *Retford and Gainsborough Times*, May 8, 1908, 5.

49. *Women's Industrial News*, March 1898, 28.

50. Edward G. Salmon, "What Girls Read," *Nineteenth Century*, October 1886, 523.

51. Stanley, *Clubs for Working Girls*, 39–41.

52. Townend, "Methods of Recreation," 139; Cadbury, Matheson, and Shann, *Women's Work and Wages*, 273.

53. Montagu, *My Club and I*, 25–26.

54. Montagu, "Popular Amusements for Working Girls," 148 (quote); Montagu, *My Club and I*, 35.

55. Dolling, *Ten Years in a Portsmouth Slum,* 38; Cadbury, Matheson, and Shann, *Women's Work and Wages,* 242.

56. LRO, *Loughborough Evening Herald,* November 11, 1905.

57. LRO, *Loughborough Evening Herald,* November 30, 1911.

58. Montagu, "Popular Amusements for Working Girls," 149.

59. LRO, *Loughborough Evening Herald,* November 9, 1905; Hobart-Hampden, "The Working Girl of To-Day," 728–729.

60. Stanley, *Clubs for Working Girls,* 232–236.

61. LRO, *Loughborough Evening Herald,* March 4, 1909.

62. Cadbury, Matheson, and Shann, *Women's Work and Wages,* 273; Montagu, *My Club and I,* 28.

63. NA, "Report for the Year 1906–1907 of the Girls' Evening Homes," 16; LRO, *Loughborough Evening Herald,* January 25, 1912.

64. For some sense of this contrast, see, for example, Reynolds, *A Poor Man's House;* Jane Ellen Panton, *From Kitchen to Garrett: Hints for Young Householders* (London: E. Nash, 1908).

65. Stanley, *Clubs for Working Girls,* 38; NA, Hyson Green Evening Home, Minute Book, October 9, 1889; NA, "Report for the Year 1906–1907 of the Girls' Evening Homes," 6.

66. LRO, *Loughborough Evening Herald,* October 8, 1891, December 7, 1893, November 17, 1904, December 15, 1904.

67. LRO, *Loughborough Evening Herald,* February 21, 1907, April 10, 1907.

68. NA, "Report for the Year 1906–1907 of the Girls' Evening Homes," 16.

69. NA, Hyson Green Evening Home, Minute Book, September 28, 1889, December 1, 1892, January 6, 1894, December 15, 1894, October 4, 1895, October 11, 1895, October 14, 1895, October 5, 1906, September 16, 1908.

70. NA, Hyson Green Evening Home, Minute Book, January 6, 1894, February 8, 1894, December 15, 1894, December 21, 1894, January 26, 1895, October 14, 1895, December 19, 1895.

71. Panton, *From Kitchen to Garrett,* 231.

72. Wills, "Recreative Evening Schools," 135.

73. NA, Hyson Green Evening Home, Minute Book, September 25, 1896, January 19, 1898.

74. Montagu, *My Club and I,* 52.

75. Ibid., 10–11, 19, 22, 26, 141–142.

76. Shrewsbury, "Prevention," 962.

77. Dolling, *Ten Years in a Portsmouth Slum,* 24, 28.

78. Townend, "Methods of Recreation," 139; Hobart-Hampden, "The Working Girl of To-Day," 728.

79. *Women's Union Journal*, July 1890, 56.

80. Cadbury, Matheson, and Shann, *Women's Work and Wages*, 268–269.

81. Stanley, *Clubs for Working Girls*, 17–18.

82. *Women's Union Journal*, October 1883, 81.

83. CCA, Wilke, manuscript draft of paper presented to the National Organisation of Girls' Clubs, October 15, 1912; Stanley, *Clubs for Working Girls*, 155.

84. Shrewsbury, "Prevention," 958–959.

85. *Retford and Gainsborough Times*, May 8, 1908, 5.

86. BRO, Bristol Association of Working Girls' Clubs, Minutes of Council Meetings and of Management Committee Meetings, 1896–1901, June 10, 1898, November 1, 1900 (quotes); NA, Hyson Green Evening Home, Minute Book, September 22, 1894, September 28, 1909, November 17, 1909.

87. *Englishwoman's Review*, January 15, 1900, 67–68.

88. *CWM*, May 1915, 1757–1759.

89. Stanley, *Clubs for Working Girls*, 145.

90. Hobart-Hampden, "The Working Girl of To-Day," 728, 729 (quotes); *CWM*, December 1911, 1198.

91. NA, "Report for the Year 1906–1907 of the Girls' Evening Homes," 11, 17; NA, Hyson Green Evening Home, Minute Book, September 28, 1889, September 29, 1890, November 15, 1894, November 26, 1895, March 6, 1896; NA, Hyson Green Evening Home, "Extracts from Reports," 1911–1912, 1912–1913. Beginning with the 1911–1912 season, the executive committee of the Hyson Green Evening Home ceased taking minutes of its meetings in favor of brief summaries of the preceding year's activities. LRO, *Loughborough Evening Herald*, November 9, 1905, April 10, 1907, October 15, 1908, November 30, 1911.

92. Montagu, *My Club and I*, 19, 43–48.

93. NA, "Report for the Year 1906–1907 of the Girls' Evening Homes," 7, 8, 16; NA, Hyson Green Evening Home, Minute Book, October 26, 1891, March 8, 1894, November 15, 1894, April 9, 1896, April 15, 1897, March 2, 1908, March 19, 1908, July 11, 1908, January 18, 1909.

94. NA, Hyson Green Evening Home, Minute Book, April 15, 1897; BRO, Bristol Association of Working Girls' Clubs, Minutes of Meetings, November 1, 1900 (quote); *Women's Union Journal*, February 1885, 14; Townend, "Methods of Recreation," 141.

95. BRO, Bristol Association of Working Girls' Clubs, Minutes of Meetings, December 12, 1901, January 31, 1901.

96. NA, "Report for the Year 1906–1907 of the Girls' Evening Homes," 9, 12, 14, 16, 21; NA, Hyson Green Evening Home, Minute Book, September 28, 1889, September 29, 1890, January 17, 1891, October 20, 1893, No-

vember 15, 1894, March 6, 1896, December 7, 1906, October 2, 1907, September 16, 1908, October 13, 1909; NA, Hyson Green Evening Home, "Extracts from Reports, 1911–1912."

97. NA, "Report for the Year 1906–1907 of the Girls' Evening Homes," 10.

98. *CWM*, May 1915, 1758.

99. Montagu, *My Club and I*, 25, 52–59; Stanley, *Clubs for Working Girls*, 49–85.

100. *CWM*, May 1915, 1757–1759; Stanley, *Clubs for Working Girls*, 29.

101. Stanley, *Clubs for Working Girls*, 27, 29; Montagu, *My Club and I*, 23, 39; *CWM*, May 1915, 1757–1759.

102. Cowper, "Work in an East-End District," 793.

103. Stanley, *Clubs for Working Girls*, 26–27.

104. Hobart-Hampden, "The Working Girl of To-Day," 729–730.

105. Stanley, *Clubs for Working Girls*, 26–27.

106. Cowper, "Work in an East-End District," 784.

107. NA, Hyson Green Evening Home, Minute Book, September 29, 1890, September 17, 1897, September 23, 1897.

108. NA, "Report for the Year 1906–1907 of the Girls' Evening Homes," 10, 11, 16, 19.

109. Montagu, *My Club and I*, 59.

110. Ibid., 24, 26–28, 35.

111. Stanley, *Clubs for Working Girls*, 16–40.

112. L. E. Crowdy, "Music and Dancing in Girls' Clubs," *Journal of Scientific Physical Training* 8 (1916): 67.

113. Stanley, *Clubs for Working Girls*, 122–130.

114. Montagu, "Popular Amusements for Working Girls," 151.

115. Crowdy, "Music and Dancing in Girls' Clubs," 68.

116. Stanley, *Clubs for Working Girls*, 124; NA, "Report for the Year 1906–1907 of the Girls' Evening Homes," 14, 15; Crowdy, "Music and Dancing in Girls' Clubs," 67; Wilke, "Physical Training in Girls' Clubs," *Girls' Club News*, November 1916, 11, 13.

117. Crowdy, "Music and Dancing in Girls' Clubs," 68, 69.

118. Montagu, *My Club and I*, 73, 75, 78, 81, 82; Stanley, *Clubs for Working Girls*, 120–125, 127, 129.

119. NA, Hyson Green Evening Home, Minute Book, March 22, 1897, April 15, 1897, April 19, 1897, September 17, 1897, December 16, 1897, January 19, 1898, October 5, 1906; NA, "Extracts from Girls' Evening Home Reports," 1911–1916.

120. Murolo, *The Common Ground of Womanhood*.

121. Walkowitz, *City of Dreadful Delight*, 52–59; Vicinus, *Independent Women*, 219–227.

122. Prochaska, *Women and Philanthropy*, 5, 10.

123. Walkowitz, *City of Dreadful Delight*, 53; Patricia Hollis, *Ladies Elect: Women in English Local Government 1865–1914* (Oxford: Clarendon Press, 1987), 11.

124. Vicinus, *Independent Women*, 220. On the themes of self-fulfillment and self-interest in women's philanthropy and social work, see Julia Parker, *Women and Welfare: Ten Victorian Women in Public Social Service* (New York: St. Martin's Press, 1989), 20, 38; Vicinus, *Independent Women*, 212; Walkowitz, *City of Dreadful Delight*, 52–59; Prochaska, *Women and Philanthropy*, 1–17; Ross, "Good and Bad Mothers," 176; Luddy, *Women and Philanthropy in Ireland*, 24, 48, 56.

125. Lilian H. Montagu, "The Responsibility of Leisure," *NCWGB, Report of Central Conference, 1912*, 125; Emily Kinnaird, "The Right Use of Leisure," *NCWGB, Report of Central Conference, 1900*, 141.

126. Hobart-Hampden, "The Working Girl of To-Day," 725; Ellen Chase, *Tennant Friends in Old Deptford* (London: Williams and Norgate, 1929), 57, 61, 106; Margaret Nevinson, *Life's Fitful Fever, A Volume of Memoirs* (London: A. & C. Black, 1926), 82; DCA, "Bergman Osterberg's College Report for 1895," 26, 29, 32; Norman MacKenzie and Jeanne MacKenzie, eds., *The Diary of Beatrice Webb*, vol. 1, 1873–1892: *Glitter Around and Darkness Within* (Cambridge, Mass.: Belknap Press, 1982), 31, 132, 185–187, 208.

192. MacKenzie and MacKenzie, *The Diary of Beatrice Webb*, vol. 1, 7.

128. Montagu, "The Responsibility of Leisure," 119.

NOTES TO CHAPTER SIX

1. Benjamin Seebohm Rowntree, *The Human Factor in Business* (London: Longmans, Green, 1921), 101.

2. Emily Rowntree, "Cookery Notes," *CWM*, June 1902, 45.

3. *CWM*, August 1905, 74; September 1905, 78–79.

4. On the industrial and social programs of the Rowntree and Cadbury families, see also Charles Dellheim, "The Creation of a Company Culture: Cadbury's, 1861–1931," *American Historical Review* 92 (February 1987): 13–23; Robert Fitzgerald, *British Labour Management and Industrial Welfare 1846–1939* (London: Croom Helm, 1988); Asa Briggs, *Social Thought and Social Action: A Study of the Work of Seebohm Rowntree, 1871–1954* (London: Longmans, Green, 1961); Edward Cadbury, *Experiments in Industrial Organization* (London: Longmans, Green, 1912).

5. *CWM*, June 1913, 1500.

6. Robert Fitzgerald, *Rowntree and the Marketing Revolution, 1862–1969* (Cambridge: Cambridge University Press, 1995), 47.

7. *CWM*, February 1904, 147–148.

8. Charles Feinstein, *York 1831–1981: 150 Years of Scientific and Social Change* (York, Eng.: Ebor Press, 1981), 123–125; Gillian Wagner, *The Chocolate Conscience* (London: Chatto & Windus, 1987), 24–30.

9. Anne Vernon, *A Quaker Businessman: The Life of Joseph Rowntree, 1836–1925* (London: Allen and Unwin, 1958), 97–98, 126–128; Fitzgerald, *Rowntree and the Marketing Revolution*, 225, 238; *CWM*, March 1902, 2 (quotes).

10. *CWM*, June 1913, 1500.

11. Chris Smith, John Child, and Michael Rowlinson, *Reshaping Work: The Cadbury Experience* (Cambridge: Cambridge University Press, 1990), 10–12, 16, 23, 42–48, 61.

12. *CWM*, September 1904, 79. See also March 1902, 7; December 1902, 111; September 1903, 82; December 1903, 122; January 1905, 143; December 1905, 115; November 1906, 260; February 1907, 301; September 1910, 944.

13. *CWM*, May 1902, 34 (quote); November 1903, 110.

14. *CWM*, May 1902, 35 (quotes); June 1902, 45; November 1903, 108–109.

15. *CWM*, September 1904, 79; November 1906, 259; January 1907, 287, 288.

16. *CWM*, April 1907, 329. D. S. Crichton was a Congregationalist minister hired by Joseph Rowntree in 1900 to manage and attend to the welfare of young male employees. He also edited the *CWM*. See Fitzgerald, *Rowntree and the Marketing Revolution*, 225, 229; Vernon, *A Quaker Businessman*, 127.

17. *CWM*, August 1908, 571.

18. *CWM*, April 1907, 329.

19. *CWM*, June 1902, 46; March 1905, 9; May 1905, 31; June 1906, 193; June 1908, 546; Fitzgerald, *Rowntree and the Marketing Revolution*, 72, 76–77.

20. *CWM*, February 1904, 140; November 1904, 102.

21. *CWM*, January 1904, 129.

22. *CWM*, December 1902, 111.

23. *CWM*, January 1904, 129.

24. *CWM*, June 1902, 46; January 1907, 287.

25. *CWM*, December 1902, 111; January 1907, 287; January 1909, 644.

26. *CWM*, August 1903, 69.

27. *CWM*, December 1902, 111.

28. *CWM*, November 1904, 104–106.

29. *CWM*, January 1904, 133–134.

30. *CWM*, November 1904, 106.

31. *CWM*, June 1907, 364.

32. *CWM*, July 1902, 53; July 1903, 54; November 1904, 104–106; August 1905, 69.

33. *CWM*, December 1911, 1198.

34. *CWM*, December 1906, 275.

35. *CWM*, June 1902, 46; December 1902, 111.

36. *CWM*, September 1902, 84; February 1903, 134; December 1902, 125; May 1905, 31.

37. *CWM*, July 1903, 54.

38. *CWM*, August 1905, 69.

39. W. David Smith, *Stretching Their Bodies: The History of Physical Education* (Newton Abbott, Eng.: David & Charles, 1974), 79–80; Sheila Fletcher, *Women First: The Female Tradition in English Physical Education 1880–1980* (London: Athlone Press, 1984), passim; Jennifer Hargreaves, *Sporting Females: Critical Issues in the History and Sociology of Women's Sports* (London: Routledge, 1994), 63–111; McCrone, *Playing the Game*, 100–126. On physical training and social reform in the United States, see Dominick Cavallo, *Muscles and Morals: Organized Playgrounds and Urban Reform, 1880–1920* (Philadelphia: University of Pennsylvania Press, 1981).

40. CCA, Dorette Wilke, manuscript of a paper presented to the National Organisation of Girls Clubs, October 15, 1912; Dorette Wilke, manuscript of a paper presented to the National Organisation of Girls Clubs, October 10, 1916.

41. S. Bradley, article in *Sidcot Quarterly* 1, no. 8 (1892), 144, quoted in Hargreaves, *Sporting Females*, 77.

42. DCA, Earl of Meath to Madame Bergman Osterberg, June 18, 1905, File C2.

43. Ibid.

44. Fletcher, *Women First*, 4 (quote); Hargreaves, *Sporting Females*, 42–87; McCrone, *Playing the Game*, 106–109, 110, 113–115, 116–118.

45. CCA, Wilke, "Physical Training for Girls," 7.

46. CCA, Wilke, manuscript of a paper presented to the National Organisation of Girls Clubs, October 10, 1916.

47. Crunden, *History of Anstey College*, 7–8, 14.

48. ACA, *Anstey Physical Training College Magazine*, Summer 1905, 8; Autumn 1905, 27, 28.

49. Crunden, *History of Anstey College*, 2, 14.

50. *CWM*, March 1902, 12; September 1902, 84; February 1903, 144; August 1903, 76; July 1904, 64; September 1905, 78–79; June 1906, 193; May 1907, 348; May 1908, 531; May 1909, 698; June 1909, 707; November 1911, 1171.

51. DCA, "Madame Bergman Osterberg's Physical Training College Report for 1896–1898"; "Register of Gymnastic Teachers and Medical Gymnasts Trained at Madame Bergman Osterberg's Physical Training College, 1913," 6; *Bergman Osterberg Physical Training College Magazine* 2, 1921, 70;

CCA, "South Western Polytechnic Institute Physical Training College for Women, Record Book 1, 1889–1912"; *CWM*, March 1902, 10; September 1910, 933; November 1911, 1184.

52. There is insufficient evidence to argue, as Shirley Reekie has, that lower-class women's sport died out in the first half of the nineteenth century. And there is suggestive, if spotty, evidence to the contrary. What is clear is that, by the turn of the twentieth century, the upper and middle classes were seeing sport as a mechanism of social and gender control to be applied to working-class women.

53. *CWM*, March 1902, 10, 12; April 1902, 22; June 1902, 41. See also McCrone, "Class, Gender, and English Women's Sport," 163; Hargreaves, *Sporting Females*, 48–49, 58, 69–74, 82.

54. *CWM*, December 1902, 130.

55. *CWM*, May 1904, 33.

56. *CWM*, May 1904, 33; August 1903, 76; December 1903, 122; February 1904, 145; April 1904, 21; December 1905, 115; November 1906, 259; February 1907, 301; March 1909, 665; December 1909, 803–804.

57. Wilke, "Physical Training for Girls," 2.

58. *CWM*, September 1911, 1156; November 1911, 1175; December 1911, 1186; April 1912, 1276; May 1912, 1295; August 1912, 1338; October 1912, 1374; January 1913, 1430.

59. *CWM*, March 1902, 7–9; April 1902, 21–22, 29–30; June 1902, 37; August 1902, 68; October 1902, 86; February 1903, 142; April 1904, 15, 23; July 1904, 63; May 1905, 31; June 1905, 46; April 1906, 167, 168; February 1911, 1028–1030; July 1911, 1111–1114; April 1912, 1266–1268; April 1914, 1664; May 1914, 1670–1671.

60. *CWM*, April 1906, 167–168.

61. Tierl Thompson, ed., *Dear Girl: The Diaries and Letters of Two Working Women 1897–1917* (London: Women's Press, 1987), 17, 21–22, 287, 289, 291, 296, 300.

62. *CWM*, May 1903, 34; April 1906, 167–168; McCrone, "Class, Gender, and English Women's Sport," 178.

63. *CWM*, April 1902, 22; June 1902, 41; May 1904, 33.

64. *CWM*, November 1908, 617; December 1908, 623–624; March 1909, 663–664; November 1909, 781–784.

65. *CWM*, May 1902, 26; May 1903, 38; June 1903, 48.

66. *CWM*, June 1903, 44.

67. *CWM*, July 1903, 62; July 1904, 64; May 1905, 38; September 1905, 81; October 1906, 243–244; October 1908, 601; October 1911, 1171.

68. *CWM*, August 1905, 74.

69. *CWM*, December 1906, 263.

70. *CWM*, December 1908, 620.

71. *CWM*, December 1909, 799, 803–804; September 1910, 933; February 1911, 1034–1035; July 1911, 1127; August 1911, 1133; November 1911, 1167; December 1911, 1194; March 1912, 1258; December 1912, 1382; June 1913, 1508, 1510–1511.

72. *CWM*, June 1913, 1505–1506.

73. *CWM*, December 1911, 1194.

74. Rowntree, *The Human Factor*, 106, 109.

75. Interview of Ethel Thompson by author, York, July 1990.

76. Interview of Ruby Pearson by author, York, July 1990.

77. Interview of Joan Sadler by author, York, July 1990.

78. McCrone, "Class, Gender, and English Women's Sport," 165–166.

79. *Boots Athletic Club Journal* (hereafter *BACJ*), December 1907, 6, Boots Company PLC Archives, Beeston, England.

80. *BACJ*, January 1908, 2–4.

81. *BACJ*, June 1908, 7.

Select Bibliography

PRIMARY SOURCES: ARCHIVES

Anstey College Archive. In the possession of Mrs. Frankie Calland, Secretary, Anstey Association, Caton, Lancashire.

Boots Archive. Boots Company PLC, Beeston, Nottingham.

Bristol Record Office, Bristol, England:
Bristol Association of Working Girls' Clubs, Minutes, 1896–1901.

Chelsea College Archive. University of Brighton, Eastbourne.

Dartford College Archive. University of Greenwich, Dartford.

Leicestershire Record Office, Wigston Magna, England:
Reports and photographs of Leicester Poor Boys' and Girls' Club, 1914–1938; Forty-First Annual Report of the Leicester Poor Boys' and Girls' Summer Camp and Institute; Newspaper Cuttings concerning Loughborough Girls' Club and Evening Home, 1891–1913; Theatre Bills for Leicester Palace Theatre of Varieties, Royal Opera House, 1901, 1897; Song Sheets, Leicester Palace Theatre of Varieties; Letters of reference for May Greaves, picture pianist, 1911, 1915; Photograph of May Greaves, 1911; Records of Glenfield Female Friendly Society, founded 1839; Papers of Miss Harriet Mason; Minute Book and Records, Leicester Branch, National Council of Women.

Lincolnshire Archives, Lincoln, England:
Files of the Lindsey Association for the Elderly (formerly Lindsey Old People's Welfare Committee); Bound volume of theatrical pamphlets, early nineteenth century.

North East Lincolnshire Archives, Grimsby, England:
National British Women's Total Abstinence Union, Grimsby Branch, Receipt and Payment Books, 1898–1980; Apprenticeship indenture for Eliza Roberts, 1891.

Nottinghamshire Archives, Nottingham, England:
  Report for the Year 1906–1907 of the Girls' Evening Homes, Talbot
  Street, Cross Street, Chelsea Street, Ruddington, and Hyson Green,
  Nottingham; Hyson Green Evening Home, Girls' Evening Home, Min-
  ute Book, 1889–1916; Papers of Sydney Race, c. 1876–1960; Burlesque
  Programme for Derby Wake Races, November 8, 1813; Rules, Orders,
  etc., of the Female Union Society, Oxton, 1824–1884; Letter, A.L.S. to
  James Worth, October 12, 1843; Letter, Hilda to Eric, April 29, 1917;
  Print of "Women's Cricket Match on Selston Common: After Removal
  of Fences in Assertion of Right of the People to Open Spaces for Recre-
  ation, etc.," c. 1877–1878; "Andy Merrilees' Armor-Clad Amazon Female Christys," publicity leaflets and letters.
Retford Local Studies Centre, Retford, England:
  Box of Theatre Bills, 1792–1835; Report of the Retford Branch of the
  National British Women's Temperance Association, 1914; Collections of
  local newspaper cuttings on Entertainment at Retford Workhouse
  (1886), Mothers' Union (1908), Working Girls' Club (1910), Alhambra
  Theatre (1886), Eldred's Comedy and Burlesque Company (1878), Jubi-
  lee Singers (1877), Olympia Cinema (1911), Electric Picture Palace and
  Varieties (1912), Circus (1875).
Rowntree Company Archives. Borthwick Institute of Historical Research,
  University of York, England.
Sheffield Archives, Sheffield, England:
  Band of Hope, Programme of Annual Gala, 1884; Women's Co-operative
  Guild Records, 1873–1878, 1902–1906; Young People's Christian En-
  deavour, Records of Cemetery Road Baptist Church Branch, 1894–1957;
  Eight Cases of Married Women Workers, Compiled for the Women's
  Industrial Council by Sister Margaret of Croft House Settlement, 1908–
  1909; Minutes of Stage Plays Licensing Committee, 1889–1892, 1896–
  1908.
Vestry House Museum, Walthamstow, England.
Victoria Girls' Club, Minutes, 1905–1918; Photographic Collection.
York Oral History Project. City Archives, York, England.

PRIMARY SOURCES: PARLIAMENTARY PAPERS

House of Commons. *First Report of the Royal Commission on Employment of
  Children, Young Persons, and Women in Agriculture.* Appendix (*Evidence from
  Assistant Commissioners*). No. 4068. Vol. 17. 1867–1868.
———. Memorials from Manchester, Salford, Birmingham, and Bristol,
  Praying for the Alteration in Law of Granting of Licenses for Sale of
  Spirits, Wine and Beer for Consumption Off-Premises. Vol. 64. 1882.

————. *Report by Miss Collet on Statistics of Employment of Women and Girls.* C. 7564. Vol. 81. 1894.

————. Royal Commission on Labour. *"Reports on Employment of Women."* C. 6894. Vol. 37. 1893–1894.

————. Select Committee on Regulation of Public Houses, Hotels, Beer-Shops, Dancing Saloons, Coffee-Houses, Theatres, and Places of Public Entertainment. *Minutes of Evidence.* Vol. 37. 1852–1853.

————. Select Committee on Regulation of Public Houses, Hotels, Beer-Shops, Dancing Saloons, Coffee-Houses, Theatres, and Places of Public Entertainment. *Minutes of Evidence.* Vol. 14. 1854.

————. Select Committee on Shop Hours Regulation Bill. *Minutes of Evidence.* Vol. 12. 1886.

————. Select Committee on Theatres and Places of Entertainment. *Evidence.* Vol. 18. 1892.

————. Select Committee to Inquire into Working of Acts for Licensing and Regulating of Theatres and Places of Public Entertainment. *Minutes of Evidence.* Vol. 16. 1866.

House of Lords. Select Committee for Inquiring into the Prevalence of Habits of Intemperance, and Effects of Recent Legislation. *Minutes of Evidence.* Vol. 10. 1878–1879.

PRIMARY SOURCES: NEWSPAPERS AND PERIODICALS

Anstey Physical Training College Magazine
Bergman Osterberg Physical Training College Magazine
Boots Athletic Club Journal
The Chartist Circular
The Cocoa Works' Magazine
The Englishwoman's Review
The Fortnightly Review
Girls' Club News
Journal of Scientific Physical Training
Loughborough Evening Herald
New Moral World
The Nineteenth Century
Northern Star
The Pioneer, or Grand National Consolidated Trades' Union Magazine
Retford and Gainsborough Times
Retford, Gainsborough, and Worksop Times
The Woman Worker
Women's Industrial News

Women's Union Journal
The Working Man

PRIMARY SOURCES: BOOKS

Acorn, George. *One of the Multitude: An Autobiography of a Resident of Bethnal Green*. New York: Dodd, Mead, 1912.

Anderson, Adelaide Mary. *Women in the Factory: An Administrative Adventure, 1893 to 1921*. New York: E. P. Dutton, 1922.

Bamford, Samuel. *The Autobiography of Samuel Bamford: Early Days*. Edited by W. H. Chaloner. 2 vols. 1848–1849. Reprint, London: Frank Cass, 1967.

Besant, Walter. *East London*. London: Chatto & Windus, 1901.

Black, Clementina. *Married Women's Work*. 1915. Reprint, New York: Garland, 1980.

———. *Sweated Industry and the Minimum Wage*. London: Duckworth, 1907.

Blundell, Nicholas. *The Great Diurnal of Nicholas Blundell of Little Crosby, Lancashire, 1712–1719*. Edited by J. J. Bagley. 2 vols. N.p.: Record Society of Lancashire and Cheshire, 1968–1970.

Booth, Charles, ed. *Life and Labour of the People in London*. 17 vols. 1889. 3d edition, London: Macmillan, 1902–1903.

Basanquet, Bernard, ed. *Aspects of the Social Problem*. London: Macmillan, 1895.

Bosanquet, Helen. *Rich and Poor*. London: Macmillan, 1908.

———. *Social Conditions in Provincial Towns*. 1912. Reprint, New York: Garland, 1985.

———. *The Standard of Life and Other Studies*. London: Macmillan, 1898.

Boucherett, Jessie, et al. *The Condition of Working Women and the Factory Acts*. London: Elliot Stock, 1896.

Bourne, Henry. *Antiquitates Vulgares*. 1725. Reprint, New York: Arno Press, 1977.

Bradley, S. A. J., ed. *Wit and Mirth: Sixty Ribald Songs from Pills to Purge Melancholy*. New York: Praeger, 1967.

Brand, John. *Observations on Popular Antiquities*. 1777. 2 vols. Revised, London: F. C. & J. Rivington, 1813.

Burnett, John, ed. *Destiny Obscure: Autobiographies of Childhood, Education and Family from the 1820s to the 1920s*. London: Allen Lane, 1982.

———. *Useful Toil: Autobiographies of Working People from the 1820s to the 1920s*. London: Allen Lane, 1974.

Butler, C. Violet. *Domestic Service: An Enquiry by the Women's Industrial Council*. London: G. Bell & Sons, 1916.

Cadbury, Edward. *Experiments in Industrial Organization.* London: Longmans, Green, 1912.

Cadbury, Edward, M. Cecile Matheson, and George Shann. *Women's Work and Wages: A Phase of Life in the Industrial City.* Chicago: University of Chicago Press, 1907.

Cadbury, Edward, and George M. Shann. *Sweating.* London: Headley Bros., 1907.

Chambers, Robert, ed. *The Book of Days.* 2 vols. London: W. & R. Chambers, 1866.

Chase, Ellen. *Tennant Friends in Old Deptford.* London: Williams and Norgate, 1924.

Cobbett, William. *Advice to Young Men, and (Incidentally) to Young Women, in the Middle and Higher Ranks of Life.* London: William Cobbett, 1829.

———. *Cottage Economy.* London: William Cobbett, 1822. Reprint, New York: Augustus M. Kelley, 1970.

Collier, John Payne, ed. *Illustration of Old English Literature.* 1866. Reprint, New York: B. Blom, 1966.

Cookson, Catherine. *Our Kate.* London: Macdonald, 1969.

Cullwick, Hannah. *The Diaries of Hannah Cullwick, Victorian Maidservant.* Edited by Liz Stanley. London: Virago, 1984.

Davies, Margaret Llewelyn, ed. *Life as We Have Known It, by Co-operative Working Women.* London: Women's Co-operative Guild, 1931. Reprint, New York: Norton, 1975.

———. *Maternity: Letters from Working Women.* London: A. R. Mowbray, 1913.

Dayus, Kathleen. *Her People.* London: Virago, 1982.

———. *Where There's Life.* London: Virago, 1985.

Defoe, Daniel. *A Tour thro' the Whole Island of Great Britain.* Edited by Samuel Richardson. 4 vols. 1742. Reprint, New York: Garland, 1975.

Dendy, Helen. "The Children of Working London." In *Aspects of the Social Problem*, edited by Bernard Bosanquet. London: Macmillan, 1895.

Dolling, Robert R. *Ten Years in a Portsmouth Slum.* London: Swann Sonnenschein, 1898.

Greenwood, James. *The Wilds of London.* London: Chatto & Windus, 1874. Reprint, New York: Garland, 1985.

Hardy, Mary. *Mary Hardy's Diary.* Norwich, Eng.: Norfold Record Society, 1968.

Hardy, Thomas. *The Mayor of Casterbridge.* 1881. Reprint, New York: Bantam, 1981.

Harland, John, ed. *Ballads and Songs of Lancashire, Ancient and Modern.* London: George Routledge & Sons, 1875.

Hone, William, ed. *The Every-Day Book: Or, Everlasting Calendar of Popular Amusements.* 2 vols. London: Hunt & Clarke, 1826–1827.

Howitt, William. *The Rural Life of England.* 2 vols. 1837. Reprint, Philadelphia: Parry & M'Millan, 1854.

Hutchins, Elizabeth L. *Women in Modern Industry.* London: G. Bell & Sons, 1915.

Hutchins, Elizabeth L., and Amy Harrison. *A History of Factory Legislation.* London: P. S. King & Son, 1926.

Kalm, Peter. *Kalm's Account of His Visit to England.* Translated by Joseph Lucas. 1753. London: Macmillan, 1892.

Kinnaird, Emily. "The Right Use of Leisure." *National Council of Women of Great Britain Handbook: The Official Report of the Central Conference of Women Workers, 1900.* Ann Arbor, Mich.: University Microfilm 458 P-135, 1980.

Laycock, Samuel. *The Collected Writings of Samuel Laycock.* London: Simpkin, Marshall, Hamilton, Kent & Co., 1900.

London, Jack. *The People of the Abyss.* New York: Macmillan, 1903; Reprint, Joseph Simon, 1980.

Lovett, William. *The Life and Struggles of William Lovett.* London: Trubner, 1876.

Lovett, William, and John Collins. *Chartism: A New Organisation of the People.* London: J. Watson, 1840. Reprint, Leicester, Eng.: Leicester University Press, 1969.

Macdonald, John. *Memoirs of an Eighteenth-Century Footman, 1745–1779.* 1790. Reprint, London: Harper & Bros., 1927.

Malcolm, James Pellor. *Anecdotes of the Manners and Customs of London during the Eighteenth Century.* 2d ed. 2 vols. London: Longman, Hurst, Rees & Orme, 1810.

Mare, Margaret L., and W. H. Quarrell, trans. *Lichtenberg's Visits to England as Described in His Letter and Diaries.* Oxford: Clarendon Press, 1938.

Masterman, C. F. G. *From the Abyss: Of Its Inhabitants, by One of Them.* 1902. Reprint, New York: Garland, 1980.

Mayett, Joseph. *The Autobiography of Joseph Mayett of Quainton, 1783–1839.* Edited by Ann Kussmaul. Aylesbury, Eng.: Buckinghamshire Record Office, 1986.

Mayhew, Henry. *London Labour and the London Poor.* London: Griffin, Bohn & Co., 1861–1862. Reprint, Harmondsworth, Eng.: Penguin, 1985.

———. *The Morning Chronicle Survey of Labour and the Poor: The Metropolitan District.* 6 vols. London: 1849–1850. Reprint, Horsham, Eng.: Caliban Books, 1980–1982.

Misson, Henri. *M. Misson's Memoirs and Observations in His Travels over En-*

gland, with some Account of Scotland and Ireland. Edited by John Ozell. London, 1719.

Mitchell, Geoffrey, ed. *The Hard Way Up: The Autobiography of Hannah Mitchell, Suffragette and Rebel.* London: Faber & Faber, 1968.

Mitford, Mary Russell. *Our Village: Sketches of Rural Character and Scenery.* 5 vols. London, 1824–1832.

Montagu, Lilian H. *My Club and I: The Story of the West Central Jewish Club.* London: Herbert Joseph, 1943.

———. "Popular Amusements for Working Girls." *National Council of Women of Great Britain Handbook: The Official Report of the Central Conference of Women Workers, 1902.*

———. "The Responsibility of Leisure." *National Council of Women of Great Britain Handbook: The Official Report of the Central Conference of Women Workers, 1912.*

More, Hannah, ed. *Cheap Repository Tracts: Entertaining, Moral, and Religious.* 8 vols. London, 1795–1798. Revised, New York: American Tract Society, 1825.

Moritz, Carl Philip. *Journeys of a German in England in 1782.* Translated and edited by Reginald Nettel. 1783. Reprint, New York: Holt, Rinehart & Winston, 1965.

Morris, Claver. *The Diary of a West Country Physician 1684–1726.* Edited by Edmund Hobhouse. London, 1934.

Morrison, Arthur. *A Child of the Jago.* London: Macgibbon & Kee, 1969.

———. *Tales of Mean Streets.* New York: Boni & Liveright, 1921.

Neville, Sylas. *The Diary of Sylas Neville, 1767–1788.* Edited by Basil Cozens-Hardy. London: Oxford University Press, 1950.

Nevinson, Margaret. *Life's Fitful Fever: A Volume of Memories.* London: A. & C. Black, 1926.

Panton, Jane Ellen. *From Kitchen to Garrett: Hints for Young Householders.* London: E. Nash, 1908.

Pinero, Arthur Wing. *Iris: A Drama in Five Acts.* Boston: Walter H. Baker, 1905.

———. *The Social Plays of Arthur Wing Pinero.* Edited by Clayton Hamilton. 4 vols. New York: E. P. Dutton, 1919.

Place, Francis. *The Autobiography of Francis Place.* Edited by Mary Thale. Cambridge: Cambridge University Press, 1972.

Reeves, Magdalen S. R. *Round About a Pound a Week.* London: G. Bell & Sons, 1913. Reprint, New York: Garland, 1980.

Reynolds, Stephen. *A Poor Man's House.* London: John Lane, 1902. Reprint, Oxford: Oxford University Press, 1982.

Ridding, Lady Laura. "The Relation of Amusements to Life." *National*

Council of Women of Great Britain Handbook: The Official Report of the Central Conference of Women Workers, 1902.

Roberts, Arthur. *Mendip Annals: Or, A Narrative of the Charitable Labours of Hannah and Martha More.* New York: Robert Carter & Brothers, 1859.

Roberts, Robert. *The Classic Slum: Salford Life in the First Quarter of the Century.* Manchester, Eng.: Manchester University Press, 1971.

———. *A Ragged Schooling: Growing Up in the Classic Slum.* Manchester, Eng.: Manchester University Press, 1976.

Rowntree, Benjamin Seebohm. *The Human Factor in Business.* London: Longmans, Green, 1921.

———. *Poverty: A Study of Town Life.* 1901. Reprint, London: Macmillan, 1908.

Russell, Charles E. B. *The Social Problems of the North.* London: A. R. Mowbray, 1913.

Scannell, Dorothy. *Mother Knew Best: Memoir of a London Girlhood.* New York: Pantheon Books, 1975.

Sherard, Robert Harborough. *The Child-Slaves of Britain.* London: Hurst & Blackwell, 1905.

Shimmin, Hugh. *Liverpool Life: Its Pleasures, Practices, and Pastimes.* Liverpool: Egerton Smith & Co., 1856. Reprint, New York: Garland, 1985.

Sims, George. *The Cry of the Children.* London: The Tribune, 1907.

———. *How the Poor Live* and *Horrible London.* 1889. Reprint, New York: Garland, 1984.

Southey, Robert. *Southey's Common-Place Book.* Edited by John Wood Warter. 4 vols. London: Longman, Brown, Green & Longman, 1850.

Stanley, Maude. *Clubs for Working Girls.* London: Macmillan, 1890.

Strutt, Joseph. *The Sports and Pastimes of the People of England.* London: Methuen, 1903. Revised, Detroit: Singing Tree Press, 1968.

Thompson, Flora. *Lark Rise to Candleford: A Trilogy.* London: Oxford University Press, 1945. Reprint, 1979.

Thompson, Thea. *Edwardian Childhoods.* London: Routledge & Kegan Paul, 1981.

Thompson, Tierl, ed. *Dear Girl: The Diaries and Letters of Two Working Women 1897–1917.* London: Women's Press, 1987.

Townend, Kathleen M. "Methods of Recreation as They Affect the Causes of Intemperance amongst Women." *National Council of Women of Great Britain Handbook: The Official Report of the Central Conference of Women Workers, 1894.* Ann Arbor, Mich.: University Microfilm 458 P-135, 1980.

Tressell, Robert. *The Ragged Trousered Philanthropists.* London: Lawrence & Wishart, 1955.

Turner, Thomas. *The Diary of Thomas Turner, 1754–1765.* Edited by David Vaisey. Oxford: Oxford University Press, 1984.

Walton, John K., and Alastair Wilcox, eds. *Low Life and Moral Improvement in Mid-Victorian England: Liverpool through the Journalism of Hugh Shimmin.* Leicester, Eng.: Leicester University Press, 1991.

Waugh, Edwin. *Poems and Lancashire Songs.* London: Whittaker, 1859.

Webb, Sidney, and Beatrice Webb. *Industrial Democracy.* 1897. Reprint, New York: Augustus M. Kelley, 1965.

Wesley, John. *The Letters of the Reverend John Wesley.* Edited by John Telford. 8 vols. London: Epworth Press, 1931.

———. *The Works of the Reverend John Wesley.* Edited by John Emory. 7 vols. New York: Eaton & Mains, n.d.

Woodforde, James. *The Diary of a Country Parson, 1758–1802: The Reverend James Woodforde.* Edited by John Beresford. 5 vols. London: Oxford University Press, 1924–1931.

Wright, Thomas. *Autobiography of Thomas Wright, of Birkenshaw. In the County of York. 1736–1797.* Edited by Thomas Wright. London: John Russell Smith, 1864.

———. *The Great Unwashed.* London: Tinsley Bros, 1868. Reprint, New York: Augustus M. Kelley, 1970.

SECONDARY SOURCES: BOOKS AND ARTICLES

Adelman, Melvin L. *A Sporting Time: New York City and the Rise of Modern Athletics.* Urbana: University of Illinois Press, 1986.

Alexander, Ruth M. *The "Girl Problem": Female Sexual Delinquency in New York, 1900–1930.* Ithaca: Cornell University Press, 1995.

Alexander, Sally. *Women's Work in Nineteenth-Century London: A Study of the Years 1820–50.* London: Journeyman Press and the London History Workshop Centre, 1983.

Anderson, Patricia. *The Printed Image and the Transformation of Popular Culture, 1790–1860.* Oxford: Clarendon Press, 1991.

Bailey, Peter. "Custom, Capital and Culture in the Victorian Music Hall." In *Popular Culture and Custom in Nineteenth-Century England*, edited by Robert D. Storch. London: Croom Helm, 1982.

———. *Leisure and Class in Victorian England: Rational Recreation and the Contest for Control, 1830–1885.* London: Routledge, 1978.

———. "Leisure, Culture and the Historian: Reviewing the First Generation of Leisure Historiography in Britain." *Leisure Studies* 8 (1989): 102–127.

———. " 'A Mingled Mass of Perfectly Legitimate Pleasures': The Victorian Middle Class and the Problem of Leisure." *Victorian Studies* 21 (1977): 7–28.

———. " 'Will the Real Bill Banks Please Stand Up?' Towards a Role Analysis of Mid-Victorian Respectability." *Journal of Social History* 12 (1979): 7–21.

———, ed. *Music Hall: The Business of Pleasure*. Milton Keynes, Eng.: Open University Press, 1986.

Barker, Hannah, and Elaine Chalus, eds. *Gender in Eighteenth-Century England: Roles, Representations, and Responsibilities*. New York: Addison Wesley Longman, 1997.

Barrell, John. "Sportive Labour: The Farmworker in Eighteenth-Century Poetry and Painting." In *The English Rural Community: Image and Analysis*, edited by Brian Short. Cambridge: Cambridge University Press, 1992.

Barret-Ducrocq, Françoise. *Love in the Time of Victoria: Sexuality, Class and Gender in Nineteenth-Century London*. Translated by John Howe. London: Verso, 1991.

Barrett, Michelle, and Maureen McIntosh. " 'The Family Wage': Some Problems for Socialists and Feminists." *Capital and Class* 11 (Summer 1980): 111–133.

Bennenson, Harold. "The 'Family Wage' and Working Women's Consciousness in Britain, 1880–1914." *Politics and Society* 19 (1991): 71–72.

———. "Victorian Sexual Ideology and Marx's Theory of the Working Class." *International Labour and Working-Class History* 25 (1984): 1–23.

Bennett, Judith. "History That Stands Still: Women's Work in the European Past." *Feminist Studies* 14 (1988): 269–283.

Benson, John. *The Penny Capitalists: A Study of Nineteenth-Century Working Class Entrepreneurs*. New Brunswick, N.J.: Rutgers University Press, 1983.

———. *The Rise of Consumer Society in Britain 1880–1980*. London: Longman, 1994.

———, ed. *The Working Class in Britain, 1850–1939*. London: Longman, 1980.

———, ed. *The Working Class in England, 1875–1914*. Bloomington: Indiana University Press, 1982.

Bienefeld, M. A. *Working Hours in British Industry: An Economic History*. London: Weidenfeld & Nicolson, 1972.

Bland, Lucy. *Banishing the Beast: Sexuality and Early Feminists*. New York: New Press, 1995.

Bradbury, Bettina. "Women's History and Working-Class History." *Labour/Le Travail* 19 (1987): 23–43.

Bradley, Harriet. *Men's Work, Women's Work: A Sociological History of the Sexual Division of Labour in Employment*. Minneapolis: University of Minnesota Press: 1989.

Brailsford, Dennis. "1787: A Sporting Year." *Research Quarterly* 52 (1981): 34–45.

Bratton, J. S., ed. *Music Hall: Performance and Style*. Milton Keynes, Eng.: Open University Press, 1986.

Braybon, Gail. *Women Workers in the First World War: The British Experience*. London: Croom Helm, 1981.

Brayton, Gail, and Penny Summerfield. *Out of the Cage*. London: Pandora, 1987.

Briggs, Asa. *Mass Entertainment: The Origins of a Modern Industry*. Adelaide: University of Southern Australia, 1960.

————. *Social Thought and Social Action: A Study of the Work of Seebohm Rowntree, 1871–1954*. London: Longmans, Green, 1961.

Bulmer, Martin, ed. *Working-Class Images of Society*. London: Routledge & Kegan Paul, 1975.

Burke, Peter. *Popular Culture in Early Modern Europe*. London: Temple Smith, 1978. Reprint, Aldershot, Eng.: Scolar Press, 1994.

Burman, Sandra, ed. *Fit Work for Women*. New York: St. Martin's Press, 1979.

Burstyn, Joan. *Victorian Education and the Ideal of Womanhood*. London: Croom Helm, 1980.

Cavallo, Dominick. *Muscles and Morals: Organized Playgrounds and Urban Reform, 1880–1920*. Philadelphia: University of Pennsylvania Press, 1981.

Chinn, Carl. *They Worked All Their Lives: Women of the Urban Poor in England, 1880–1939*. Manchester, Eng.: Manchester University Press, 1988.

Clark, Alice. *Working Life of Women in the Seventeenth Century*. 3d ed. London: Routledge and Kegan Paul, 1982.

Clark, Anna. *The Struggle for the Breeches: Gender and the Making of the English Working Class*. Berkeley: University of California Press, 1995.

Clark, Peter. *The English Alehouse: A Social History, 1200–1830*. London: Longman, 1983.

Clarke, John, and Chas Critcher. *The Devil Makes Work: Leisure in Capitalist Britain*. London: Macmillan, 1985.

Clarke, John, Chas Critcher, and Richard Johnson, eds. *Working Class Culture: Studies in History and Theory*. London: Hutchinson, 1979.

Coffin, Judith G. "Credit, Consumption, and Images of Women's Desires: Selling the Sewing Machine in Late Nineteenth-Century France." *French Historical Studies* 18 (1994): 759–783.

Colley, Linda. *Britons: Forging the Nation, 1707–1837*. New Haven: Yale University Press, 1992.

Constantine, S. "Amateur Gardening and Popular Recreation in the Nineteenth and Twentieth Centuries," *Journal of Social History* 14 (1981): 387–406.

Copelman, Dina M. *London's Women Teachers: Gender, Class and Feminism 1870–1930*. London: Routledge, 1996.

Crunden, Colin. *A History of Anstey College of Physical Education*. Sutton Cold-field, Eng.: Anstey College of Physical Education, 1974.

Cunningham, Hugh. *Leisure in the Industrial Revolution, c. 1780–c. 1880*. London: Croom Helm, 1980.

Curran, James, and Vincent Porter, eds. *British Cinema History*. London: Weidenfeld & Nicolson, 1983.

Davidoff, Leonore. "Gender and Class in Victorian England: The Diaries of Arthur J. Munby and Hannah Cullwick." *Feminist Studies* 5 (1979): 87–141.

———. "The Separation of Home and Work? Landladies and Lodgers in Nineteenth and Twentieth Century England." In *Fit Work for Women*, edited by Sandra Burman. New York: St. Martin's, 1979.

Davidoff, Leonore, and Catherine Hall. *Family Fortunes: Men and Women of the English Middle Classes, 1780–1850*. London: Hutchinson, 1987.

Davidoff, Leonore, and Belinda Westover, eds. *Our Work, Our Lives, Our Words: Women's History and Women's Work*. Basingstoke, Eng.: Macmillan Education, 1986.

Davidson, Caroline. *A Woman's Work Is Never Done: A History of Housework in the British Isles, 1650–1950*. London: Chatto & Windus, 1982.

Davies, Andrew. *Leisure, Gender and Poverty: Working-Class Culture in Salford and Manchester, 1900–1939*. Buckingham, Eng.: Open University Press, 1992.

Davin, Anna. "Imperialism and Motherhood." *History Workshop Journal* 5 (1978): 9–65.

Dawick, John. *Pinero: A Theatrical Life*. Boulder: University Press of Colorado, 1993.

Deem, Rosemary. *All Work and No Play? The Sociology of Women and Leisure*. Milton Keynes, Eng.: Open University Press, 1986.

———. "Women, Leisure and Inequality." *Leisure Studies* 1 (1982): 29–46.

de Grazia, Victorian, with Ellen Furlough, eds. *The Sex of Things: Gender and Consumption in Historical Perspective*. Berkeley: University of California Press, 1996.

Dellheim, Charles. "The Creation of a Company Culture: Cadbury's, 1861–1931." *American Historical Review* 92 (February 1987): 13–23.

Delves, Anthony. "Popular Recreation and Social Conflict in Derby, 1800–1850." In *Popular Culture and Class Conflict 1590–1914: Explorations in the History of Labour and Leisure*, edited by Eileen Yeo and Stephen Yeo. Brighton, Eng.: Harvester Press, 1981.

Demers, Patricia. *The World of Hannah More*. Lexington: University of Kentucky Press, 1996.

Donajgrodzki, A. P., ed. *Social Control in Nineteenth Century Britain*. London: Croom Helm, 1977.

Dyhouse, Carol. *Girls Growing Up in Late Victorian and Edwardian England.* London: Routledge & Kegan Paul, 1981.

Earl, John. "Building the Halls." In *Music Hall: The Business of Pleasure,* edited by Peter Bailey. Milton Keynes, Eng.: Open University Press, 1986.

Ewen, Elizabeth. *Immigrant Women in the Land of Dollars: Life and Culture on the Lower East Side, 1890–1925.* New York: Monthly Review Press, 1985.

Feinstein, Charles. *York 1831–1981: 150 Years of Scientific and Social Change.* York, Eng.: Ebor Press, 1981.

Ferguson, Moira. "Resistance and Power in the Life and Writings of Ann Yearsley." *Eighteenth Century* 27 (1986): 247–268.

———. "The Unpublished Poems of Ann Yearsley." *Tulsa Studies in Women's Literature* 12 (1993): 13–29.

Fitzgerald, Robert. *British Labour Management and Industrial Welfare 1846–1939.* London: Croom Helm, 1988.

———. *Rowntree and the Marketing Revolution, 1862–1969.* Cambridge: Cambridge University Press, 1995.

Fletcher, Sheila. *Women First: The Female Tradition in English Physical Education 1880–1980.* London: Athlone Press, 1984.

Fraser, W. Hamish. *The Coming of the Mass Market, 1850–1914.* Hamden, Conn.: Archon Books, 1981.

Gaskill, S. M. "Gardens for the Working Class: Victorian Practical Pleasure." *Victorian Studies* 23 (1980): 479–501.

Giles, Judy. *Women, Identity, and Private Life in Britain, 1900–50.* New York: St. Martin's Press, 1995.

Girouard, M. *Victorian Pubs.* London: Studio Vista, 1975.

Golby, J. M., and A. W. Purdue. *The Civilisation of the Crowd: Popular Culture in England, 1750–1900.* London: Batsford, 1984.

Gomersall, Meg. *Working-Class Girls in Nineteenth-Century England: Life, Work, and Schooling.* Basingstoke, Eng.: Macmillan, 1997.

Gourvish, Terence R. "The Standard of Living, 1890–1914." In *The Edwardian Age: Conflict and Stability 1900–1914,* edited by Alan O'Day. Hamden, Conn.: Archon Books, 1979.

Gray, Robert. "Factory Legislation and the Gendering of Jobs in the North of England, 1830–1860." *Gender and History* 5 (Spring 1993): 56–80.

Guttmann, Allen. *Women's Sports: A History.* New York: Columbia University Press, 1991.

Hall, Catherine. "The Tale of Samuel and Jemima: Gender and Working-Class Culture in Nineteenth-Century England." In *E. P. Thompson: Critical Perspectives,* edited by Harvey J. Kaye and Keith McClelland. Philadelphia: Temple University Press, 1990.

Hargreaves, Jennifer. *Sporting Females: Critical Issues in the History and Sociology of Women's Sports.* London: Routledge, 1994.

Harrington, Maureen, Don Dawson, and P. Bolla. "Objective and Subjective Constraints on Women's Enjoyment of Leisure." *Loisir et Société* 15 (1992): 203–222.

Harris, Tim, ed. *Popular Culture in England, c. 1500–1850.* New York: St. Martin's Press, 1995.

Harrison, Brian. *Drink and the Victorians: The Temperance Question in England 1815-1872.* Pittsburgh: University of Pittsburgh Press, 1971.

———. "For Church, Queen and Family: The Girls' Friendly Society 1874–1920." *Past and Present* 61 (1973): 107–138.

———. "Religion and Recreation in 19th Century England." *Past and Present* 38 (1968): 98–125.

Hart, Nicky. "Gender and the Rise and Fall of Class Politics." *New Left Review* 175 (1989): 19–47.

Henderson, Karla A. "The Contribution of Feminism to an Understanding of Leisure Constraints." *Journal of Leisure Research* 23 (1991): 363–377.

Henderson, Karla A., and K. R. Allen, "The Ethic of Care: Leisure Possibilities and Constraints for Women." *Loisir et Société* 14 (1991): 97–114.

Henderson, Karla A., and Deborah M. Bialeschki. "A Sense of Entitlement to Leisure as Constraint and Empowerment for Women." *Leisure Sciences* 13 (1991): 51–65.

Henderson, Karla A., et al. *A Leisure of One's Own: A Feminist Perspective on Women's Leisure.* State College, Pa.: Venture Publishing, 1989.

Henderson, Robert W. *Ball, Bat and Bishop: The Origin of Ball Games.* New York: Rockport Press, 1947.

Hill, Bridget. *Women, Work and Sexual Politics in Eighteenth-Century England.* Oxford: Basil Blackwell, 1989.

Hill, Jeffrey. "British Sports History: A Post-Modern Future?" *Journal of Sport History* 23 (1999): 1–19.

Hoggart, Richard. *The Uses of Literacy: Aspects of Working-Class Life.* London: Chatto & Windus, 1957.

Hollingworth, Brian, ed. *Songs of the People: Lancashire Dialect Poetry of the Industrial Revolution.* Manchester, Eng.: Manchester University Press, 1977.

Holt, Richard. *Sport and the British: A Modern History.* Oxford: Clarendon Press, 1989.

Holton, Sandra Stanley. "Silk Dresses and Lavender Kid Gloves: The Wayward Career of Jessie Craigen, Working Suffragist." *Women's History Review* 5 (1996): 129–149.

Horgan, D. M. "Popular Protest in the Eighteenth Century: John Collier (Tim Bobbin), 1708–1786." *Review of English Studies* 158 (1997): 310–329.

Howkins, Alun. "The Taming of Whitsun: The Changing Face of a Nineteenth-Century Rural Holiday." In *Popular Culture and Class Conflict 1590–1914: Explorations in the History of Labour and Leisure*, edited by Eileen Yeo and Stephen Yeo. Brighton, Eng.: Harvester Press, 1981.

Hufton, Olwen. "Women in History." *Past and Present* 101 (1983): 125–141.

Humphries, Jane. "Class Struggle and the Persistence of the Working-Class Family." *Cambridge Journal of Economics* 1 (1977): 241–258.

————. "Protective Legislation, the Capitalist State and Working-Class Men: The Case of the 1842 Mines Regulation Act." *Feminist Review* 7 (1981): 1–33.

Jones, Jennifer. "*Coquettes* and *Grisettes*: Women Buying and Selling in Ancien Régime Paris." In *The Sex of Things: Gender and Consumption in Historical Perspective*, edited by Victoria de Grazia, with Ellen Furlough. Berkeley: University of California Press, 1996.

Jones, Stephen G. *Workers at Play: A Social and Economic History of Leisure 1918–1939*. London: Routledge & Kegan Paul, 1986.

Jordan, Thomas E. *The Degeneracy Crisis and Victorian Youth*. Albany: State University Press of New York, 1995.

Joyce, Patrick. *Visions of the People: Industrial England and the Question of Class 1848–1914*. Cambridge: Cambridge University Press, 1991.

Kift, Dagmar. *The Victorian Music Hall: Culture, Class and Conflict*. Translated by Roy Kift. Cambridge: Cambridge University Press, 1996.

Klein, Lawrence E. "Gender and the Public/Private Distinction in the Eighteenth Century: Some Questions About Evidence and Analytic Procedure." *Eighteenth-Century Studies* 29 (1995): 97–109.

Kneale, James. " 'A Problem of Supervision': Moral Geographies of the Nineteenth-Century British Public House." *Journal of Historical Geography* 25 (1999): 333–348.

Kowaleski-Wallace, Beth. "Women, China, and Consumer Culture in Eighteenth-Century England." *Eighteenth-Century Studies* 29 (1995–1996): 153–167.

Langford, Paul. *A Polite and Commercial People: England, 1727–1783*. Oxford: Oxford University Press, 1989.

Lenskyj, Helen. "Measured Time: Women, Sport and Leisure." *Leisure Studies* 7 (1988): 233–240.

Lewis, Jane. *Women in England, 1870–1950: Sexual Divisions and Social Change*. Brighton, Eng.: Wheatsheaf Books, 1984.

Lowerson, John, and John Myerscough. *Time to Spare in Victorian England*. Brighton, Eng.: Harvester Press, 1977.

Lown, Judy. *Women and Industrialization: Gender at Work in Nineteenth-Century England*. Minneapolis: University of Minnesota Press, 1990.

Luddy, Maria. *Women and Philanthropy in Nineteenth-Century Ireland*. Cambridge: Cambridge University Press, 1995.

Maidment, Brian. *The Poorhouse Fugitives: Self-Taught Poets and Poetry in Victorian England*. London: Carcanet, 1987.

———. "Prose and Artisan Discourse in Early Victorian Britain." *Prose Studies* 10 (1987).

Malcolmson, Robert W. *Popular Recreations in English Society, 1700–1850*. Cambridge: Cambridge University Press, 1973.

McCarthy, Kathleen D., ed. *Lady Bountiful Revisited: Women, Philanthropy, and Power*. New Brunswick, N.J.: Rutgers University Press, 1990.

McCrone, Kathleen E. "Class, Gender, and English Women's Sport, c. 1890–1914." *Journal of Sport History* 18 (1991): 159–182.

———. *Playing the Game: Sport and the Physical Emancipation of English Women, 1870–1914*. Lexington: University of Kentucky Press, 1988.

McKibbin, Ross. *The Ideologies of Class: Social Relations in Britain, 1880–1950*. Oxford: Clarendon Press, 1990.

———. "Why There Was No Marxism in Great Britain." *English Historical Review* 99 (1984): 121–135.

Meacham, Standish. *A Life Apart: The English Working Class, 1890–1914*. Cambridge, Mass.: Harvard University Press, 1977.

Meyerowitz, Joanne J. *Women Adrift: Independent Wage Earners in Chicago, 1880–1930*. Chicago: University of Chicago Press, 1988.

Mitchell, Sally. *The New Girl: Girls' Culture in England, 1880–1915*. New York: Columbia University Press, 1995.

Murolo, Priscilla. *The Common Ground of Womanhood: Class, Gender, and Working Girls' Clubs, 1884–1928*. Urbana: University of Illinois Press, 1997.

Myers, Mitzi. "Reform or Ruin: 'A Revolution in Female Manners.' " *Studies in Eighteenth-Century Literature* 11 (1982): 199–216.

Nord, Deborah Epstein. *Walking the Victorian Streets: Women, Representation, and the City*. Ithaca: Cornell University Press, 1995.

Oldfield, Sybil. *This Working-Day World: Women's Lives and Culture(s) in Britain 1914–1945*. London: Taylor & Francis, 1994.

Parker, Julia. *Women and Welfare: Ten Victorian Women in Public Social Service*. New York: St. Martin's, 1989.

Parratt, Catriona M. " 'The Making of the Healthy and the Happy Home': Recreation, Education, and the Production of Working-Class Womanhood at the Rowntree Cocoa Works, York, c. 1898–1914." In *Sport and Social Identity in the North of England*, edited by Jack Williams and Jeff Hill. Keele, Eng.: University of Keele Press, 1996.

Pedersen, Susan. "Hannah More Meets Simple Simon: Tracts, Chapbooks, and Popular Culture in Late Eighteenth-Century England." *Journal of British Studies* 25 (1986): 84–113.

Peiss, Kathy. *Cheap Amusements: Working Women and Leisure in Turn-of-the-Century New York City*. Philadelphia: Temple University Press, 1986.

Pennybacker, Susan. " 'It Was Not What She Said, But the Way in Which She Said It': The London County Council and the Music Halls." In *Music Hall: The Business of Pleasure,* edited by Peter Bailey. Milton Keynes, Eng.: Open University Press, 1986.

Pinchbeck, Ivy. *Women Workers and the Industrial Revolution 1750–1850.* London: Routledge, 1930. Reprint, London: Frank Cass, 1969.

Poovey, Mary. *Uneven Developments: The Ideological Work of Gender in Mid-Victorian England.* Chicago: University of Chicago Press, 1988.

Prendergast, Shirley. "Stoolball—the Pursuit of Vertigo?" *Women's Studies International Forum* 1 (1978): 15–26.

Prochaska, Frank K. *Women and Philanthropy in Nineteenth-Century England.* Oxford: Clarendon Press, 1980.

Purvis, June. *Hard Lives: The Lives and Education of Working-Class Women in Nineteenth-Century England.* Cambridge, Eng.: Polity Press, 1981.

Purvis, Martin. "Societies of Consumers and Consumer Societies: Co-operation, Consumption and Politics in Britain and Continental Europe c. 1850–1920." *Journal of Historical Geography* 24 (1998): 147–169.

Rappaport, Erika Diane. *Shopping for Pleasure: Women in the Making of London's West End.* Princeton, N.J.: Princeton University Press, 2000.

Reekie, Shirley M. "A History of Sport and Recreation for Women in Great Britain, 1700–1850." Ph.D. dissertation, Ohio State University, 1982.

Reid, Douglas. "The Decline of St. Monday, 1766–1876." *Past and Present* 71 (1976): 76–101.

Rendall, Jane. *Women in an Industrializing Society: England 1750–1880.* Oxford: Basil Blackwell, 1990.

Roberts, Elizabeth. *A Woman's Place: An Oral History of Working-Class Women, 1890–1940.* Oxford: Basil Blackwell, 1984.

Roberts, Mary Louise. "Gender, Consumption, and Commodity Culture." *American Historical Review* (1998): 817–844.

Rogers, Nicholas. "Carnal Knowledge: Illegitimacy in Eighteenth-Century Westminster." *Journal of Social History* 23 (1989): 355–375.

———. *Crowds, Culture, and Politics in Georgian Britain.* Oxford: Clarendon Press, 1998.

Rose, Sonya O. "Gender Antagonism and Class Conflict: Exclusionary Strategies of Male Trade Unionists in Nineteenth-Century Britain." *Social History* 13 (1988): 191–208.

———. *Limited Livelihoods: Gender and Class in Nineteenth-Century England.* Berkeley: University of California Press, 1992.

Rosman, Doreen M. *Evangelicals and Culture.* London: Croom Helm, 1984.

Ross, Ellen. "Good and Bad Mothers: Lady Philanthropists and London Housewives before the First World War." In *Lady Bountiful Revisited:*

Women, Philanthropy, and Power, edited by Kathleen D. McCarthy. New Brunswick, N.J.: Rutgers University Press, 1990.

―――. *Love and Toil: Motherhood in Outcast London 1870–1918.* New York: Oxford University Press, 1993.

―――. "Survival Networks: Women's Neighbourhood Sharing in London Before World War I." *History Workshop Journal* 15 (1983): 4–27.

Ruane, Christine. "Clothes Shopping in Imperial Russia: The Development of a Consumer Culture." *Journal of Social History* 28 (1995): 765–782.

Rule, John. "Methodism, Popular Beliefs and Village Culture in Cornwall, 1800–50." In *Popular Culture and Custom in Nineteenth-Century England,* edited by Robert D. Storch. London: Croom Helm, 1982.

Schiebinger, Londa. "Why Mammals Are Called Mammals: Gender Politics in Eighteenth-Century Natural History." *American Historical Review* 98 (1993): 382–411.

Schwarzkopf, Jutta. *Women in the Chartist Movement.* New York: St. Martin's Press, 1991.

Scobey, David. "Anatomy of the Promenade: The Politics of Bourgeois Sociability in Nineteenth-Century New York." *Social History* 17 (1992): 203–227.

Seccombe, Wally. "Patriarchy Stabilized: The Construction of the Male Breadwinner Norm in Nineteenth-Century Britain." *Social History* 11 (1986): 53–76.

Seleski, Patty. "Women, Work and Cultural Change in Eighteenth- and Early Nineteenth-Century London." In *Popular Culture in England, c. 1500–1850,* edited by Tim Harris. New York: St. Martin's Press, 1995.

Sharpe, Pamela. *Adapting to Capitalism: Working Women in the English Economy, 1700–1850.* New York: St. Martin's Press, 1996.

Shaw, Susan M. "Gender and Leisure: Inequality in the Distribution of Leisure Time." *Journal of Leisure Research* 17 (1985): 266–282.

―――. "Gender, Leisure, and Constraint: Towards a Framework for the Analysis of Women's Leisure." *Journal of Leisure Research* 26 (1994): 8–22.

Shiman, Lilian Lewis. "The Band of Hope Movement: Respectable Recreation for Working-Class Children." *Victorian Studies* 17 (1973): 49–74.

Smith, Chris, et al. *Reshaping Work: The Cadbury Experience.* Cambridge: Cambridge University Press, 1990.

Smith, W. David. *Stretching Their Bodies: The History of Physical Education.* Newton Abbot, Eng.: David & Charles, 1974.

Spelman, Elizabeth V. "Woman as Body: Ancient and Contemporary Views." *Feminist Studies* 8 (1978): 108–131.

Stansell, Christine. *City of Women: Sex and Class in New York 1789–1860.* Urbana: University of Illinois Press, 1987.

Stone, Lawrence. "Money, Sex and Murder in Eighteenth-Century England." In *Women and Society in the Eighteenth Century*, edited by Ian P. H. Duffy. Bethlehem, Pa.: The Lawrence Henry Gipson Institute, c. 1983.

Storch, Robert D., ed. *Popular Culture and Custom in Nineteenth-Century England*. London: Croom Helm, 1982.

Strange, Carolyn. *Toronto's Girl Problem: The Perils and Pleasures of the City, 1880–1930*. Toronto: University of Toronto Press, 1995.

Strasser, Susan. *Never Done: A History of American Housework*. New York: Pantheon, 1982.

Taylor, Barbara. *Eve and the New Jerusalem: Socialism and Feminism in the Nineteenth Century*. New York: Pantheon, 1983.

Tebbutt, Melanie. *Making Ends Meet: Pawnbroking and Working-Class Credit*. Leicester, Eng.: Leicester University Press, 1983.

———. *Women's Talk? A Social History of "Gossip" in Working-Class Neighbourhoods, 1880–1960*. Aldershot, Eng.: Scolar Press, 1995.

Thompson, Derek. "Courtship and Marriage in Preston between the Wars." *Oral History* 3 (1975): 39–44.

Thompson, Dorothy. *The Chartists*. London: Temple Smith, 1984.

Thompson, E. P. *The Making of the English Working Class*. New York: Pantheon, 1964.

———. "Patrician Society, Plebeian Culture." *Journal of Social History* 7 (1974): 63–81.

Thompson, Peter. *The Edwardians: The Remaking of British Society*. Bloomington: Indiana University Press, 1975.

Tilly, Louise A., and Joan W. Scott. *Women, Work, and Family*. New York: Holt, Rinehart & Winston, 1978.

Valenze, Deborah. *The First Industrial Woman*. New York: Oxford University Press, 1995.

———. *Prophetic Sons and Daughters: Female Preaching and Popular Religion in Industrial England*. Princeton, N.J.: Princeton University Press, 1985.

Valverde, Mariana. *The Age of Light, Soap and Water: Moral Reform in English Canada, 1885–1925*. London: McClelland & Stewart, 1985.

———. "The Love of Finery: Fashion and the Fallen Woman in Nineteenth-Century Social Discourse." *Victorian Studies* 28 (1989): 169–170.

Vamplew, Wray. *Pay Up and Play the Game: Professional Sport in Britain 1875–1914*. Cambridge: Cambridge University Press, 1988.

Vicinus, Martha. *Independent Women: Work and Community for Single Women, 1850–1920*. Chicago: University of Chicago Press, 1985.

Vickery, Amanda. *The Gentleman's Daughter: Women's Lives in Georgian England*. London: Yale University Press, 1998.

———. "Golden Age to Separate Spheres? A Review of the Categories and

Chronology of English Women's History." *Historical Journal* 36 (1993): 383–414.

Vinson, Adrian. "The Edwardians and Poverty: Towards a Minimum Wage." In *Edwardian England*, edited by Donald Read. London: Croom Helm, 1982.

Wagner, Gillian. *The Chocolate Conscience*. London: Chatto & Windus, 1987.

Wahrman, Dror. "Percy's Prologue: From Gender Play to Gender Panic in Eighteenth-Century England." *Past and Present* 159 (1998): 113–160.

Walby, Sylvia. *Patriarchy at Work*. Cambridge, Eng.: Polity Press, 1986.

Walkowitz, Judith R. *City of Dreadful Delight: Narratives of Sexual Danger in Late-Victorian London*. Chicago: University of Chicago Press, 1992.

Walton, John K. *The English Seaside Resort: A Social History 1750–1914*. New York: St. Martin's, 1983.

Walvin, James. *Beside the Seaside: A Social History of the Popular Seaside Holiday*. London: Allen Lane, 1978.

———. *Leisure and Society, 1830–1950*. London: Longmans, 1978.

Wearing, Betsy, and Stephen Wearing. " 'All in a Day's Leisure': Gender and the Concept of Leisure." *Leisure Studies* 7 (1988): 111–123.

Webb, Ida M. "The History of Chelsea College of Physical Education with Special Reference to Curriculum Development, 1898–1973." Ph.D. dissertation, University of Leicester, Leicester, Eng., 1977.

Williams, Raymond. *Marxism and Literature*. Oxford: Oxford University Press, 1977.

Wimbush, Erica, and Margaret Talbot, eds. *Relative Freedoms: Women and Leisure*. Milton Keynes, Eng.: Open University Press, 1988.

Wood, Andy. "The Place of Custom in Plebeian Popular Culture: England, 1550–1800." *Social History* 22 (1997): 46–60.

Yeo, Eileen, and Stephen Yeo, eds. *Popular Culture and Class Conflict 1590–1914: Explorations in the History of Labour and Leisure*. Brighton, Eng.: Harvester Press, 1981.

Zlotnick, Susan. " 'A Thousand Times I'd Be a Factory Girl': Dialect, Domesticity, and Working-Class Women's Poetry in Victorian Britain." *Victorian Studies* 35 (1991): 7–27.

Index